VERDUN
—— 1916 ——
Malcolm Brown

OTHER BOOKS BY MALCOLM BROWN

Scapa Flow
(with Patricia Meehan)

Tommy Goes to War
(Re-issued Tempus 1999)

Christmas Truce
(with Shirley Seaton)

A Touch of Genius:
The Life of T.E. Lawrence
(with Julia Cave)

The Letters of T.E. Lawrence
(Editor)

Secret Despatches from Arabia,
and Other Writings by T.E. Lawrence
(Editor)

The Imperial War Museum
Book of the First World War

The Imperial War Museum
Book of the Western Front

The Imperial War Museum
Book of the Somme

The Imperial War Museum
Book of 1918: Year of Victory

Cover illustration: German soldier assaulting the French lines at Verdun (The Imperial War Museum)

VERDUN

— 1916 —

Malcolm Brown

TEMPUS

First published 1999
Paperback edition published 2000

PUBLISHED IN THE UNITED KINGDOM BY:

Tempus Publishing Ltd
The Mill, Brimscombe Port
Stroud, Gloucestershire GL5 2QG

PUBLISHED IN THE UNITED STATES OF AMERICA BY:

Tempus Publishing Inc.
2A Cumberland Street
Charleston, SC 29401

Tempus books are available in France, Germany and Belgium
from the following addresses:

Tempus Publishing Group	Tempus Publishing Group	Tempus Publishing Group
21 Avenue de la République	Gustav-Adolf-Straße 3	Place de L'Alma 4/5
37300 Joué-lès-Tours	99084 Erfurt	1200 Brussels
FRANCE	GERMANY	BELGIUM

British Library Cataloguing in Publication Data.
A catalogue record for this book is available from the British Library.

ISBN 0 7524 1774 6

Typesetting and origination by Tempus Publishing.
PRINTED AND BOUND IN GREAT BRITAIN.

Contents

Acknowledgements

I first visited Verdun in 1978 in the course of researching and filming for the BBC TV Documentary *Armistice and After*, in the company of that programme's outstanding presenter, the historian and biographer John Grigg. Some years later I went there again in high-quality company, when researching for the BBC TV series *Soldiers*. In this case my companion and consultant was Richard Holmes, now justly celebrated as the Western Front's best contemporary interpreter on television. Add Frederick Forsyth to the list, with whom I filmed a memorable sequence in the dripping depths of Fort Douaumont for the *Soldiers* series, and the reader will correctly assume that the responsibility for any shortcomings or errors in this book must be mine and mine alone. A fourth presence should be acknowledged, in this case someone I have never met, except through the pages of his masterly account of Verdun, *The Price of Glory*. I refer of course to Alistair Horne. His book, first published in 1962 and still going strong, is of such a calibre that re-telling the story of Verdun can almost seem the equivalent of re-writing Shakespeare. Yet such must be attempted, if only because new material continues to emerge even from such a well-known holocaust as Verdun, and because each new generation needs to make its own assessment of the great sagas of the now departed twentieth century. At a time when Antony Beevor's account of the epic story of Stalingrad is throwing up horrors previously unknown, it is worth claiming that Verdun is now giving off vibrations which can genuinely be described as almost hopeful. *Plus ça change, ce n'est pas toujours la même chose.* We are so used to cynicism, it is good to be able to record a possible advance.

Such luminaries apart, this book would not have been possible without the benign and talented help of very many people, who in the present context might best be described as prisoner's friends. I am immensely grateful to all of them. Prominent among them are the three comrades with whom I undertook a vital return visit to Verdun in the summer of 1999: Roderick Suddaby, Keeper of the Department of Documents at the Imperial War Museum, with whom every conversation was a serious tutorial and quite rightly so; his wife Jenny who took many of the photographs with which this book is illustrated; and Neil Smith, schoolmaster of the highest quality, whose greatest virtue is to ask the vital, challenging question. Next I must list my fellow-translators, who responded benignly, indeed eagerly, to my request to render often very obscure and intensely powerful French, or German, into fluent and palatable English: Sylvia Newberry, Hilary Hamilton (assisted by Graham Hayter), and, bearing the biggest burden and producing work of consistent vigour and style, my wife Betty, while Kate Tildesley produced some admirable translations from German.

A number of scholarly French colleagues encountered through other areas of work, notably my writings on T.E. Lawrence, expressed great interest when they knew that I was attempting a book on Verdun and offered to send me their comments on how they see Verdun today. To Dr Maurice Larès, Christophe Leclerc, Marie-Laure Blay-Gilbert and Philippe Braquet, therefore, my sincere thanks for caring enough about a British historian's effort to enrich it with their special insight and wisdom; they have added an important element which would otherwise have been difficult to obtain. Another French friend whose contribution is greatly appreciated is the artist and journalist Mme Françoise Eyraud; she supplied the text of her 1993 interview with the Verdun survivor Pierre Rouquet, quoted in Chapters 12 and 19, and the photograph of him reproduced as illustration 50, showing him as a young *poilu* before his baptism of fire in 1916.

For help in the matter of producing valuable, indeed vital, contemporary material I wish to thank Jan Mihell, newly retired from the Imperial War Museum, who carried out some highly valuable research into newspaper files, discovering evidence which much enriched the book's narrative quality and range. Former BBC colleague Jane Callander, now a researcher in archaeology, provided material which led me to give much greater prominence than I had previously intended to that outstanding figure Pierre Teilhard de Chardin: towering twentieth-century intellect and, remarkably, humble stretcher-bearer at Verdun. I defy anyone to read his statement in the aftermath of terrible fighting at Froideterre in August 1916, as quoted on page 162, and not be moved, even awed. What he wrote in 1916 vibrates through all our conflicts today. This is, as it were, a Galileo among so many of lesser quality, and I am proud, and humbled, to be able to offer him as contributor to this retelling of the story of Verdun.

One most important category requiring very special acknowledgement is that of the copyright holders who have kindly allowed me to use their material, whether previously published or unpublished, to enrich the book's text or to add to the range and quality of its illustrations. The latter are acknowledged in the captions: the former are acknowledged either explicitly or by implication in the Bibliography. All sources noted are included not merely to convey necessary and, it is hoped, useful information but also as a gesture of gratitude.

Others I am pleased to thank for their much valued help are: Michael Paterson, who provided me with valuable material on Crown Prince Wilhelm and the contemporary postcard-portrait here reproduced as illustration 9; his wife Sarah, of the Imperial War Museum's Department of Printed Books, who cast a strict, professional eye over my Source notes and Bibliography, making numerous improvements; Julie Robertshaw of the same department, first to read the manuscript from end to end with a view to assessing its clarity and narrative drive; and Roderick Suddaby, already named, whose sharp and scholarly criticisms of the book's initial draft ensured that the one which went to the printers was markedly superior. I have had much help too from the Museum's Photograph Archive, especially Hilary Roberts and the staff of the Archive's reading room, and from Mike Moody and Pauline Allwright of the Department of Art, while Mike Hibberd, of the Department of Exhibits and Firearms, left me much in his debt for his expert advice on artillery matters. As ever I have been able to call on the knowledgeable and good-humoured aid of the Department of Documents, which has now been host to me as a free-lance historian for over ten years. The support of Jane Carmichael, Assistant Director, Collections, and of Dr Christopher Dowling, Keeper of Museum Services, is also warmly acknowledged; thanks to them, both this book and Tempus's recent remake of my *Tommy Goes to War* are published 'in association with the Imperial War Museum'.

My sincere thanks also to: my son-in-law James Rowles, whose skill in scanning often obscure documents into Word 97 saved hours of tedious typing, and to whose coolness and wise counsel during moments of serious computer malfunction (there were several) I am deeply indebted; my wife Betty for her hours of careful proof-reading; Ian D. Crane for his most valuable index; and Kate Adams and Anne Phipps of Tempus Publishing who between them saw the book through from MS to publication. My gratitude finally to Alan Sutton and Jonathan Reeve of Tempus Publishing for the honour of appearing for the second time in their lists.

Malcolm Brown, Autumn 1999

Preface

Anyone who has been moved by the saga of the Battle of the Somme cannot but be aware of the longer struggle going on throughout almost all of 1916 over 150 miles away to the south-east at Verdun. Yet for the English-speaking reader, especially perhaps the British, Verdun is all too often dismissed as 'noises off', as a *doppelgänger* lookalike which seems to have only a marginal bearing on what they see as largely an Anglo-German ordeal running from July to November in the region of the Somme. But 1916 was dominated by the battle fought in distant Lorraine and it should never be forgotten that a prime reason for the Somme's controversial continuance from high summer to the edge of winter was that it should relieve pressure on Verdun.

I have been interested in the awesome, multi-faceted drama of 1916 for many years and as someone who has wrestled with the Somme both as documentary film-maker and latterly as historian I welcome the opportunity given me by Tempus to write about its Franco-German parallel. From the moment the idea of a short but, it was hoped, a pungent and scholarly book on the subject was put on the table I realized that this volume would represent the fulfilment of a distinct, if to that point all but undeclared, ambition. Though different in length and format, it will, I hope, take its place alongside my *Imperial War Museum Book of the Somme* published in 1996.

A deliberate hallmark of my books on the First World War has been their concentration on the experience of the individual and this one is no exception. In great conflicts which can look from a distance like armies of ants fighting in a huge ant-hill such a focus is surely both legitimate and necessary in that otherwise it is all too easy to see monumental events of this kind merely in terms of the amount of ground gained or lost, the number of guns captured or, on the human level, in terms of the statistics of the wounded, the prisoners and the dead. Never was there such an ant-hill as Verdun and with the added hazard of the language barrier (though it is good to be able to state that there are a handful of notable contributors to this book whose natural tongue was English) it can seem all but impossible to turn the telescope onto the actual people involved. Every attempt has been made to breach this barrier and I am most grateful to those translators past and present, known and unknown, who have assisted me in the vital task of bringing a significant number of those people into focus. Their efforts (my debt to those known to me is already acknowledged on page 7) combined with the remarkable candour with which participants on both sides recorded their experiences will I, hope, help to make this book as fascinating and moving to read as I have found it to research and write.

One question that might arise from that statement is worth anticipating here. How was it that in the midst of all the anxiety, stress and suffering of Verdun, men still found the time, and more importantly the will, to write long and detailed letters, or personal diaries, in which they often gave extremely frank accounts of their experiences? And did such outpourings represent an exception or a rule? A recent German historian of Verdun, German Werth, believes it to be the former; indeed, in his view, letter writing was extremely rare and such letters as came out from Verdun were terse, perfunctory and gave only the minimum of information. The battle was too overwhelming; more, its effect would continue long after it was over:

> Most of the soldiers who returned from the front were silenced by the 'hell of the matériel battle'. Few kept diaries; as a rule only reminiscences of events were produced. In positions close to the line, in areas that were not altogether peaceful, there was practically no opportunity to exchange shovel or rifle for a pencil. Letters home restricted themselves to the barest essentials, were primarily a sign that the soldier was still alive, the pages of diaries recorded only the coarsest of impressions. They could not provide a perspective on the 'sense' of the action that was left to the memoirs of the generals and commanders, who, for their part, knew little of the lives of the ordinary men in the trenches.

Fortunately the exceptions, determined to communicate or record what they were going through and, in the case of letters, eager to hold contact with the world beyond the battlefield, have left some remarkable evidence. Additionally, particularly on the French side, there was much collecting of first-hand accounts in the interwar period and there has been more research of a similar kind since, with an inevitable surge in respect of recent First World war anniversaries. In fact, from one source or another, the material relating to Verdun is verging on the encyclopaedic. One massive repository of personal material is the volume *Verdun 1916* edited by Jacques Péricard, originally published in a huge volume in1933 and now happily available in a convenient softback, while another, *Verdun* by Jacques-Henri Lefebvre, published in 1960, gives away the reason for its scholarly weight by its subtitle: *'la plus grande bataille de l'Histoire'*: 'the greatest battle in History'. More recently, the best-selling *Paroles de Poilus,* published in 1998 by Librio in association with Radio France, has brought to light another crop of high-quality letters from both sides of the battle-lines. I am most grateful for the opportunity of including material from these sources, and from numerous others, some of them published while the battle was in progress or within a very short time of its conclusion.

The title *Paroles de Poilus* raises another subject: that of the name *poilu*. Strictly it means 'hairy one', or 'bearded one'; the French infantryman was traditionally bearded which was why tradition was offended when men had to shave off their beards to wear gas masks. Much as British soldiers were not enthusiastic about being called 'Tommy', French soldiers did not like being called *'poilus'*; to them it savoured too much of journalistic slang. They generally referred to each other as *'les bonhommes'*, of which probably the best British equivalent is 'the lads'.

Chronology

1916

21 February	Start of German attack on the right bank of the River Meuse
22 February	Death of Lieutenant-Colonel Driant
25 February	Seizure of Fort Douaumont★
26 February	General Philippe Pétain takes command at Verdun
6 March	German attack on the left bank of the Meuse
5-10 April	General German assault on both banks
10 April	Pétain's message: *'Courage: on les aura!'*
1 May	General Robert Nivelle takes over as Verdun commander; Pétain becomes Commander, Army Group Centre
22 May	Failed attempt to retake Fort Douaumont
7 June	Fall of Fort Vaux
23 June	German attack on Fleury and Fort Souville Nivelle's message 'You will not let them pass!'
1 July	Opening of the Battle of the Somme
12 July	Germans briefly reach Fort Souville: furthest point of German advance
24 October	Recapture of Fort Douaumont
2 November	Reoccupation of Fort Vaux
18 November	End of the Battle of the Somme
15-18 December	Final French right bank attack at Verdun

1917

April	Nivelle offensive, Chemin des Dames
August	Second Battle of Verdun: recapture of Mort-Homme, Côte 304, Avocourt

1918

November	American troops reclaim remainder of Verdun battlefield

★ *Strictly Fort Douaumont should be referred to as Fort de Douaumont. This book follows normal English practice from 1916 onwards by deleting the 'de'; hence Fort Douaumont, Fort Vaux, Fort Souville etc.*

1 The name

Certain places are fated to be permanently marked by what happened in them or in their vicinity at one particular moment of history. The name is enough: mention it and the connotations gather around, the reputation clicks instantly into place. The twentieth century was rich in such names and in its own particular category Verdun stands high. The battle to defend that garrison town in north-eastern France from 21 February to 18 December 1916 has become a symbol almost without parallel of the awfulness of modern industrialised conflict. Perhaps only Stalingrad, famous for the six-months-long siege-battle in Soviet Russia which became the turning point of the Second World War, can invite serious comparison. So much was implicitly acknowledged by the man who more than anyone caused the Stalingrad débâcle, Adolf Hitler, when in November 1942 he assured his Nazi Old Guard in a speech at Munich that it would never become 'a second Verdun'. It did, with himself and his country as the losers.

Verdun had its Russian connotations even while the battle was being fought. The German Supreme Commander on the Russian Front (himself to be closely associated with Hitler's rise to power) was General Paul von Hindenburg. He would later write:

> 'Verdun!' The name was continually on our lips in the East from the beginning. . . As time went on. . . doubts gradually began to prevail, though they were but seldom expressed. They could be summarised shortly in the following question: Why should we persevere with an offensive which exacted such frightful sacrifices and, as was already obvious, had no prospects of success?

The Russians — allies of France and Britain at this time, their defection under Lenin still almost two years away — looked on the French response to the German attack on Verdun with something approaching awe. M. Maurice Paléologue, the French ambassador at the court of the Tsar, had been aware that for some time the Russian people had tended to sneer at the French contribution to the war. Now he sensed a different mood. 'The Battle of Verdun,' he noted in his diary as early as 28 February, 'has changed all that. The heroism of our army, the skill and coolness of our High Command, our enormous resources in *matériel* and the splendid attitude of our public opinion are admired by everyone.'

Britain also watched with admiration, if with frustration in military circles because 1916 was meant to be the year of a great Anglo-French offensive, not a German one. The intended attack went ahead, if with reduced French participation. It became known as the

Battle of the Somme, itself a kind of Verdun replica, not dissimilar in level of sacrifice if fortunately shorter in duration.

For the French, Verdun would become a lasting symbol. When Henry Bordeaux, who doubled as soldier and patriotic writer, produced the first of his two books about the battle, *The Last Days of Fort Vaux* — published in 1917 — he began his Preface with the paragraph:

> *VERDUN* — those two syllables that have already become historic ring out today like the brazen tones of a trumpet. In France, no one can hear them without a thrill of pride. In England, in America, if any speaker utters them, the whole audience rises as one man.

If one were to nominate a British parallel, it would not be associated with the Somme, but with that other sector of the former Western Front where the British have long had a special link, Flanders, where between 1914 and 1918 there took place no fewer than four Battles of Ypres. The city of Ypres, determinedly defended with the kind of 'they shall not pass' mentality which pertained at Verdun, is the only possible British equivalent. In August 1915, a young British private, Rifleman P.H. Jones of the Queen's Westminster Rifles, wrote in his diary:

> One feels that this City of the Dead is infinitely greater, infinitely more sublime in the hour of its ruin than it could ever have been in the past. It seems to be a symbol, not only of the mad destruction against which we are fighting but also of the ideals for which we struggle. We hold this place for moral effect only (our troops would be better off behind the Canal) for an ideal, in short. We have paid a heavy price for our ideal, two great battles and Heaven knows how many more to come. There is nothing sordid in this place, in holding it men have died for a dream, sacrificed themselves for a heap of ruins.

The French would have recognized such sentiments for they reflect what they themselves felt instinctively in relation to Verdun. There was, however, a major difference. The British were fighting abroad. The French, like the Belgians, were fighting on their own ground, their *patrie*. More, substantial areas of that *patrie* were under occupation. As far back as the first weeks of the war a British Cavalry officer, Captain E.W.S. Balfour, Adjutant of the 5th Dragoon Guards, had sensed the fury his allies felt at the loss of so much territory to the enemy. In a letter to his family he wrote:

> To the French it is their own home and it makes them mad. We somehow fight on with no increased animosity. If we were ordered to retire again tomorrow, I don't believe we should lose morale. The French really are giving everything and it makes one wonder if people in England realize what the advance of an invading army over a country means.

1.   L'Enfer — *'Hell': Georges Leroux's vision of Verdun, (Imperial War Museum Department of Art)*

It was because of such attitudes that when the Germans attacked Verdun in 1916 it was defended in so furious a manner. The French had yielded enough heartland already; to lose more would inflict yet more humiliation. In Balfour's phraseology, it made them mad and forced them to give everything rather than concede.

The result was what rapidly became known as the 'Hell of Verdun'. Significantly the most famous painting of the battle, by Georges Leroux, is called *'L'Enfer'*: 'Hell'. With its depiction of smoke, fire, mud, shattered trees, and pygmy figures in gas-masks attempting to crawl out of a flooded trench it is almost like a science-fiction version of a Gustave Doré illustration to Dante or a painting by Hieronymous Bosch. Small wonder that Verdun's reputation once fixed became so enduring.

There was further fighting there in the following year, if smaller in scale; even the thought of it could act as a reminder of what had happened in the preceding one. In the late summer of 1917 a sixteen-year-old American, Julian Green (born in Paris, with French as his chief language, and a future novelist of distinction), then working as a volunteer ambulance-driver, found himself in the wooded hill country of the Argonne, not many miles from Verdun. Soon after his arrival a fellow member of his unit called him out on to the terrace of the building they were using as a headquarters and invited him to listen, to a low, distant, incessant rumbling. His first thought was that he was hearing a storm. 'No' said his colleague. 'If it were thunder the noise would stop occasionally. This noise is constant. It's Verdun.' Green would write of his reaction:

> I shuddered at the mention of this sinister yet fascinating name. There, I knew I really would have been frightened. There, my intestines would certainly have turned to liquid like those of King David in the Psalms. Verdun was a hell, and the noise I heard in the distance was the ghastly rattle of death, the vast black hole where the armies of two nations were being swallowed up. I could not utter a word. . . .

How Verdun came to be attacked and how it was defended, and how, against the odds, it has now become a remarkable symbol of international reconciliation is the subject of this book, published at the onset of a century in which it is hoped that such massive human tragedies as those that took place at Verdun, the Somme, Ypres and Stalingrad will join the list of what the poet William Wordsworth called 'old unhappy far-off things and battles long ago'.

Above and below: The Combatants of Verdun:
2.   German troops marching to the front (Q 23761)

3.   French troops marching to the front (Q 58154)

2 The background

Verdun is a town — now more frequently referred to as a city — of the Department of Meuse, itself part of the ancient province of Lorraine. The annual Michelin guide notes its distance from other notable centres: Paris 262 kilometres, Metz 66, Châlons-sur-Marne 87, Nancy 110, Reims 119. In terms of its situation in 1916 it might have added: approximate distance from German front line, 18 kilometres.

Verdun is surrounded by a circle of hills, the Meuse Heights, with beyond them to the east the marshy Woevre Plain; Metz lies at its extreme edge. Not far to the north is the uphill country of the Ardennes (through which Hitler to the amazement of his enemies sent his invasion forces in 1940), while to the west are the forests of the Argonne. Further west lie the plains, and the vineyards, of Champagne. The reason for the town's existence is that it stands at the point where the main route from Metz to Paris crosses the river Meuse.

The Meuse has none of the obvious glamour of the Loire or the Seine, but its course is nevertheless a fascinating one, and one with much history. Flowing 885 kilometres from its source in the department of Haute-Marne, it passes Domrémy-la-Pucelle, famous as the birthplace of Joan of Arc, on its northward progress to Verdun. Moving on from Verdun it next claims Sedan, scene of an ignominious French surrender in 1870, before entering Belgium, where its name changes to the Flemish version, Maas. Then, in the course of a long eastward parabola towards the North Sea, it passes the Belgian towns of Namur and Liège and the Dutch town of Maastricht before linking up with the Waal, part of the supreme river of the German cultural imagination, the Rhine. Even then it manages to reach the sea in several outlets and under several aliases. Among the rivers feeding into it is the Sambre; devotees of Britain's war poets will recall that the best of them, Wilfred Owen, lost his life in November 1918 on the banks of the nearby Sambre-Oise Canal. Much of the course of the Meuse was fought over in numerous actions in both the twentieth-century's world wars.

A river's banks are labelled in relation to its progress to the sea. Thus when in the context of the Verdun battle the Meuse's right bank is mentioned, the reference is to the eastward side (at this point it flows, if with several severe loops, almost due north); its left bank, therefore, is that to the west.

Verdun has long been a bone of contention. In that huge area of northern France, Belgium and constantly changing border country which none other than General Charles de Gaulle (himself a combatant there in 1916) was to call a 'fatal avenue', Verdun was a place that was frequently in the wars.

There was a Gallic settlement here and then a Roman: 'Virodunum Castrum', hence, by the easiest of mutations, Verdun. Attila the Hun attacked it in 450, leaving it 'like a field ravaged by wild beasts'. In 843 a treaty signed here annexed Verdun to the ancient kingdom of Lorraine. From 870 for a time it became part of France, but in 923 it was incorporated in the then German Empire. Moving on several centuries we find Verdun seized in 1552 by Henri II, King of France. Over time it would acquire the distinction of being subjected to at least ten sieges.

One of the most famous was that of 1792, during the wars that broke out subsequent to the French Revolution. The siege produced one of those ringing exhortations at which the French have always been adept, when Danton, then supreme revolutionary leader, urged the town's populace to hold out against the investing Prussians with the message: *'il nous faut de l'audace, encore de l'audace, toujours de l'audace'*: 'we need audacity, more audacity, always audacity'. It was not enough, for the town capitulated, but it started a trend. There would be more such slogans when Verdun was under siege once again in 1916.

Verdun came well out of the disastrous Franco-Prussian War of 1870-71. At a time of deep national disgrace, it refused to open its gates to the victorious armies of Kaiser Wilhelm I, spiritedly repelling an attack in August 1870 and only conceding in November, when its garrison was allowed to surrender with the honours of war. Paris had been under siege for months before Verdun gave in. In the harsh political settlement that followed, while Alsace and most of Lorraine were annexed to Germany, Verdun was excepted. It thus became in effect a frontier town, with the new border barely a day's march away. As a result it could easily have been an early victim in 1914, when the impetuous French advance into Alsace-Lorraine was brushed aside by the superbly trained forces of Kaiser Wilhelm II. But the troops of the Crown Prince Wilhelm's Fifth Army were held up before it by fierce resistance and so when the lines congealed and trench warfare began, it remained in French hands, if with the Germans ominously close.

Verdun had another distinction. It was a town exceptionally well-defended in the style associated with one of the great masters of seventeenth century warfare, Marshal Sebastian de Vauban.

Vauban (1633-1707) is a key figure in the history of modern Europe but one whose name is relatively unknown, largely because his speciality, fortifications, makes for less exciting reading than that other matter which dominates the writing of history, fighting. Everybody knows who lost and won the siege of Troy, but who were the superb military architects who made that city so impregnable that it could only be seized after ten years through the basically unsporting ruse of the wooden horse? Vauban's stock in trade was the creation of a Trojan-style security: in effect, walls to forestall wars.

His principal role was that of specialist military adviser to one of the most bellicose leaders of the last millennium, King Louis XIV of France. Famous now most of all for his splendid palace, Versailles, and secondarily for his mistresses, the so-called 'Sun King' was in his lifetime seen above all as a human Mars, a bringer of war. This he himself acknowledged when on his deathbed in 1715 he confessed to his young successor, Louis XV, that he had 'loved war too much'.

Under Louis XIV's almost quixotic lust for glory was a need for security. What drove him to almost constant warfare was the fear that the alternative might lead to defeat and therefore disgrace. In such circumstances Vauban might easily have been a compliant

4.   *The Citadel of Verdun, designed by Vauban, with statues of French generals (Mrs Jenny Suddaby)*

5.   *One of the entries into the Citadel (Mrs Jenny Suddaby)*

Two Seré de Rivières forts:

6.   *(above) Fort de Génicourt – left to the depredations of nature (Author)*
7.   *(below) Fort de Vaux – having suffered at the hand of man (Author)*

toady, but on the contrary he presented him with what has been described as 'a method of waging war elegantly and with a minimum of bloodshed'. Vauban proposed, in effect, a frontier of interconnected and brilliantly designed strongholds which an enemy would find virtually impossible to penetrate. Thus was begun a philosophy of defence which links Vauban directly across the centuries with that supreme icon of the 1930s, (alas, also to be dubbed a supreme white elephant) the Maginot Line.

Vauban's creations can be seen far and wide today: at Mont-Louis in the Pyrenees, at St Malo in Brittany, where the Fort National offers a Vauban 'first' to visitors from Britain, in the great Citadels of Lille and Arras, and at numerous other places along the northern and eastern frontier such as Montmédy, whose 'majestic citadel' (as described by the historian Richard Holmes in his *tour de force* celebration of this crucial zone of Europe, rightly called *Fatal Avenue)*, 'scrapes the skyline long before the town itself is visible'. There is even one of his creations, more a forward bastion than part of any obvious plan of defence, at Neuf-Brisach on the left bank of the Rhine. Verdun was of course bound to be included high in his list, as is evident from the town's massive Citadel, which bears the master's unmistakable hallmark.

The experience of 1870, however, had left the French with the feeling that Vauban's legacy along their eastern frontier was not enough. Thus an expert in fortification of a similar school, General Seré de Rivières, was entrusted with the construction of a whole new defence system which effectively created a series of 'entrenched camps'. Each consisted of a town and an outlying ring of forts. Belfort, Toul, Épinal and Verdun made up, as it were, the front line, while Langres, Dijon and Besançon lay in reserve. Between Épinal and Toul a gap was deliberately left, in the hope that in the case of another invasion it might act as a kind of mouse-trap, to lure an unwary enemy to come in and be destroyed. There was a similar, much less developed system along the Belgian border, though there was less urgency over this sector, as it was not perceived as a main point of danger. In the region of Verdun, the scheme was at its most sophisticated. Thus when the Germans began to plan their assault there in 1916 they found their maps marked with no fewer than twenty major and forty minor obstacles in the way of their possible lines of attack.

Many of these would survive the coming battle intact, and some remain more or less in their original condition to this day, if, as in the case of Fort de Génicourt south of Verdun, so transformed by decades of abandonment to nature as to seem like a castle out of a story by the Brothers Grimm. Others, such as Fort Douaumont and Fort Vaux, on the Meuse Heights to the north-east of the town, would be changed over the months of fighting into monstrous hulks, themselves in their own way to become icons of French mythology almost as potent as Verdun itself.

Ironically, at the moment when it might have seemed that de Rivières' forts were about to come into their own, they suddenly fell out of fashion. But perhaps this is scarcely surprising in a story with as many twists as that of Verdun.

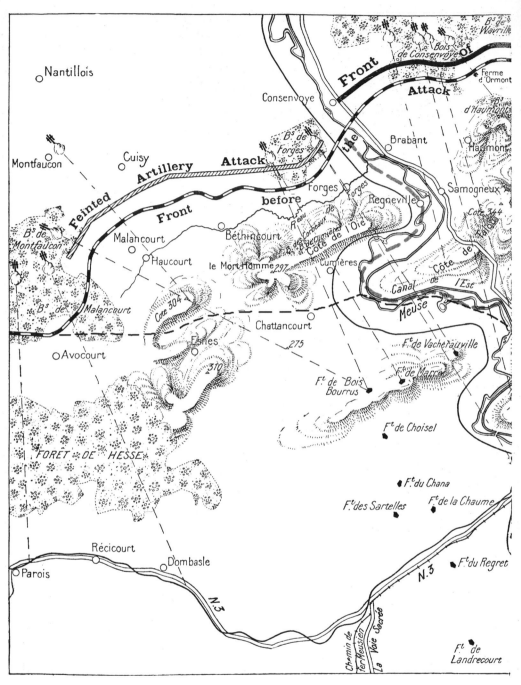

The following labels appear on the map:

Nantillois · Bᵈ de Wavrille · Bois de Consenvoye · Front Of · Attack · Ferme d'Ormont · Consenvoye · Bᵈ d'Haumont · Brabant · Bᵈ de Forges · Haumont · Montfaucon · Cuisy · Artillery Attack · the · Samogneux · Forges · Forges · Regneville · Cote 344 · Feinted · Front · before · Réau de Forges · Cote de l'Oie · Ruisseau de Corbeaux · Béthincourt · Cote de · Bᵈ de Montfaucon · Malancourt · le Mort-Homme 297 · Cumières · Côte de · Haucourt · Côte de l'Est · Bᵈ de Malancourt · Cote 304 · Canal de · Meuse · Chattancourt · Fᵗ de Vacherauville · Avocourt · Esnes · 275 · 310 · Fᵗ de Marre · Fᵗ de Bois Bourrus · FORÊT DE HESSE · Fᵗ de Choisel · Fᵗ du Chana · Fᵗ des Sartelles · Fᵗ de la Chaume · Récicourt · Dombasle · Fᵗ du Regret · N.3 · Parois · N.3 · Chemin de Fer Meusien · La Voie Sacrée · Fᵗ de Landrecourt

THE BATTLEGROUND OF VERDUN:
as shown in the 1919 Michelin Guide adapted
to show the limit of the German advance and the
frontline at the end of the battle

PLAN OF THE GERMAN

"*Concentrate an all-powerful artillery, cut with gun-fire the only defences, isolating their occupants with heavy artillery barrages crushing the last vestiges of resistance,*"—*such was the "kolossal"*

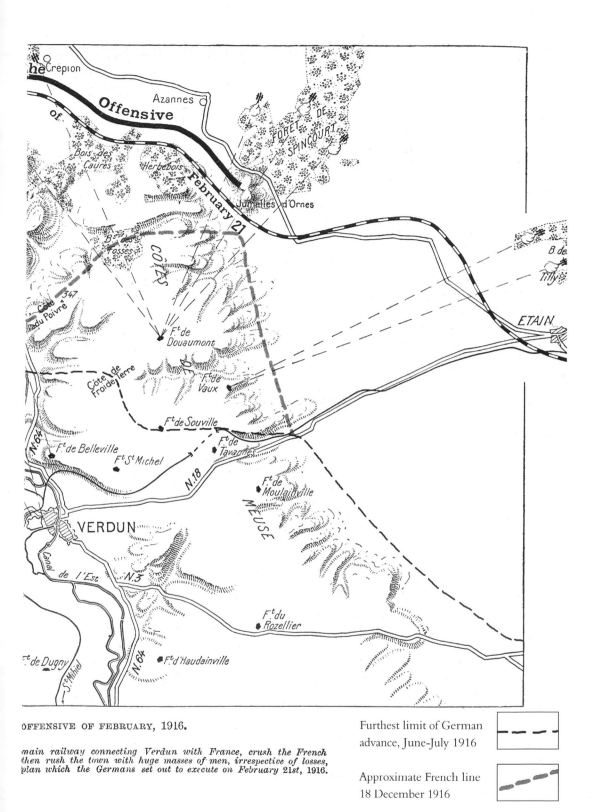

OFFENSIVE OF FEBRUARY, 1916.

main railway connecting Verdun with France, crush the French
then rush the town with huge masses of men, irrespective of losses,
plan which the Germans set out to execute on February 21st, 1916.

Furthest limit of German
advance, June-July 1916

Approximate French line
18 December 1916

3 The plan

Verdun lies so deep in French territory that it can seem somewhat incredible that the deviser of the strategy that subjected it to ten months of terror in 1916 had as his prime aim the defeat of Great Britain: or more precisely, of England. Conditioned by long years of imperial rivalry, Germany's Chief of the General Staff, General Erich von Falkenhayn, saw France, above all, as 'England's best sword'. If only that sword could be knocked out of her hand, England would herself surely concede and admit defeat. The destruction of France's will to resist, by whatever means, was seen as the vital step to that end. Ironically, indeed inevitably, 'England' was to be merely a fascinated spectator of the resultant encounter, while the huge casualty lists to which it gave rise were primarily French, though there were also massive losses on the German side.

Falkenhayn's attitude towards England was not, however, unique to him. German public opinion was far more anti-English than anti-French. France was the old enemy, beaten in previous wars. England was the heart of the Empire which should have been friendly — were not the two countries linked through their royal families? — but seemed determined, casually, almost arrogantly, to bar Germany from her place in the sun.

To produce the result required Falkenhayn proposed that Germany should attack France at a point where the wound would be so hurtful that she would defend to the last, no matter what the scale of sacrifice. As he himself would put it (in a document attributed to December 1915 which would become known as the 'Christmas Memorandum'):

> Within our reach behind the French sector of the Western Front there are objectives for the retention of which the French General Staff would be compelled to throw in every man they have. If they do so the forces of France will bleed to death — as there can be no question of a voluntary withdrawal — whether we reach our goal or not. If they do not do so, and we reach our objectives, the moral effect on France will be enormous. For an operation limited to a narrow front, Germany will not be compelled to spend herself as completely.

Falkenhayn went for the option of an inland battle in his struggle against England because he saw no alternative. Flanders, the obvious area of attack, would probably only produce a military log-jam, as indeed would be the case in 1917. A naval battle was far too risky; when one was attempted later in 1916, at Jutland, the Germans were fortunate to get away with a kind of score-draw. Unrestricted submarine warfare was a possible option — indeed, having been called off after the sinking of the *Lusitania* and other such ships the previous year, it would be restarted in February 1916 as a second string to the initiative against Verdun. But it would obviously be slow to take effect. If, however, France could be so destabilized that she was forced to sue for peace, England would surely conclude that she too must withdraw from the war. On first consideration this might seem a bizarre gamble, but the German attacks of 1918 were launched on a very similar premise. They were meant to break the Anglo-French forces apart, force the French to give up and send the British back across the Channel, before the arrival of the Americans. Falkenhayn's policy was basically an earlier variation on the same theme.

The German supremo had two names in his short-list of places appropriate for attack: Belfort and Verdun. But Belfort, at the eastern end of the front close to the Swiss border, offered restricted scope for manoeuvre; more, any advantage gained there would be too peripheral. Verdun, by contrast, had much to recommend it, not least because, he argued, its closeness to German railway communications offered a point of attack for the French whereby they could make the whole German front in France and Belgium untenable.

Verdun had a number of other advantages from the German viewpoint. The fighting of earlier months had left it in a salient, overlooked, in the style associated in British minds with Ypres, on three sides and therefore ripe to be pinched out. Additionally, its links to the rest of France were minimal. The main railway line between Verdun and Paris's Gare de L'Est via Ste Menehoulde ran so close to the enemy's lines as to be at the mercy of his guns. There remained one narrow-gauge railway and one road, linking Verdun with the departmental capital, Bar-le-Duc, almost sixty kilometres away. On the German side, by contrast, fourteen railheads were available through which the men and the *matériel* required might be brought to the points of attack.

A valuable aid to the understanding of the concept of the Verdun battle is the 1919 Michelin Guide, entitled *Verdun and the Battle for its Possession*. Produced, like all the others in this emotive series, 'in memory of the Michelin employees and workmen who died gloriously for their country', it is a volume of commemoration, a guidebook, and a thumbnail history. The following is its graphic caption to a double-page map entitled 'Plan of the German offensive of February, 1916':

> 'Concentrate an all-powerful artillery, cut with gun-fire the only main railway connecting Verdun with France, crush the French defences, isolating their occupants with heavy artillery barrages then rush the town with huge masses of men, irrespective of losses, crushing the last vestiges of resistance' — such was the 'kolossal' [sic] plan which the Germans set out to execute on February 21st, 1916.

This, in a nutshell, was the essence of the German intention, though it is significant that it takes for granted that the Germans wished actually to *take* Verdun whereas in fact there was, and there still remains, considerable ambiguity as to precisely what it was that lay at the heart of Falkenhayn's strategy.

The key question to be asked is: what would best serve Falkenhayn's purpose? The seizure of Verdun would be a great coup, but would that lead to the destruction of the French army? Would it not be better to turn the Verdun sector into a kind of open wound, which the French would keep pouring men and resources into to staunch? In other words,

8. (left) General Erich von Falkenhayn, instigator of the Battle of Verdun (Q 23726)

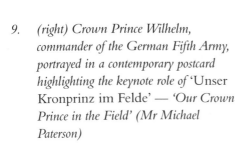

9. (right) Crown Prince Wilhelm, commander of the German Fifth Army, portrayed in a contemporary postcard highlighting the keynote role of 'Unser Kronprinz im Felde' — 'Our Crown Prince in the Field' (Mr Michael Paterson)

would it not be more productive to make attrition the purpose of the offensive, rather than victory?

That, however, was not how an offensive could be sold to the soldiers to be involved. There was nothing 'dulce et decorum' in dying for so arid and ruthless a policy.

Thus it was necessary that Crown Prince Wilhelm's Fifth Army, which was to carry out the attack, should believe that Verdun itself was the target. In his Army Orders the Prince defined his aim as *'to capture the fortress of Verdun by precipitate methods'*. Confirmation that his troops assumed that such was the basic intention occurs in the memoirs of a French commander whose reputation was soon to be made in the forthcoming struggle, the future Marshal Pétain. He wrote of the pre-battle period: '[N]umerous letters found on prisoners mentioned an early action to be led by the Crown Prince, also a military review scheduled to be held toward the end of February on Verdun's parade-ground, and even predictions of the ensuing peace'. With such prospects in view, the Germans would contemplate the ordeal facing them in a better frame of mind than would have been the case had they known they were to take part in a kind of timeless killing-match.

A caveat must be entered, however, before the story continues. Recent research has questioned the whole basis of the Falkenhayn view of the Verdun battle. The text of his so-called 'Christmas Memorandum' only occurs in his book *General headquarters 1914-1916 and its Critical Decisions,* written in 1919. The German Official History quotes it, but obviously uses the autobiography as source, since it states that no copy was found in the official archives. It has therefore been suggested that the Memorandum too was written in 1919, to justify in retrospect why Verdun was never captured, the argument being: 'it never fell; I never meant it to fall'. Some students have therefore taken the view that the standard explanation view of the origin of the battle is no longer valid. By contrast, a recent highly respected scholar in this field, Holger H. Herwig, accepts that the document might have been written later but nevertheless believes it still reflected Falkenhayn's overall intention in 1916. The situation remains suspicious but not proven; indeed it could be argued against a revisionist interpretation that Falkenhayn was doing little for his own reputation in the wake of Germany's defeat in aligning himself with a deliberate policy of attrition for attrition's sake, just at the time — 1919 — when at last the belligerent nations were able to look back on the war and count its terrible cost.

But another question has been raised: why was Falkenhayn so sure that an attack on Verdun would persuade France to pour out her life-blood to hold the breach? Looking back on Verdun 1916, do we not invest it retrospectively with the status it would shortly acquire? Was Falkenhayn in fact so surprised at the amazing French response and tenacious resistance that he had to invent his 'bleed France white' philosophy to explain it?

A historian and politician, and indeed soldier, of the time who saw Falkenhayn's strategy as primarily one of attrition was Winston Churchill. While the battle was still in progress he wrote an article for the *London Magazine* (published in its November edition) which he subsequently quoted in his influential book *World Crisis.* In that book he stated:

> Writing in August 1916, I tried to penetrate and analyse the probable motives which animated the Germans in their attack on Verdun.

'. . . . Suppose your gap is blasted — what then? Are you going to march to Paris through it? What is to happen, if you break the line of an otherwise unbeaten army? Will you really put your head into the hole?

'No,' say Main Headquarters; 'we are not so foolish. We are not seeking Verdun. . . We seek to wear down an army, not to make a gap; to break the heart of a nation, not to break a hole in a line. We have selected Verdun because we think the French will consider themselves bound to defend it at all costs; because we can so dispose our cannon around this apex of their front as to pound and batter the vital positions with superior range and superior metal, and force our enemy to expose division after division upon this anvil to our blows.'

In brief, Churchill saw the attritional explanation of Verdun (whether that was the case or not) as the only one that made military and strategic sense.

There is perhaps a third option; that Falkenhayn was unsure as to his own motives. A memorable comment relating to the pre-battle period occurs in the diary of Crown Prince Rupprecht of Bavaria, head of the German Sixth Army (which was serving on the Somme at this time) and a soldier of impressive record throughout the war. Having been told of certain discussions involving Falkenhayn as to how the French and the British might react elsewhere along the front to the Verdun attack, he stated: 'General von Falkenhayn was himself not clear as to what he really wanted, and was waiting for a stroke of luck that would lead to a favourable conclusion'. It is tempting to suggest that that might be applied to the Verdun scheme overall, that there was, indeed, an opportunist as well as a strategist — even a touch of Mr Micawber — lurking under Falkenhayn's iron-hard Prussian exterior.

Whatever Falkenhayn's strategic intentions overall, there was what would emerge as a fatal flaw in his tactics from the start. The Michelin history's so-called 'kolossal' plan envisaged an attack of shattering intensity, but it would be targeted at one bank of the Meuse only, not both. In effect Falkenhayn's strike would be with just one mailed fist, when he might with better wisdom have used two. He believed he could achieve his goal with nine divisions; it was to prove a crucial miscalculation — in the end the Germans used over fifty — without which events might well have taken an entirely different course.

Crown Prince Wilhelm, commanding the Fifth Army, which was to make the attack, was deeply unhappy about this aspect of the plan. So was his Chief of Staff, General Schmidt von Knobelsdorf. The two had been yoked together since 1914, as part of the deal whereby the prince had been allowed a field command in the first place. The young Wilhelm had been summoned by his father, the kaiser, who had informed him:

I have entrusted you with the supreme command of the Fifth Army. You get Lieutenant-General Schmidt von Knobelsdorf as Chief of the General Staff. Whatever he advises you, you must do.

10. *The Crown Prince reviewing his troops (Q 23775)*

This powerful if somewhat shadowy figure was a confidant of Falkenhayn in a manner entirely unavailable to the Kaiser's son. Thus when Falkenhayn, having won agreement to his proposed offensive from the Kaiser himself at Christmas 1915, returned from Potsdam to his operational headquarters at Charleville-Mézières, it was von Knobelsdorf, not the Crown Prince, who boarded his train at Montmédy to hear the good news. The official commander of the Fifth Army was subsequently given the information second hand. With regard to the coming attack, however, for once the Crown Prince and his Chief-of-Staff were agreed. But Falkenhayn would not be moved.

Crown Prince Wilhelm, notoriously mocked as 'Little Willie', and not helped by his almost dandyish appearance, has always had a bad press. He had, however, a supporter in Winston Churchill, who wrote of him:

> He has been represented at once as a fop and a tyrant, as a callow youth and as a Moloch; as an irresponsible passenger and as a commander guilty of gross and disastrous military errors. None of these contradictory alternatives fits the truth. . . .   [N]o group of armies was more consistently successful than his; and there is evidence that his personal influence — whatever it may have been — was often thrown into the right side of the scales.

He would certainly be proved correct in regard to his views on a one-bank only attack. When later the second bank was drawn into the frame, Crown Prince Rupprecht commented in his diary: 'I hear that at Verdun the Left Bank of the Meuse is to be attacked now, too. It should have been done at once; now the moment of surprise is lost.'

The Germans needed a code-name for the operation about to be launched. The names they selected for the offensives of 1918 were oddly bland: 'Michael' for the great attack in March, 'George', subsequently downgraded to 'Georgette', for the one in April, with perhaps a little more stiffening when it came to 'Blücher' in May and 'Gneisenau' in June. For Verdun they chose 'Gericht'. The word has several translations: court of justice, law court, tribunal; *vor Gericht stellen* is to arraign, to bring to trial; the phrase *das Jüngste Gericht* means Judgement Day, the Last Judgement, Doomsday. Historians have been tempted to extrapolate from such a richness of meaning: hence 'execution place' has been suggested as a possible translation, or even 'scaffold'. Whatever gloss might be put on it, there is no doubt that the name was grimly appropriate to the operation for which as 1915 moved into 1916 the preparations were in full swing.

4 The preparations

If there was ambiguity in Germany's basic plan, there was great precision in the assembling of her guns. The bombardment that would open the Verdun offensive would be the greatest in military history. And that at least would target both banks of the Meuse.

Altogether 1220 artillery pieces were in position when the attack began. But more important than the number was the nature of the weapons brought up by road or train in the weeks of countdown.   At the lighter end of the scale were the 77mm field guns, almost as effective in dealing with enemy infantry as the French 75s, that legendary French artillery piece recognized throughout the war by ally and enemy as a quality performer. When it came to heavier weapons, however, Falkenhayn's forces had a clear and ominous superiority. First, there were the 13cm guns, which fired shells which flew fast and low like a flat stone thrown at water, while by contrast there were mine throwers whose missiles could be seen approaching in slow and clumsy spirals, though such forewarning was of little use as they could wreak destruction over a wide area. While these weapons would target the infantry, the larger long-muzzled 15cm guns would hammer at artillery positions and at the routes of supply. Next in scale were the 21cm guns, formidable, quick-firing and easy to move, described by Alistair Horne as 'for the French *poilu*. . . the most familiar and feared weapon at Verdun'. Seventeen Austrian 'Skoda' 30.5cm mortars added to the array, while there were also two 38cm (equivalent to 15-inch) naval guns, concealed in deep woodland from which they could hurl their long-range projectiles virtually undetected. At the top of the scale was the 42cm howitzer, the biggest artillery piece to be used in the war. a product, like the naval guns, of the famous armaments firm of Krupp of Essen.

This 'sawed-off bloated giant' (to quote the historian Barbara Tuchman) had been developed 'in iron secrecy' as far back as 1909. In its original form it had to be transported by rail in two sections each requiring its own locomotive. For its intended use as a siege gun it had to be embedded in concrete with a clearance several yards deep in the rear to absorb its recoil. Once thus installed, it could only be released from its concrete standing by blasting. Now modernised and capable of being moved by road, and with a range of between 9.3 and 12.5 kilometres, thirteen of these monsters would take part in the coming offensive.

It would not be incorrect to say that they had already played a key role in the Verdun battle before a salvo was fired.

When the Germans marched into Belgium in August 1914, they found their hoped-for rapid advance frustrated by the Belgian fortresses of Liège and Namur. The Krupp 42cms, assisted by the Skoda 30.5cms, were called up to take out the forts defending these two

11. 42cm German howitzer, popularly known as 'Big Bertha' (Q 65817)

historic towns and proceeded to do so with devastating effect. A prominent citizen of Liège who saw one of the Krupp guns dragged into the town in order to reduce one of its remaining bastions, Fort Loncin, described the awesome scene:

> The monster advanced in two parts, pulled by 36 horses. The pavement trembled. The crowd remained mute with consternation at the appearance of this phenomenal apparatus. . . . Hannibal's elephants could not have astonished the Romans more! The soldiers who accompanied it marched stiffly with an almost religious solemnity. . . [I]t was carefully mounted and scrupulously aimed. Then came the frightful explosion; the crowd was flung back, the earth shook like an earthquake and all the window panes in the vicinity were shattered. . . .

Expected to hold up the German advance by two weeks, the defence of Liège did so by only two days. Similar execution was subsequently wrought on the forts of Namur. Overall those apparently brief delays would prove highly significant, in that they helped to force the fatal adaptation of Germany's strategic plan whereby her then military Chief, General von Moltke — nephew of the Field Marshal of that name who had masterminded the Prussian victory in 1870 — abandoned the attempt to encircle Paris and pulled his forces across to the north instead. This offered the French, assisted by the British, the

Original-Aufnahme vom Kriegsschauplatz.
Die durch ein einziges 42 cm Geschoss zerstörten Betondecken
eines Panzerturmes des Forts Loucin.

Kr. 86.
VERLAG VON
GUSTAV LIERSCH & C?
BERLIN, S.W.

12. *Fort Loncin, Liège; official German photograph showing the results of 'Big Bertha's' attentions, August 1914 (Q 65817)*

chance to strike hard at the faltering Germans in the crucial battle of early September which became known as 'the miracle of the Marne'. But before that, to the French, watching from across the frontier, the fate of Liège and Namur had seemed to offer an important military lesson — a lesson reinforced nearer home when France's own biggest and most modern fort, Manonviller, south east of Nancy, was forced into surrender in similar fashion. Forts were clearly not what they had been cracked up to be. They were obvious targets, which could be easily pinpointed and mercilessly destroyed. A serious reappraisal began as a result of which the carefully laid, long nurtured schemes by de Rivières out of Vauban fell into disfavour. There thus came about the curious paradox that the sophisticated defences of the fortress targeted by Falkenhayn as France's pride and joy were not primed and ready when the vital hour struck but were undermanned, stripped of most of their guns and generally in serious disarray.

The change took some time to bring about. It was on 5 August 1915 that Verdun ceased to be a fortress in its own right and became instead the centre of *Région Fortifiée de Verdun,* which stretched from the edge of the Argonne in the west down to St Mihiel in the south. Over the following months forty-three heavy and eleven foot artillery batteries were withdrawn, while most of the forts' counterscarp machine-guns and cannon were given to the field armies. Not that Verdun was now a pushover, but it was not the proud cordon bleu fortress it had been.

Ironically, the French general most associated with this switch of emphasis was the one who had come with the highest credit out of the 'miracle of the Marne', General Joseph Jacques Césaire Joffre.

13. General Joffre, portrayed as 'Organizer of the Victory': a tribute to his fame in 1914 as the hero behind 'the miracle of the Marne' (Imperial War Museum Department of Art)

As it happened, Joffre's declining faith in forts coincided with an increasing belief in himself. The Marne had made him not merely a French but also an international hero. Jean de Pierrefeu, editor of the daily communiqué issued from Joffre's headquarters, has left a striking account of the cult that grew up around this overweight, heavily moustached, humbly-born soldier from the Pyrenees following his stemming of the German tide in 1914:

> For two years, the whole world all but idolized the victor of the Marne. . . . There came boxes of candies from leading confectioners all the world over, crates of champagne, wines from the best vintages, fruits, game, clothes, all kinds of articles and tools, smokers' items, ink wells, and paper-weights. Every country was sending its speciality. . . .
>
> The letters, too, written in all sorts of writings and styles, came from all over the world. They were full of emotion, and overflowed with thankfulness, love and adoration. People called him 'Saviour of the World', 'Father of the Country', 'Executor of God's Will', 'Benefactor of Mankind', etc. These attributes were given him not only by the French, but also by Americans, Argentines, Australians, etc. Thousands of children, without telling their parents, wrote to him and sent him their love: most of them called him 'Our Father'! . . . To all these childish minds, Joffre appeared like Saint George slaying the dragon. It can be said that he actually embodied the victory of good over evil, of light over darkness in the conscience of men.

Such adulation seems hard to credit. Central to it, undoubtedly — though this hardly explains the international response — was the awareness that a mere forty or so years earlier Germany (or rather at that time Prussia) had reached out a long arm towards Paris and had completely encircled it. A city which saw itself as an Athens of high culture was then subjected to a degrading siege in which its citizens had been reduced to eating cats, rats and mice. This had been followed by the divisive episode of the Commune, which had culminated in what became in effect a one-city civil war, in the course of which twenty thousand Parisians were slaughtered by their fellow countrymen in a shameful act of political (as opposed to ethnic) cleansing. This two-fold disaster had left a deep wound on the French psyche. By his success at the Marne 'Papa' Joffre, as he became widely known, had saved the nation from a recurrence of such dreadful, all too recent horrors. The fact that he had served as a junior gunner officer in the 1870-71 siege, during which he had helped man the Paris ramparts, could only give him an extra cachet. He had suffered with his people and so was well qualified to lead them to, or in this case preserve the integrity of, the promised land.

His quasi-Biblical gloss did not affect his eating habits, however. On Good Friday, 1915, he noticed that a meatless meal had been put on his table. He flew into a rage and demanded meat at once, saying 'I am a republican general!' 'Which, of course', wrote Pierrefeu, who tells the story, 'did not prevent him from being very tolerant regarding the personal convictions of his officers'.

However, the year 1915, following 'entrenchment' and the establishing of the situation of virtual siege-warfare, which would pertain until the war's last nine months, had not been a good one for Joffre, nor for any other commander on the Western Front. All attempts to break the military log-jam had failed. Meanwhile the atmosphere of the war had been worsened, in fact had been literally polluted, by the advent of poison gas. But 1916, Joffre devoutly hoped, would promise better things: a miracle on the Somme, perhaps, to equal that on the Marne, with the British, hitherto in his view seriously under-engaged, helping the cause by matching their French partners man for man and blow for blow.

He was therefore less than pleased when reports began to circulate to the effect that the Germans might strike first, and at Verdun: a sector which he had decided was not one of great importance and which had now been relieved of much of its artillery for use elsewhere. The Head of the French Intelligence Services, General Dupont, appeared to have strong evidence of German preparations in the vicinity of Verdun. Enemy units and batteries were being steadily reinforced; élite divisions were massing; heavy Austrian howitzers were arriving transferred from the Eastern front; extensive field works were being undertaken. However, as Pierrefeu would state in his remarkably honest and forthright account:

> With their habitual scepticism towards the Second [Intelligence] Bureau, whom they accused of taking too dramatic a view of the situation, the Third [Operational] Bureau, refused to allow themselves to be hypnotized by Verdun. Champagne and Artois were equally possible as theatres of operations. Did the commanders in these sections not express the same fear of being attacked as those round Verdun? Was it not the habit of all to believe themselves the objective of the enemy?

14. *German naval gun, mounted on a field-gun carriage, being brought to the front by special train (Q 23798)*

Meanwhile, behind the German front, as well as the trains bringing up the heavy artillery, and all the other necessities of battle, from bombs to barbed wire or from sandbags to cement, the troop trains were running.

Railways in Germany had been built from the start with a view to their military potential. In the event of war their prime purpose was to get the armies to the frontiers as rapidly as possible. As well as train and station staff they employed a highly trained corps of telegraphists whose task was to ensure excellent communication. Railways had played their part in 1870 and in 1914 they had done so again, bringing the troops to their points of invasion with stunning efficiency and speed. Now they were to make their vital contribution to the solution of the immense logistical problems facing those organizing the offensive against Verdun.

In his account of the battle (which at times reads more like a documentary novel than a straight history) the French historian Georges Blond tried to peer inside those trains, packed with German soldiers, rolling slowly towards the Verdun front in the weeks before the fighting began:

> In the passenger cars, which carried commissioned and non-commissioned officers, gas jets were burning. Airplanes might easily have spotted the caterpillar-like motion of the train, but in February 1916, few airplanes flew by night. In the freight cars, in defiance of orders, the soldiers had set up lanterns on the straw in order to play cards. . . Someone occasionally peered through a crack in the side of the car and tried to make out the features of the landscape. Wooded hills and valleys and trees. . . 'Is that a French tree or a German tree?' The landscape was very much the same, the same clods broken by the same

15. *Narrow gauge railway behind the German front; the one shown was in the Argonne region but there were numerous such railways built behind the Verdun front in 1916 (Q 45541)*

plow, the same foliage, the same dog barking in the farmyard at night. . . .

Sometimes the trains came to a stop in a station. They stopped at Sedan, Neufchâteau, Bastogne, Arlon, Luxembourg, Longwy, Thionville, Briey, Conflans, Chambley, and Thiaucourt. The men nearest the doors leaped to the platform, looking for a drinking fountain, a canteen, a latrine, anything that might furnish an excuse to stretch their legs and ask questions, although their sergeants warned them not to go too far because the train would leave soon. Officers made hasty purchases of cigars and then returned to their seats. The canteens were taken by storm. When several trains arrived simultaneously at the same station, the men shouted to one another, their warm breath forming a mist in the cold air; even the officers leaned out of their windows to exchange greetings.

As the trains rumbled on, the inevitable questions were raised. Where were they going, and for what purpose? Were they perhaps merely reinforcing a key sector against a possible French attack? The nearer they got to their points of disembarkation, the surer they were that they were there for something more positive and dangerous than that. Meanwhile, in the minds of the soldiers glancing nervously at the passing landscape, increasingly the focus appeared to be — Verdun; and that, they knew, would be no easy target:

Most of them felt that the dark lodestar which had drawn men out of the heart of Germany and even from the Russian front was going to turn into a furnace. Verdun had been the great block to the 1914 invasion, untouched and untouchable even when the German troops had nearly reached Paris, and ever since, on a semi-circle stretching northward and eastward, it had held them at bay, like a crouching dog, by its growl alone. An attack on the strongest point of the enemy line must have some strategic reason. Every officer, even the most close-mouthed, foresaw a colossal bloodletting.

First-hand documentary evidence is somewhat harder to come by, though hints of what it must have been like to be a German soldier heading for the front in early 1916 occurs in the brief but eloquent diary of Reserve Lieutenant W. Weingartner, 38th *Minenwerfer* (Minethrower) Company, 38th Jaeger Division, XI Corps. (It was found in an abandoned German dugout in Palestine in 1918, probably — it must be presumed — following the death of its author.) He started it on his arrival in France, on 4 January. He was not involved in the Verdun action in the first stage, but knew that he might be drawn into serious fighting at any time. His diary also serves as a reminder that the British and French were not the only nationalities to fight convinced that they were doing so in a righteous and honourable cause:

> Now the war has started for me. I shall know it very soon.
> I left Berlin very early in the morning of December 30th feeling very depressed and everyone rather overwrought and many mothers in tears. The bells of a church in Berlin were ringing and the thought of it is always in my mind.   I feel so proud of my country and even Dora [his horse] seems to know how I feel.
> There were three trainloads of us and it took some hours to get settled. We went through many Berlin stations and stopped at each a long time. Every station was crowded with people — young and old — some very cheerful and some very sad. It was an unforgettable sight.
> Quicker and quicker we went towards the west. On the 31st in the morning we arrived at Oberhausen. We shall always remember it because of the good breakfast we had there. In Düsseldorf we had a short rest which we were glad of. Next day we went towards the Rhine and it was a beautiful sight with the sun shining. We crossed the bridge singing *Die Wacht am Rhein* and it sounded lovely and one cannot describe our thoughts as we remembered our ancestors.

Once in France he was soon aware of the animosities, on both sides, that underlay the current war situation; he found himself in a town apparently bombarded by the French to disrupt its use by the Germans who had occupied it (though it should be added that it would be more thoroughly 'wasted' by the Germans when they withdrew from the area a year or so later):

> The first thing we saw were the ruins of Coucy le Château — France, why did you do this? Because of your rage and hatred of us? Well for all you do to us we will repay you!

16. German 30.5cm howitzer being prepared for action (Q 5556)

Minor skirmishes were all that he experienced in his first weeks at the front — the full horror would come later — but even these produced their fatalities and their angry response. Having recorded the funeral of a fellow officer he commented:

> There is one Lieutenant called Marten, who hates the French. He says 'May the devil take them, it is they who have made an end to all peace'.

In the period of relative calm before the battle, various other characters appeared briefly on the stage, to make, or fail to make, their point, and then disappear.

One who had already gone some months before was the former Governor of Verdun, General Coutanceau. When the commander of the Group of Armies East, General Dubail, had expressed the now prevailing doctrine that forts such as those at Verdun had no value, Coutanceau had demurred and been promptly dismissed. His successor, General Herr, was firmly informed by Dubail on his appointment: 'Strongholds, destined to be invested, have no longer a rôle to play'. All this might have been of less significance if a serious attempt had been made to substitute sound trench defences, of a kind that pertained over most of the Western Front, for the now disregarded forts. But that was not the case. Trench lines had been prepared in front of the forts but they were distinctly less than adequate; certainly they were not primed to face a sophisticated attack. The last weeks before the battle even saw the unhappy General Herr desperately trying to construct some reasonable reserve defences *to the rear of Verdun,* first on the left and then on the right bank of the Meuse. At least if the Germans struck there would be some means of preventing a

17. French 105mm gun, Verdun sector, 1916 (Q 69619)

walkover. However, the men available to carry out the work were, for the most part, the battle-worn, cast-off soldiery of other fronts, who expected an easy rather than a hard-working life on being moved to what was now widely perceived as a backwater sector. Appeals to French Headquarters — the *Grand Quartier Général*, or G.Q.G. — produced neither sympathy nor help; on the contrary they were likely to prompt requests to give away yet more batteries.

Enter one of the tragic hero-figures of the Verdun story, commemorated and honoured because he foresaw the disaster which was about to happen and then fell victim to it.

A dozen kilometres to the north of Verdun, in a clearing a hundred metres into woodland from a minor road rising into the Meuse Heights, stands a small stone memorial, unusual among the many public remembrances of the Verdun battle in that it refers just to one man. It bears the message: '*Ici est tombé le Lt Col Driant*': 'Here fell Lieutenant-Colonel Driant'. Émile Driant had been an outstanding infantry officer but failure to achieve the promotion he expected and believed he deserved had prompted him to resign his commission. He had then become a parliamentary Deputy, for the Lorraine town of Nancy, in which role he devised the draft bill which instituted the Croix de Guerre. He had also written several books on war, futuristic and anti-British in tone, under the anagrammatized pen name of Captain Danrit. In 1914 he rejoined as a reserve officer and 1916 found him, now over sixty, commanding the 56th and 59th battalions of *Chasseurs à Pied* — roughly the equivalent of the rifle regiments of the British Army or the Jaeger regiments of the German — at a peacetime beauty-spot called the Bois des Caures. The wood, being on the right bank, constituted part of the front line directly facing the projected German attack.

As far back as August 1915 Driant had begun a campaign of protest, using his political connections to rattle complacency in high places. The poverty of the French defences in front of Verdun were, in his view, plain to see, and he saw no virtue in pretending otherwise. In a letter to the President of the Chamber of Deputies, who was also a personal friend, he warned: '[W]e are doing everything, day and night, to make our front inviolable. . . but there is one thing about which one can do nothing; *the shortage of hands.* . . . If our front line is carried by a massive attack, our second line is inadequate and we are not succeeding in establishing it; *lack of workers* and I add: *lack of barbed wire.*' He succeeded only in bringing on his head the wrath of Joffre, furious at serving soldiers, even distinguished ones, 'bringing to the Government, by channels other than the hierarchic channel, complaints or protests concerning the execution of my orders. . . . It is calculated to disturb profoundly the spirit of discipline in the Army'. Commenting on this subject and on the subsequent outcome, Alistair Horne has written: 'Probably only Driant's heroic death saved him from the ignominy of a court martial, securing for him instead immortality among the French martyrs.'

Meanwhile on the far side of the now neglected forts the German preparations continued. Ironically, while the French showed increasing disinterest in their own concrete earthworks, the Germans were constructing *Stollen*; elaborate, shell-proof underground chambers which would house the infantry until the time came for them to move forward to the jumping-off trenches. The hapless General Herr got wind of these from deserters, often Alsatians with no sympathy for the German cause, but when he passed on the information to G.Q.G. it was dismissed as being of little importance. Doubtless they were for defensive purposes only.

So the stage, prepared with prodigious attention to detail on one side, and almost ignored on the other, was now set. Indeed, the Operational 3rd Brigade, irritated by interference by the Government and such lobbyists as former Deputy Driant, was inclined to welcome a strike against Verdun should the Germans be so unwise as to make one. As Jean de Pierrefeu put it:

> As a matter of fact, there was complete confidence. . . [T]he Staff longed for the attack to take place. 'If only those confounded Boche would attack it would at least silence the agitators in Parliament and the War Office.'

There was more such arrogance to come:

> At last on the eve of the famous day an increase of artillery fire became noticeable on the whole Verdun sector. I remarked upon it in the *communiqué* which I submitted to Colonel Renouard. He nodded with the calm and smiling air he assumed when big things were in the wind. Turning to the officers present, he said: 'It is coming now, but if the Germans attack at Verdun, what a hornet's nest they'll fall upon!'

18. 'Poilus':
*French
soldiers in a
dug-out, late
1915
(Q 49296)*

19. 'Les Boches': *German
troops emerging from their
quarters en route for the
front (Q 29942)*

5 The battle: first phase

The assault was scheduled for 12 February, but a bout of severe wintry weather forced repeated postponements. There were thus several eves before battle, the traditional time for men to write what might well become last letters home. On the 18th, a young German soldier, Otto Heinebach, a former student of philosophy, wrote to his family in Berlin, with what he thought would be one full day of anxious waiting before action, though in the event it turned out to be two. The sentiments he expressed were not especially German; they might have been written by men of any nationality involved in that war — there would be many such written later in 1916 on the British front in the countdown to the Somme:

> In the dressing-station dugout, where we are all lying for a day in reserve, it is stiflingly hot. The place is crammed with men. Outside it is raining as usual. A little while ago we heard that the attack had again been postponed for twenty–four hours, and just now came word that it was fixed for the 20th. That seems to be the final decision, though there is no sign of any improvement in the weather. Packs are to be worn, but everything not absolutely necessary is to be left behind.
>
> I say good-bye to you, my dear Parents and Brothers and Sisters. Thanks, most tender thanks for all that you have done for me. If I fall, I earnestly beg of you to bear it with fortitude. Reflect that I should probably never have achieved complete happiness and contentment. Perhaps my life would, to the very end, have been cleft by the impossibility of reconciling desire and fulfilment, struggle and attainment, yearning and actuality. . . .
>
> And so, in imagination, I extinguish the lamp of my existence on the eve of this terrible battle. I cut myself out of the circle of which I have formed a beloved part. The gap which I leave must be closed; the human chain must be unbroken. I, who once formed a small link in it, bless it for all eternity. And till your last days remember me, I beg you, with tender love. Honour my memory without gilding it, and cherish me in your loving faithful hearts.

Frequently such letters had no need to be sent — if they survived they did so as curiosities; but in this case the letter would be delivered.

Monday 21 February 1916. A dry still winter morning. Not a mouse stirring on the Meuse Heights. In the French lines the usual routines were under way. It seemed a day like any other. The Allied communiqués had nothing extraordinary to report: in Belgium a failed attempt by

20.   *German heavy gun firing from deep cover (Q29970)*

the Germans to cross the Yser Canal; on the distant Eastern front hard fighting with some Russian gains. However, the famous phrase *Im Westen Nichts Neues* — 'Nothing New in the West' — immortalized by the Germans novelist Erich-Maria Remarque and translated into English as 'All Quiet on the Western Front', was not to apply to 21 February 1916.

The first shell of the battle was aimed not at the front but at Verdun itself. Fired by a 38 cm naval gun concealed in the Forest of Spincourt thirty kilometres away, it failed to find its intended target, a key bridge over the Meuse, and exploded in the courtyard of the Bishop's palace, knocking off a corner of the cathedral. This would now be labelled (and explained away as) collateral damage, but as in the case of recent examples of that phenomenon, it would not be good for the reputation of those responsible for it. It was seen and would be denounced as yet another example of German 'frightfulness'. A more defensible salvo followed which hit the Verdun railway station; lines of communication have long been recognized as a legitimate military target, so against that strike there could be no complaint. These opening shots signalled a tactic that would continue. Steadily, sporadically, the shells kept falling. They would continue to do so, slowly beating the town into the ground, so that ultimately Verdun would become a city of destruction almost, if not quite, in the style of Ypres.

The real action of 21 February took place elsewhere. Crown Prince Wilhelm later recorded the progress of events:

> Shortly before 8 a.m. on February 21st the General Commanding the Artillery, General Schnabel, and the corps commanders received their instructions to

21. *The Cathedral of Notre Dame, Verdun, showing damage from German shelling (HU 82678)*

open fire. In the clear winter air the thunder of the howitzers opened the chorus, which rapidly swelled to such a din that none of those who heard it had ever experienced hitherto.

The enemy, surprised by the annihilating volume of our fire, only shelled a few villages at random. At 5 p.m. our barrage jumped on to his second line, and the skirmishers and shock troops of all the corps left their trenches. The material effect of our bombardment had been, as we discovered later, rather below our expectations, as the hostile defences in the wooded country were in many cases too well concealed; the moral effect, however, was immense. Everywhere the infantry encountered only slight resistance.

The Crown Prince's cool, understated description covered a fearsome reality. Between 7 a.m. and 4 p.m. French time (which will be used throughout this narrative), lay nine hours of the most severe and sustained bombardment, with each of the long list of German guns seeking out its particular targets. This is how the start of the battle was described by the French historian Jacques Péricard:

Six German observation balloons direct the firing. Several French aircraft appear, but they soon have to make a getaway before the vast numbers of German planes which fill the sky. 'There are gun-batteries everywhere,' they report on their return; 'they follow each other non-stop; the flames from their shells form an unbroken sheet,'

The woods of Consenvoye, Étrayes, Crépion, Moirey, Hingrey, Le Bretuil, le petit de Gremilly, the forests of Mangiennes and of Spincourt, the hillsides of Romagne, of Morimont, the woods of Tillale-Baty, seem to be blowing a gale of flame without interruption. From now on, the expression, 'the bombardment of Verdun', will live on in the language of the combatants to describe, not a rain of shells, but a hailstorm, a cataract.

Péricard's account carries an important implication; that Verdun above all would be a gunners' battle. This shattering opening bombardment was the first of countless others. The French infantry would spend far more time cowering under what the Germans called *Trommelfeuer* — 'drumfire' — than fulfilling the role they had trained for. The Germans would suffer in their turn. This description by a liaison officer of the 164th Regiment of Infantry, G. Champeaux, who was at Herbebois on the right flank of the battle-front, records the kind of experience that was almost universal in the French lines on 21 February 1916:

The trees are cut down like wisps of straw; some shells come crashing out of the smoke; the dust produced by the upheaval of the earth creates a fog which prevents us from seeing very far. All day, we are bent double. We have to abandon our shelter and go to ground in a deep crater; we are surrounded by wounded and dying men whom we are totally unable to help.

An officer of the 243rd Regiment, H. Hovine, was just to the west of Champeaux, in the Bois de Wavrille:

By 3 o'clock in the afternoon, the section of the wood which we occupied and which, in the morning, was completely covered with bushes, looked like the timber-yard of a saw-mill; a little later, I had lost most of my men.

The bombardment was such that men could feel that they were being attacked, not so much by a mass of individual shells, as by one powerful force. So it seemed to the soldier-writer Maurice Genevoix:

Above all, the dominant sensation is of the *weight* of the thing coming down. . . . A monstrous creature sweeps towards us, so heavy that its flight alone flattens us in the mud.

The opening bombardment was directed at both banks of the Meuse. The whole Verdun region, in a great arc from Malancourt in the west to Les Éparges to the south, was severely pounded. Thus it is not surprising that just as the great bombardment preceding the

Somme would be heard in London, so the thunder at Verdun was distinctly audible from almost a hundred miles off in the Vosges. But the heaviest artillery fire was directed at the eight-mile zone on the right bank where the infantry were to make their attack. Here the bombardment was virtually blanket in its coverage and the Germans were lavish in the expenditure of shells. Thus no fewer than 80,000 fell that day on the Bois de Caures, where, as one historian put it, 'trees were shattered, uprooted and hurled aside like skittles'. The sight of such a massive, non-stop barrage could leave remarkable images in the minds of those who survived. For Corporal Maurice Brassard, of the 56th Chasseurs, the front line under fire reminded him of 'the linked chains of a gigantic rosary, of which the beads were formed by the explosions of the shells.' But on a grimmer note he added, recording the fate of one small group of his men: 'Out of five *poilus*, two have been buried alive in their shelter, two are more or less wounded, and the fifth is waiting his turn.'

Corporal Brassard was one of the NCOs of Lieutenant-Colonel Driant. At his Command Post in the wood, Driant, having written his final orders, received absolution from his chaplain and waited resignedly for his premonitions to be justified. Sometime that day he also managed a last letter to his wife. 'The hour is near,' he wrote: 'I feel very calm. . . In our wood the front trenches will be taken in a few minutes.' His main concern was for his men: 'My poor battalions, spared until now!'

At 4 p.m. the German infantry attacked. In contrast to the intensive nature of the bombardment, it was curiously tentative. Patrols and probing parties, accompanied by flamethrower detachments, felt their way forward, investigating the results of the barrage rather than trying to capitalize on them. Thus Driant's battalions were spared the instant infantry assault he feared. There was an exception in one sector where, conforming to what had become by this time expected Western Front practice, storm troops were thrown forward following the cessation of the bombardment. This was near the extreme western end of the front where the commander was General von Zwehl, heading the VII Reserve Corps. He had won the highest German award — the *Pour le Mérite* — for his capture of the French frontier fortress of Maubeuge in 1914 and had later performed outstandingly during the crucial Battle of the Marne. He was therefore aware that a touch of independence in the running of affairs in his sector would not be held against him, particularly if he met with success. He did so, though it took five hours to wrest control of the Bois d'Haumont, which lay just to the north-west of Driant's Bois des Caures.

In fact, despite the awesome nature of the opening bombardment, 21 February did not prove quite as successful as the German commanders had hoped. The assumption was that their infantry would find nothing but corpses in the French front line. In numerous areas they were in for a swift disillusion, so that a day in which losses were expected to be light nevertheless managed to produce a 600 casualty count by midnight. For there were many among the French who had come safely through the *Trommelfeuer* unharmed and with their motivation unaffected, so that the advancing German troops frequently found themselves surprised by machine-gun bullets or grenades from groups of men holding a fragment of undestroyed trench or a defiant defence position in a corner of a shattered wood.

Few woods had suffered more by the end of the day than Driant's Bois des Caures. Now generously re-endowed with a rich covering of trees the wood almost effortlessly conceals its grim contact with history, so that it is difficult to imagine it in the state in which Driant and his men found it when during lulls in the bombardment they emerged to contemplate their changed surroundings: broken stumps, devastated ground, here and there fragments of broken men. That they were able to emerge at all was largely due to Driant's wisdom in laying out his defences in small redoubts and strongholds, not in a continuous line of trenches as was now normal practice along most of the Western Front.

They even managed a counter-attack that evening in the course of which they captured some soldiers of a Hessian Regiment who had been so confident following their circumspect advance that they had settled for the night in a section of the former French front line. The success, however, brought daunting information, one prisoner divulging that there would be a major attack at noon on the following day. As if to underline the accuracy of the intelligence received, the German guns opened up again at nightfall. Driant sent a brief message by runner to his divisional commander, General Bapst: 'We shall hold against the Boche, although their bombardment is infernal'.

Abandoning their position being out of the question, Driant's Chasseurs awaited their almost inevitable fate. Duly on the following afternoon, after a further heavy bombardment, the Germans, now clearly meaning more serious business than they had done the previous day, stormed the Bois des Caures. Seeing the situation was becoming hopeless, Driant instructed the survivors to break up into three groups and make their way through the wood to the village of Beaumont-en-Verdunois, a little over a kilometre to the rear. As Driant himself was about to leave, one of his men, Chasseur Papin, was struck by a bullet. Driant took a dressing from his pocket and put it on the wound. A Sergeant Pioneer of the 58th Chasseurs, Jules Hacquin, described what happened next:

> I had just fallen in a shellhole when a sergeant who was accompanying Colonel Driant and was walking a pace or two in front of him fell in the same hole. This sergeant, he told me afterwards, was called Coisnes and he belonged to the 56th Chasseurs.
>
> After having seen the sergeant jump in the hole, I distinctly saw Colonel Driant on the edge of the same hole throw out his arms exclaiming: 'Oh! my God!', then he made a half turn and collapsed behind the hole, facing the wood.
>
> His body being stretched out flat, we could not see it from inside the hole, owing to the amount of earth that had been thrown up all around.
>
> Realizing the Colonel had been wounded, Coisnes and I at once made what efforts we could to remove with our bare hands the earth which concealed the colonel from us. We wanted to get him down into the shell-hole with us without leaving the hole ourselves.
>
> When we had cleared enough earth to be able to look out, we could see the colonel. He gave no sign of life, blood was flowing from a wound in his head and also from his mouth. He had the colour of a dead man and his eyes were half closed.
>
> The time must have been about 16.30 hrs.

As the historian Richard Holmes has written, the battle had its first hero.

But it also had its other anonymous heroes. Driant's soldiers were not young recruits; they were mostly reservists who had served their time, had then joined the territorial reserve and had returned to the colours at the outbreak of war. Since their re-enlistment they had rarely been out of the line, and many of them carried the extra burden of being citizens of the occupied territories, where they had families of whom they had heard no news for over one and a half years. It is small wonder that they fought with a fierce determination and wrote a page in the history of the Verdun battle for which they have long been honoured.

A hint of their gallantry and commitment survives in the curiously eloquent inscription carved on the reverse side of the monument marking the point where Driant was killed: *'Ils sont tombés silencieux sous le choc comme une muraille'*. The word *'choc'* in this context implies the shock of the attack, *'silencieux'* expresses their stoic fortitude; while *'muraille'* is perhaps best translated in this context as 'a high defensive wall'. Thus a rough, if inelegant translation might be: 'They fell without complaint like a great wall': a not unfitting epitaph for the heroic defenders of the Bois des Caures.

There were other losses on the 22nd: the village of Haumont, and two woods, the Bois de Champneuville and, down by the Meuse, the Bois de Brabant. On the 23rd the litany of loss continued: Herbebois, Wavrille and Brabant village. Samogneux, also a riverside village, was the next to fall. Here, in the confusion of battle and with the best of intentions, a tragic mistake led to Frenchmen killing Frenchmen. Hearing that the Germans had taken it, General Bapst ordered its immediate recapture. But when General Herr, trying desperately as overall commander to cope with a situation changing by the hour, assembled his guns on the other side of the river with a view to avenging the village's seizure, he was unaware of the efforts being made to reclaim it. The French retook the village to find themselves being targeted with pinpoint accuracy by their own artillery. 'Cease fire' rockets fired to call off the bombardment had no effect. Begun at 0.15 on the 24th, the French barrage cleared the way for the Germans with amazing speed and thoroughness and by 3 a.m. Samogneux was ready for German re-occupation. It was a sad but far from unique example of what has come to be known, not without a touch of irony, as 'friendly fire'.

Samogneux would rise from its ashes, but these first days of fighting saw the destruction of a number of villages which would never be resurrected. They would become officially described as *'villages détruits'* and would ultimately be honoured with the epitaph standard to the crosses of all France's dead: *'Mort pour la France'*. Haumont, seized on the 22nd, was the first to fall, taken by General von Zwehl's VII Corps. Next came Beaumont, to which Lieutenant-Colonel Driant had ordered his troops to retreat in the last moments before his death on the 22nd. It fell on the 24th, but not before the French had cut swathes through the German 18th Corps by sustained machine-gun fire. Some of the village's defenders managed to fall back on Louvemont, which itself would join the list of the officially destroyed in due course.

On the eastern side of the battle zone, where Ornes, another doomed village, was already in German hands, a further one fell after bitter fighting on the 25th. This was Bezonvaux, which had had a hard history from the war's first month. On 22 August 1914, with Verdun under threat from the approaching German Army, refugees from the north had streamed through Bezonvaux and the village's inhabitants had felt compelled to join them. When the Germans subsequently seized nearby Ornes and Étain, Bezonvaux had become part of the French front-line and had been subjected to substantial bombardments. Now again in 1916 it was under murderous fire, with soldiers of the 44th Infantry Regiment, who were attempting to defend it, falling victim one by one. Their commander being wounded, their adjutant-major, Captain Dumas, assumed command. Recording the event, the Regimental History would describe how, seizing a rifle, Dumas leapt on to a wall to get a better view of the battle scene and was instantly struck by a bullet which went through both his thighs. His men wanted to evacuate him, but, in the words of the History, *'il n'est pas de ceux qu'une blessure arrête'* — 'he was not of the sort to be deterred by a mere wound'. The Germans rushed towards him, but he eluded them and made his way across the village to new lines where elements of the regiment were still maintaining a fierce resistance. Their cause, however, was hopeless; by nightfall almost all the members of the 44th had succumbed and what was left of the village was in German hands.

Bezonvaux would be reclaimed by the French at the end of the year, though by then it would be merely a smoking ruin, soon to be judged as beyond resuscitation. Haumont and Beaumont by contrast would be under German occupation until the Americans fought their way through the area in the course of the final advance of the war in November 1918.

Bezonvaux's seizure on 25 February, however, was a mere footnote to a day which would become legendary, indeed infamous, in French military history. For that day a few kilometres to the west the mighty Fort Douaumont was taken by the Germans, with scarcely a hand being raised in its defence.

6 The seizure of Fort Douaumont

No visitor to Verdun today can be left in any doubt as to the central role of Douaumont in the region's recent history. All roads, it can seem, lead to Douaumont. If there is time to go to one site only, Douaumont it has to be. The tall tapering tower of the Douaumont Ossuary dominates the horizon for miles around, much as the Thiepval Memorial catches the eye of the visitor to the Somme, except that the Douaumont landmark can be seen from further off. But the Ossuary and the immaculate cemetery in front of it are only where they are because of the fort which made Douaumont famous. That lies under a kilometre away to the north east. It is a strange sight, certainly it bears little resemblance to the massive, geometric structure it once was. It is a sprawling wreck, a beaten hulk, pummelled and distorted by artillery fire on such a scale that it is easy to accept the claim that Fort Douaumont is almost certainly the most shelled place on earth. In total, between the outbreak of war and November 1917 the fort was hit by at least 120,000 shells, of which 2000 were of the calibre of 270 mm or above.

Started in 1885 but not completed until 1913 it was conceived as the linchpin of Verdun's defences. The cost of building it, including the armour and armaments, came to a total of 6,100,000 gold francs. It was the largest of Seré de Rivière's constructions in the area, and the most prestigious.

To explore its long gloomy galleries today is a macabre experience; they drip with moisture so that one's eye is perpetually caught by myriads of tiny white stalactites hanging from the roof, their colour an unhealthy livid white. The gallery floor is never dry and there is the perpetual sound as of distant trickling water. Gaunt metal-sprung bunk-beds, three layers high, loom in dank barrack-rooms, confirming one's instinctive assumption that garrisoning such establishments was no picnic even in peacetime. A side room of lavatories — each one with its two footprints around a central hole, of a style once common in France but now happily a rarity — confirm the grim impression, even more so because of the fact that, incredibly, they were only added in 1917. Little wonder that throughout its grim heyday in 1916 the fort was plagued by a permanent unhealthy smell. Surprisingly, for a fortress vaunted for its strength, it seems singularly lacking in armament, there being only two turrets for guns of consequence, one 75mm and one 155mm, the remains of which, now half wrecked, are available for public view.

It is when one stands on the fort's sprawling battered roof — of special concrete 2.5 metres high, plus a substantial layer of earth, with a scatter of dalek-like gun-turrets jutting dramatically out of the ground — that one gets some idea of its huge dimensions and of its key position. It was a superb observation post, and it is strangely moving to look north and east over the long landscape, now forested to the horizon and almost beautiful, over which the Germans advanced in 1916. Somewhere off to the left is what remains of the village from which the fort took its name, another in the list of the *villages détruits*.

23.   Fort Douaumont in the early stages of the battle (Henry Dugard, The Battle of Verdun*)*

It is also instructive to see it from a distance, for example from the roof of its neighbouring, if smaller, defence work, Fort Vaux. Douaumont's long high profile is unmistakable on the skyline — oddly reminiscent of some great prehistoric earthwork — its tall flagpole and tricolour flag still asserting the place's importance as a symbol of French pride.

On 25 February 1916 it fell to the Germans almost by chance, and in a way that made its loss seem to those on the French side who knew the facts to be so unacceptable that from the moment the news came through it was subjected to creative re-interpretation. In short, there was a 'cover-up', a swift invocation of the 'fog of war'.

In 1914 Fort Douaumont had a garrison of six officers and 417 men. But the new policy instituted on 5 August 1915 stripped it of most of its defenders and much of its capacity for defence. Moreover, in the weeks before the battle began, the Corps of Engineers of the Verdun fortified region were implementing orders to prepare the destruction of the main works of the fort — the gun turrets, the Bourges casemates and the escarp casemates. A supply of gunpowder and explosives was prepared for this purpose and the plan to incapacitate the fort was approved on 8 February. In the meantime it was home merely to a tiny garrison of fifty-seven territorial gunners under the command of a warrant-officer, who saw their role more as one of staying where they were and surviving than in engaging in any active warfare. In fact, on 25 February the majority of them were taking cover against the prevailing shellfire in the bowels of the fort.

Thus it came about that a handful of soldiers of the German 24th Brandenburg Regiment, ignoring orders to halt on a line 750 yards to the northeast of the fort, advanced cautiously towards its outer defences, encouraged by the fact that the only obviously active

24. The battered hulk of Fort Douaumont today, with tricolour (Mrs Jenny Suddaby)

gun in the fort, its one 155mm, was firing at some distant target. Their own approach appeared not to have attracted the slightest notice. Finding an opened embrasure leading into one of the galleries a Sergeant Kunze, hoisted up by a human pyramid formed by his soldiers, ventured inside. Now the story almost touches the edge of farce, for Kunze arrested the 155mm gunners single-handed, only to see them escape in the maze of the fort's numerous underground galleries. Undeterred, he carried on exploring until the discovery of a well-provisioned mess-room provided him with a welcome late lunch. Meanwhile three officers, Lieutenants Radtke and Brandis and Captain Haupt, had also independently penetrated the fort together with a number of their men. In short order the garrison was arrested and the fort secured. First out with the astonishing good news, Brandis would ultimately win the *Pour le Mérite,* as would Captain Haupt. Radtke would fare less well, being rewarded with a signed photograph of the Crown Prince, while Kunze, the first of these few, would eventually win promotion to police inspector.

But whatever honours might accrue to the Germans involved, on the French side there was utter confusion and dismay. When deciding on the downgrading of Douaumont and, especially, on the plans for its possible destruction, the French High Command had not deemed it necessary or advisable to confide in the French people. Thus when Germany celebrated the news *'Douaumont ist Gefangen'* — 'Douaumont is Captured' with banner headlines, the ringing of church bells all over the country and a special holiday for the nation's schoolchildren, the French leadership, both military and political, had an acute public relations problem on their hands.

With hindsight, one can ask why the French did not have the courage to say that the Germans had achieved nothing of any consequence, that because Douaumont had been deliberately deprived of military significance all the enemy had done was to capture a folly,

25. One of the Fort's numerous galleries, with stalactites. *(Cliché Editions MAGE)*

a husk left to entice them, even, as it were, a decoy. But such a course was simply not possible in the political climate of the time. The casualty-less coup had to be turned into a desperate, hard-fought battle, making it inevitable that the commitment would be made that, whatever the cost, Douaumont would be reclaimed. In a telling and emotive phrase by one French historian, Douaumont became '*la forteresse défaillante que le Poilu de Verdun dut remplacer par ses poitrines*': 'the defiant fortress for which the soldiers of Verdun had to substitute their own breasts'. It has been estimated that they did so at the cost of 100,000 lives.

The tone of response when the deadly news came through was set immediately by France's Prime Minister, Aristide Briand. His statement on the subject is worth quoting at length, in that it is clear that once such an enriched version of events had been put about, and from such a high authority, there could be no going back:

> In the afternoon [of the 25th], at the very moment when the Germans thought they had obtained possession of this formidable position, at the cost of an enormous sacrifice of men, a violent counter-attack was made by one of our army corps (40,000 men) which had been held in reserve. The Germans were caught between frightful curtains of fire, 'feux de barrage', and swept by machine guns on all sides. They were taken by surprise, their advance was stopped dead. The fighting assumed Titanic proportions. Three times the Germans gained possession of their objective, and three times they were driven out. Our heroic troops fought with absolute frenzy. Our artillery, heavy and light, ploughed bloody furrows in the enemy's close ranks. At last, exhausted, mown down, their lines gradually thinning more and more, the German

armies gave way in their turn. They abandoned Champ Neuville, the Poivre Hill (two miles west of Douaumont) and the Douaumont position.

What was not denied in this farrago of invention and exaggeration, however, was that the Germans were still in the fort and had not been removed. If by the phrase 'Douaumont position', Briand had meant the *actual fort*, he would surely have said so.

Contradictory messages from official sources — from German Headquarters on the one side, and in communiqués from Paris on the other — inevitably sowed confusion in the minds of observers elsewhere. Thus on 28 February the *Daily Mirror* came out with the headline: MYSTERY OF THE FATE OF THE FORT OF DOUAUMONT, its editors clearly being baffled by the range of opposing claims. Lesser headlines clearly betrayed their uncertainty. Hence 'Verdun Fort Retaken' in one column contradicted an earlier column's 'Berlin Says French Failed to Reconquer Lost Verdun Fort'. In the event the Berlin version proved correct, and those who had been responsible for misinformation on the French side would regret their rashness in attempting to spin a clear defeat into a quasi-victory. By implying that Douaumont was under siege, and therefore liable for imminent recapture, they had done little for their cause. Jean de Pierrefeu would write:

> The truth was that there was no question of a siege. We had been compelled by the terrible fire of the enemy to withdraw our troops gradually to the rear. Besides, the Germans had dug a communication trench on the northern side of the work leading to their own lines. This incident proved to us how dangerous it was in a *communiqué* to arouse hopes that were not certain of being realized.

Meanwhile at Verdun the news had created a mood of near desperation. The sight of a rocket fired from Douaumont requesting the German artillery to hold its hand, and thus indicating that it was no longer in French hands, so dismayed the commander of the 37th African Division, General de Bonneval, whose troops had been thrown piecemeal into the battle over the preceding days with a disastrous impact on morale, that he ordered a retreat to the Belleville Ridge, the last spur of the Meuse Heights before Verdun. It was as though he were admitting the cause was all but lost. More, German aircraft lost no time in dropping leaflets on the French lines with the message: 'Douaumont has fallen. All will soon be over now. Don't let yourselves be killed for nothing.' In the town itself there was panic in the streets. One lieutenant ran amok with the cry *'Sauve qui peut!'* — the equivalent of 'every man for himself'; he was arrested for his pains. The sight of refugees pushing their pathetic prams piled with household belongings had been a commonplace in the vulnerable parts of France in 1914; now the same scenes were re-enacted at Verdun.

As for the Germans, their sense of triumph knew no bounds. The Crown Prince himself would later write that he felt that they were within a stone's throw of victory. The Kaiser himself lost no time in descending on the Crown Prince's headquarters at Stenay, clearly conveying the almost Biblical message that Wilhelm was his beloved son in whom he was well pleased. And the battle was only in its fifth day.

22. *The Battlefield of Verdun, as shown in* The Sphere, *4 March 1916. The line indicating the German advance shows Driant's Bois des Caures, left, well inside captured territory and Fort Douaumont, right, under heavy French bombardment following its seizure on 25 February. The picture also gives some idea of the difference in terrain between the right and left banks of the Meuse. (Courtesy* Illustrated London News *Picture Library)*

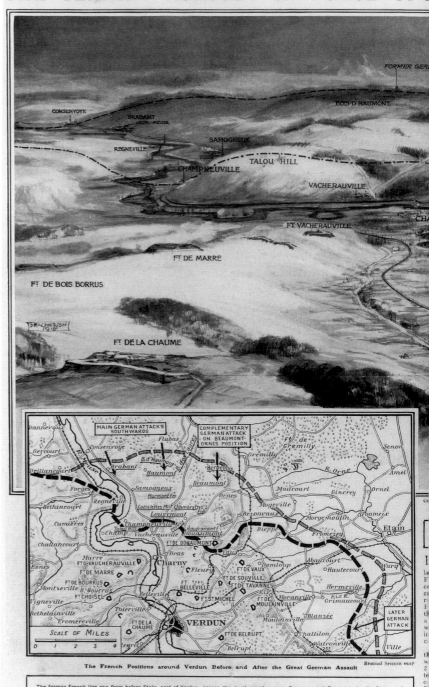

The French Positions around Verdun Before and After the Great German Assault

Special SPHERE *map*

The former French line ran from before Etain, east of Verdun, across the level country near Fromezey and Bezonvaux to the Ornes and Herbebois positions on the north. Here the country becomes more hilly as it reaches the wooded heights of the Meuse. The fighting line ran formerly along the line formed by the hills which rise towards the river from Ornes to Brabant. This line has now been withdrawn to the more southerly line around Louvemont and Douaumont, and now stretches across the Talou and Poivre hills, linking up with the former line in the flat country near Fromezey. Arrows indicate the positions of the main German attacks, the supplementary attack on Beaumont, and also of the later attack which developed south of Etain and Warq. The German attack on the Woevre forced the French line to withdraw for a short distance in the direction of Watronville and Chattilon

THE VERDUN POSITION : Special "Sphere" View and Map.

Assault on Verdun Through Brabant and Herbebois—The French Retirement to the Talou-Poivre-Douaumont Line

DRAWN BY D. MACPHERSON, 19

was also abandoned by the French. On the evening of February 23 fresh German reinforcements advanced to the support of the attacking troops, and the battle raged through the night and the following morning. In the result the French were compelled to abandon Brabant, and at the close of the day their line ran south of Samogneux and Beaumont to Ornes.

During the night of February 24 snow fell heavily; the battles of the succeeding day—Friday, the 25th—were fought in a snow-storm. As the prevailing winter winds in this corner of France are from the north-east it will easily be seen what an advantage the Germans—with their meteorological stations all behind them in the direction from which the storm would come, and with the snow beating in the face of their opponents—really had. The most desperate of all the Verdun battles was fought on this day. Fort Douaumont, on a height to the north of Verdun, was captured by the 24th Regiment of Brandenburgers, but was re-gained the following afternoon by the French.

The line held by the French on Saturday afternoon, February 26, was held inviolate against all further assaults. From Forges it ran near the railway skirting the Meuse, describing a double curve between Regneville and Champneuville. From south of the latter place the line ran over the Talou hill, north of Vacherauville, to the Poivre plateau, which was held firmly by the French against many German assaults. Around Douaumont fort—recaptured from the Germans—the line continued south-eastwards towards Hill 255, where a German subsidiary attack was threatened during the main attacks to the north. Here the French line has been withdrawn somewhat after a heavy bombardment and outpost assaults, but no big action comparable to the attack on Douaumont took place.

VERDUN—Showing the Cathedral and the Houses Lining the Meuse

Verdun is a fortress of the first class on the banks of the Meuse some thirty-five miles west of Metz. The town has an important place in European history by reason of the famous Treaty of Verdun in 843, when the possessions of Charlemagne were divided amongst his three grandsons. In 1792 the town was bombarded by the Prussians and surrendered within a few hours; in the Franco-Prussian War the town was again bombarded, but gallantly resisted for three weeks before giving way to the enemy

7 The nights of the generals

Jean de Pierrefeu's account of life at French Headquarters records a regular late night telephone conversation at this time:

> 'Well, how are things?' inquired M. Étienne. 'What does the General say?'
> 'The General is asleep,' was the invariable reply.
> 'Capital!' exclaimed M. Étienne, completely reassured. 'If things were going badly he would not sleep.'

The General in question was Joffre, and M. Étienne was a former Minister and a personal friend. It was his habit to ring French Headquarters, the G.Q.G., at Chantilly every night about eleven o'clock to enquire about the progress of the war. The General always retired to bed at ten, and only in the direst emergency did anyone dare to wake him. When such crises occurred there was an agreed procedure: after several knocks the General would awake and ask what was the matter. If persuaded that the call was of sufficient importance he would get out of bed, put on his slippers and unlock the door. If papers were handed to him he would immediately return to bed to read them. His views having been made clear, he would lock the door again and go back to sleep. All this was done without the slightest sense of crisis or stress. Thus Jean de Pierrefeu could write of the Commander-in-Chief that 'during the whole of the Verdun drama he never abandoned his serenity of manner'. If Joffre slept, France could sleep too.

On the night of 24 February it was considered imperative that the general's sleep should be disturbed. The person who insisted on rousing him was his remarkable Chief of Staff, Major-General de Castelnau. There are variant interpretations as to why he did so. One merely suggests that de Castelnau considered the situation had suddenly become much more urgent than it might have seemed and that therefore he needed immediate authority to implement certain contingency plans already agreed. A more dramatic interpretation has it that Joffre, with his known disinterest in Verdun, had virtually agreed, without consulting de Castelnau, to give up the city and let it fall, and that the latter's purpose in interrupting his C-in-C's sleep was to make him change his mind. According to the account offering this interpretation, a ridiculous scene took place with the duty officer refusing the Major-General access to the General's bedroom. At last de Castelnau was allowed to pass a brief message — 'un petit mot' — to his chief. The latter, having woken up, replied: 'Qu'il fasse comme il veut': 'Let him do what he wants.' From that moment any thought that Verdun would be abandoned as a free trophy for the enemy became history. Falkenhayn's gamble had paid off. His challenge was accepted. France would be prepared to bleed herself white in Verdun's defence.

26. Generals and
veterans. Left,
General de
Castelnau,
Chief of Staff in
1916; centre,
General Joffre,
Commander in
Chief; right,
General Pau,
commander of
the armies of
Alsace in 1914.
All three had
fought in the
Franco-Prussian
War, in which
General Pau
had lost his right
arm.
(Q 53625)

What seems indisputable is that de Castelnau left General Headquarters that night with permission to drive to Verdun there and then to sort out the crisis in person and in accordance with his own views.

Who was this man in the speeding staff car hurrying along the night-time roads in the direction of Verdun? Noël Marie Joseph Edouard, Vicomte de Currières de Castelnau, like Joffre, hailed from the Pyrenees. Like Joffre, he had served in the Franco-Prussian War; sixty-five in 1916, he was one year older than his chief. Unlike Joffre, he came from an aristocratic, military family of long standing. His intervention in the Verdun story was brief but crucial. Everything in his background and experience made him believe that a withdrawal from Verdun, even a carefully calculated one to save unnecessary bloodshed, was not an option. He, even more so than Joffre, had taken to heart the lesson of France's defeat in 1870; that once a retreat began it could become a rout; that one day the Germans might be at the gates of Verdun, the next they might be at the gates of Paris. Yet he was no mindless hawk. Earlier he had been a prime advocate of France's policy of outright attack — of *'l'offensive à outrance'* to give its formal, technical title — which proved so disastrous

THE SPHERE

AN ILLUSTRATED NEWSPAPER FOR THE HOME With which is incorporated "BLACK & WHITE"

Volume LXIV, No 843.   {REGISTERED AT THE GENERAL POST OFFICE AS A NEWSPAPER}   London, March 18, 1916.   Price Sixpence.

Copyrighted in the U.S.A.

DRAWN BY F. MATANIA FROM MATERIAL SUPPLIED, MARCH, 1916

GENERAL PETAIN—THE FRENCH COMMANDER AT VERDUN

From photographic material just received "The Sphere's" artist has been able to construct this impression of General Petain among the ruins of a battered village on the Meuse heights. General Henri Philippe Petain was born April 24, 1856, at Cauchy-à-la-Tour (Pas de Çalais), and became a lieutenant in 1883. He made steady progress in his profession, and from the command of an army corps he has passed to the command of an army engaged in one of the most herculean tasks which the present war has brought about. He is very popular with the poilus, and there is a refrain around Verdun which runs, "V'la Petain, Gare au potin"

27.   *The soldier summoned to save Verdun; General Philippe Pétain, as portrayed in* The Sphere, *18 March 1916. (Courtesy* Illustrated London News *Picture Library)*

in 1914, but when that failed he had been swift to revise his views. He had emerged from the first eighteen months of the war with his reputation intact; indeed there were some in the higher ranks of the army who would have been delighted to see de Castelnau in Joffre's place as C-in-C.

But de Castelnau saw himself more as kingmaker than king. An essential element of his mission to Verdun was to stiffen the will of those caught up in the fighting, but almost more so to prepare the way for the general whom he believed to be the best available candidate for the vital role of man of the hour. This was the then commander of the 2nd French Army, which had the virtue at that time of not being engaged in the front line because certain sectors had recently been handed over to the British. The commander in question, who would cast a long shadow over the history of twentieth-century France, was General Henri Philippe Omer Pétain.

Pétain had been a man apart for much of his career. He had never subscribed to the idea of the war of dash and *élan* which had attracted so many of his fellow officers. Taciturn, thoughtful, from the cold Nord as opposed to the more heady south, he believed, given the new kind of warfare evolving in 1914 and '15, in a strategy of realistic defence rather than one of subliminal attack, with much emphasis on artillery support and on the guaranteeing of all necessary supplies. He was also unusual among French commanders in that he was prepared to give ground where it was tactically necessary rather than to hold on to every last metre of French soil simply out of sentiment. De Castelnau sensed that Pétain's steady hand was appropriate for the present crisis, but with the key proviso that withdrawal from Verdun was not among his options. When, before dawn on the 25th, he broke his journey at the Headquarters of General Langle de Cary, Commander of Army Group Centre, at Avize, east of Châlons-sur-Marne, he wrote a brief but unambiguous order to be handed to Pétain in person on his arrival:

> The Meuse must be held on the right bank. There can be no question of any other course than of checking the enemy, cost what it may, on that bank.

Pétain told this story, quoting the above order, in his own account of the battle published in 1929, adding that 'General de Castelnau then continued on his way to Verdun, in order to draw his conclusions on the spot and to study the conditions under which the Second Army should there be employed.' His narrative continued:

> As I was available at Noailles with my staff, I thought it extremely probable that I should be assigned to the Verdun front, where the importance of the struggle and the numbers of reinforcements sent would justify the entrance into the line of a new army. On my own initiative, I had already sent the head of my intelligence service to obtain precise information concerning the course of events. Consequently I was not in the least surprised on the evening of February 24th to receive orders to send my headquarters Staff immediately on its way to Bar-le-Duc and to report in person to General Joffre on the morning of the 25th.

In a curious way, as has been deftly described by Verdun's best British chronicler, Alistair Horne, nocturnal behaviour was very much part of the equation at this early stage of the drama. Aware as he was that he might be summoned in the nation's hour of need, General Pétain, a 59-year-old bachelor but with no aversion to the pleasures of the flesh, had designated the night of Thursday 24-25 February to non-military activities. Thus while Joffre slept solo behind his locked door and de Castelnau's motorcade rumbled rapidly eastwards along the roads of Champagne, Pétain was not at his Headquarters at Noailles, but fifty kilometers to the south in a Paris hotel near the Gare du Nord, with his mistress. It was the inspired guess of his aide-de-camp, Captain Serrigny, who sped by fast staff-car down the roads to the French capital to inform the general of his date with destiny, that ensured that Pétain would be present and correct at Chantilly at eight o'clock the following morning. As in the case of Joffre, there was the discreet midnight knock on the bedroom door, the whispered messages given and received, the decision made. Pétain's characteristic response was not to panic, but to take things as they came. As Horne describes the outcome: 'Pétain, impassive, decisive, tells Serrigny he must find a bed in the hotel. In the morning they will journey together to G.Q.G. Meanwhile the night imposes its own duties. To these Pétain now returns.'

So Pétain reported to Chantilly as required, and was immediately admitted to the office of the Commander-in-Chief. The atmosphere of G.Q.G. was feverish and excited, though Joffre was his usual calm self. The General briefly summed up the situation, which seemed to him 'serious but not alarming'. He then ordered Pétain to proceed with all speed to meet with General de Castelnau, who would give him all necessary instructions. There followed yet another hurried journey, this time one held up by snow and sleet, so that it was a long and tedious one. Pétain had been told to head for Bar-le-Duc but to save time he went straight on to the village of Souilly, almost half way between Bar and Verdun, where de Castelnau was awaiting him.

If when he left Chantilly the situation had seemed serious but not alarming, by the time he reached Souilly at seven p.m. it was to face one which had taken a distinct turn for the worse. Fort Douaumont — 'the tangible expression of our reasons for confidence', as he would later describe it — had fallen to the enemy. Verdun had changed from a problem to a crisis. France could be staring into an abyss. For Pétain the nights of dalliance were over, though Joffre as ever would continue to sleep serenely in his bed at G.Q.G, while M. Étienne, presumably, would continue to telephone and continue to feel reassured.

8 The holding of the line

Pétain's arrival at Souilly was undramatic, low key, but impressive. There were no stirring speeches, no histrionics, just a quiet purposeful assumption of command. Louis Madelin, then a sergeant attached to the Souilly headquarters, recorded the event:

> On 26 February, on the staircase which goes up from the ground-floor of Souilly town hall to the first floor, which — for so many months — would house the nerve-centre of the battle, I passed a big man, pale, with very clear blue eyes beneath heavy eyelids, a firm mouth beneath a moustache whose redness was turning white, a figure straight and strong beneath the greatcoat of a soldier, brisk legs in woollen puttees. The orderlies jostled to see him: 'The new chief!' Our 'chief' he will remain, the man of Verdun, Pétain, he who said, 'We shall beat them!' ['*On les aura!*'] — and who beat them.
>
> He went right into the great hall, shook a few hands, went straight to the large map 'assembled' on the panelling, took a stick of charcoal and traced some of the sectors with as much calm as if he were savouring a landscape on a halcyon morning. Everything had culminated, after the last fighting, in confusion on the battlefield; it was necessary, above all, that order should be re-established by a rigorous delimitation of responsibilities, dividing up zones of action: 'Here, Bazelaire. Here, Guillaumat. Here, Balfourier. Here, Duchêne.' And he gave the No.1 order by which he would define the role of his army: 'To check, at all costs, the effort which the enemy is delivering on the Verdun front. Every parcel of land which might be seized by the enemy will give rise to an immediate counter-attack.' Bazelaire would be in command from Avocourt to the Meuse; Guillaumat, from the Meuse to the village of Douaumont; Balfourier, from Douaumont to Eix; Duchêne, from Eix to the Meuse downstream to Saint-Mihiel. Never had the expression, 'to seize a battle in one's hand', seemed more just to me. To see this hand seizing the reins made one feel inspired by a new warmth.

The town hall — or '*mairie*' — at Souilly remains much as it was in the First World War. Stone-built, with a steep roof and high windows, fronted by a double-sided, balustraded stone staircase almost worthy of a château, and giving directly on to the main road from Bar to Verdun, it is a place of dignity and unshowy authority. Normally assigned to the minutiae of local administration, it was of world importance for ten crucial months in 1916, and though it was established as headquarters before Pétain assumed command, it is remarkably appropriate to the man whose spirit still seems to inhabit it. His modest upper-floor command office is retained as a kind of shrine, with chair, desk and tricolour,

28. Souilly Town Hall, Headquarters of the commanding general, Verdun sector, throughout the battle (Author)

and it is easy, and moving, to think of him working there to the accompaniment of the non-stop day and night fracas from the road outside, as his men and the *matériel* of war passed below on their way to or from the battlefield. Famously he would describe how, empathizing with his soldiers in a manner not always associated with Western Front commanders, he would go down to watch them pass, with a particular affection for the younger among them:

> [M]y heart bled when I saw our young twenty-year-old men going under fire at Verdun, knowing as I did that with the impressionability of their age they would quickly lose the enthusiasm aroused by their first battle and sink into the apathy of suffering, perhaps even into discouragement, in the face of such a task as was theirs. As I stood on the steps of the Town Hall of Souilly, my post of command, which was excellently situated at the crossing of the roads leading to the front, I singled them out for my most affectionate consideration as they moved up into the line with their units. Huddled into uncomfortable trucks, or bowed under the weight of their packs when they marched on foot, they encouraged each other with songs and banter to appear indifferent. I loved the confident glance with which they saluted me. But the discouragement with which they returned! — either singly, maimed or wounded, or in the ranks of their companies thinned by their losses. Their eyes stared into space as if transfixed by a vision of terror. In their gait and their attitudes they betrayed utter exhaustion. Horrible memories made them quail. When I questioned them, they scarcely answered, and the jeering tones of old poilus awakened no response in them.

29. *Troops on the march away from the battlefront passing Souilly Town Hall watched by General Guillaumat (courtesy Souilly Town Hall)*

But that lay ahead. The first task was to make sure that he had a battle to wage, and that he had not come merely to make the best of what could all too easily have developed into an ignominious retreat.

The fighting over the next days was crucial. The Germans were determined to press home the advantage, both psychological and military, of their easy seizure of Fort Douaumont. The feeling grew that there could be a major breakthrough with even bigger prizes. But the French, stung by the Douaumont fiasco and finding that bombardments could be survived, were giving the Germans the kind of machine-gun experience that the British would later suffer on the Somme. French losses had been huge; now the German ones were beginning to catch up. And there was another factor, stemming directly from Falkenhayn's decision to concentrate on the right bank of the Meuse only. Effectively this gave the French a free artillery platform on the left bank, and the new commander at Souilly, with his strong belief in the importance of the artillery, immediately packed that left bank with batteries which poured withering fire into the flanks of the advancing Germans. In particular, General von Zwehl's VII Reserve Corps, which had achieved so much in the first phase of the battle and whose sector was closest to the river, suffered heavily. This was not an example of the new-style artillery technique usually defined as firing 'over the hill', in which guns aimed at targets that were out-of-sight in accordance with instructions from forward observers. The French gunners could see exactly what they were aiming at across the river and could note the devastating effect of their shells. This was war of an almost Napoleonic style, and the largely out-of-fashion non-recoiling

30. *The guns that hammered the Germans from the Meuse's left bank; a battery of French 155mm guns moving up to forward positions (Q 78040)*

French 155s, which had to be re-sited after each salvo, had one of their finest, if also one of their final, hours. Von Zwehl sent his Chief of Staff post-haste to the Crown Prince to urge that the left bank should be attacked and at once. Thus though it could seem further east in the centre of the Crown Prince's advance that the door to Verdun was almost on the edge of being prized open, to the west there was evidence of considerable disarray. For this the forward commanders knew precisely where the blame lay: with the man whose strategy had dictated the course of the battle so far. In a powerful passage in his book on Verdun, Alistair Horne wrote: 'Thus Falkenhayn through his pusillanimity, his passion for half-measures and his obsession with the "bleeding white" experiment. . . lost the opportunity of bringing off one of the greatest triumphs of the war. It was one that would never recur. Little did he know then, but he had thrown away probably the last good chance that Germany had of winning the war.'

Meanwhile elsewhere there was a growing curiosity as to the character, background and style of the man who had emerged into the limelight to assume a central role in the story currently filling the newspaper headlines. It was not unlike those occasions in the Second World War, when personalities hitherto comparatively obscure were suddenly vested with high responsibility: the case of General Montgomery, or, perhaps even more appropriately, of General Dwight D.Eisenhower, appointed Allied Generalissimo for the Second Front without having fought in a single battle, come to mind. Thus on 4 March 1916 *The Times* published a story headed 'The Defender of Verdun' which attempted to answer the inevitable questions in its readers' minds; (M. Poincaré, it should be stated, was the then President of France and — a fact which can be correctly construed as indicating a deep commitment to the Verdun cause — a native of Lorraine, having been born in Bar-le-Duc in 1860):

> The Republic seeks to enshroud the identity of its generals in some mystery, and it was only yesterday that the public learned from M. Poincaré's visit to the Verdun region that the active command of the Verdun field army has been entrusted to a man who on the eve of the war was about to retire from the Army, having reached the rank of colonel at an age when a military career could not hold out much promise of promotion. Colonel Pétain did useful work during the retreat from Charleroi, and was marked out for promotion by General Joffre when the Generalissimo was purging the Army of elderly incompetents. He very rapidly became Brigadier-General. Then, after the brilliant handling of his men during the Artois offensive of May last year, he was appointed to command the army which General de Castelnau's new duties in the centre left without a leader. The thrusting powers he displayed in Artois made it quite natural that in selecting a general for the important part of the French offensive in Champagne last September the choice should fall on him.
>
> Now after the first days' engagements General Pétain has been given the command under General Joffre of the field defence of Verdun.

There was perhaps some polishing of a hitherto rather modest reputation in the above testimonial, but there was certainly justice, and some human colour, in the sentences which followed:

> He is a general with an extraordinary capacity for work and a master of scientific tactics. He ardently believes that it is among the duties of a soldier to keep physically fit, and numberless stories are related of his methods of so doing. He is well liked by his men, who, for instance, during the Champagne fighting when he covered three miles at the double, were able to see that their chief was able and willing to share their fatigues.

Yet however much the new commander might feel for his troops, they could not be spared the ordeal of the intensive fighting which the situation required and which the tenacity of both sides made inevitable. The overview at Souilly and the close focus of the soldier at the front were worlds apart. Captain Georges Kimpflin, a French officer who fought in the war, if not at Verdun, wrote as follows in his 1920 war memoir *Le Premier Souffle*:

> The fighting man is short-sighted, he marches in blinkers and these blinkers shut him in all the more because he occupies a less elevated rung on the ladder of the hierarchy; but because his vision is narrow, it is precise; because it is restricted, it is clear. He does not see much, but what he sees he sees very well. Because his own eyes and not those of others inform him, he sees what is there.

Few participants in the Verdun battle confirm the accuracy of such a statement more than Paul Dubrulle, an unusual and remarkable witness in that he combined the functions of both soldier and Jesuit priest. His account — published posthumously; he would survive Verdun and the Somme but die in the Aisne offensive in 1917 — has an eloquence and an immediacy which marks it out as something very special. With that close, almost myopic soldier's vision as described by Kimpflin, he spent the day of panic in which Douaumont fell and generals rushed hither and thither across northern France in almost total unconcern:

> For our chiefs, the anxiety was great; as for us, modest troopers, we were in complete ignorance of the real situation and we passed the day in a kind of indifference, and even in a certain tranquillity.

When the order came to move forward he and his comrades had no clear idea as to where they were going or for what precise purpose:

> We are marching. An interminable and miserable slog. We wander down valleys, across fields, into ravines; we follow the lines of a railway; we stumble on the bodies of dead horses, we fall into shell holes.

At last they arrived at some sort of destination; they found themselves near Haudromont Farm, to the west of Douaumont, where they were to 'occupy' (the inverted commas are Dubrulle's) some trenches dangerously placed, too near the crest of a ridge for any soldier's liking. His captain went forward, after instructing him — he was a senior NCO at this time, the equivalent of an assistant quartermaster — to follow in due course and to meet him at an agreed point. He was soon to see something of the reality of the battle in which he was now engaged:

> I leave my men at their post and set off on the road towards the west. In the half-light of the still distant dawn, a heart-breaking scene meets my eyes. There in front of me are the manifest signs of a headlong retreat: abandoned vehicles, heavy mortars, gun-carriages, cases of ammunition, a dead horse. Further off, a living horse, motionless on the side of the road, his eyes dull and despondent. I take pity on him, stroke him, fondle him. He makes no response. I take his halter-rope to lead him away: he refuses to budge. I pull, he resists. I use force, threats, persuasion. No use. Discouraged, I leave him to his unhappy fate and move on.
>
> A little further beyond this, I stumble over some bodies; at once, despite the half-darkness, I see or guess there must be about thirty of them. They lie there, stretched out, stiff and grinning, in all sorts of positions. I examine their badge numbers: they are from four or five regiments. What does this mix signify?
>
> Suddenly, I hear a muffled cry in the distance. 'Who's there?' A long time later, another cry. This time, I make it out: '*À boire!*' ['A drink!'] 'Where are you?' The voice calls again: 'A drink!' I go forward in what seems the right

direction, but see nothing. I call again: 'Where are you?' The voice, this time, seems to come out of the earth. I search at random, and soon I find some shelters hollowed out in the side of the ridge. I discover there about twenty wounded men. They have been there for three days, left in the care of a stretcher-bearer who has sacrificed himself to stay with them. This scene is so heart-breaking that it brings tears to my eyes. I share out my water-bottle between them and, after several words of encouragement, and after promising to send them stretcher-bearers from my regiment, I continue my exploration.

Thus his concern for the wounded; Dubrulle's dual role came most into prominence when he came across the dying, French or German, friend or stranger, to whom he would give comfort and absolution. He was shortly to be called on to fulfill that function in relation to someone much loved and admired by both him and all his comrades, the battalion commander. The first intimation came as his company was about to withdraw from the line:

At about that time, sinister news reaches us. A liaison-officer approaches the captain of the relieving company and, in an official tone, says to him: 'Captain, you are ordered to take over the command of the battalion, in place of Commanding Officer Gaby, killed by shrapnel.'

Commandant Gaby killed! No other catastrophe would have caused more consternation. Commandant Gaby had been with us for only a month, but by his calm, his fatherly kindness, by several actions which raised the spirits of the men, he had gained, not just the respect but the affection, I could even say the adoration of the battalion. The news of his death is, for everyone, a terrible blow and we are in a daze.

After a moment of confusion, I question the messenger: 'The C.O. — he's dead?' — 'No, but he has lost consciousness!' My duty as a priest calls me over there. I go down the ridge as quickly as possible and arrive at the command post. There I find all the staff in tears. I speak to the adjutant: 'Where is the Commandant?' He doesn't answer me — his sobs prevent him — he shows me with a gesture. I raise the tent-cloth which covers him and see him sitting there, his head bandaged. The blood seeps slowly from a ghastly wound and stains his fine uniform. His breathing is slow and deep.

The sight is pitiable; in my turn, I feel my chest heaving with sobs. I call to him: 'Commandant! Can you hear me? I'm the assistant quarter-master from the 6th!' There is no response. It is useless to persist. I take a moment to collect my thoughts, then, sobbing, I recite the words of the rite of absolution.

During this time, all the men present had spontaneously come together in a semi-circle and, kneeling, heads uncovered, they prayed and wept.

I prayed for several minutes for this wonderful man, so good, so generous, and then immediately returned to my post.

My captain, fearing to sadden his troops in the middle of a battle, had wanted to keep back the news from them. But by the time I returned, the rumour, mysteriously, had already leaked out. All along the line, men were whispering about it, and gloom remained on their faces after that. The men felt that they had lost a father.

Dubrulle, being both fighting man and priest, represents a phenomenon non-existent in the British Army but not uncommon in the French. There are accounts of an influx of clergy, who had been living abroad hurrying back to join the colours in 1914, in whom a love of God was equalled by a passionate love of country. His descriptions, vivid, compassionate and, as in the case of the incident just described, at times brimming with emotion, should perhaps be put in the context of a moving prayer he wrote that would be included in the preface to the book of his experiences both at Verdun and on the Somme which would appear in 1917 under the title *Mon Régiment: Impressions de guerre d'un prêtre soldat*:

> Perhaps, oh Jesus, you ask us to shed all our blood for France, just as you shed all yours for humanity on the cross of your Calvary. . . . Being unable to die for you, we are ready to die for that which you love and which loves you – *la France!*'

While Paul Dubrulle was undergoing his initiation on one side of the line, on the other Karl Gartner, a *Feldwebel* (the German equivalent of a sergeant-major, though he was actually serving as officer) of the 243rd Regiment, from Pomerania, was undergoing his, if initially more as observer than participant. His account came to light in a curious way. Over the course of some three weeks, he wrote a letter, in diary form, to his mother, which was still in his pocket-book, unfinished, when he lost his way on 14 March while on a night patrol near Vaux and strayed into a French trench. He was instantly taken prisoner, the letter was seized and subsequently appeared in translation in a book about the first weeks of the battle published under a Verdun imprint later in 1916. Before the year was out it was published in English by a publisher in London. What makes it particularly interesting is that Gartner assumed it would be posted in Germany by a friend due to return there for a home appointment and therefore he had no compunction in expressing his doubts and disclaimers. As the chronicler who publicized it, Henry Dugard, stated when describing how it was found, it is notable for its 'simple, direct style, the complete absence of brag and [its] absolute freedom'. Its special value is that it shows how rapidly the mood on the German side changed from one of easy confidence to an awareness that the promised success was not going to happen, and that the price of such limited advances as had been made was a horrendous one. The following is a shortened version:

> My dear Mother,
> I am sending these lines by Otto Bilsen, who is shortly to go to the depôt to train the latest recruits. I can therefore speak more freely knowing that this letter will not go through the post. We have to send our letters always open.
> *February 21st*. There is a violent artillery duel on our front. We are in reserve and will not take part in this attack, as we are being kept for the final rush on Verdun.

February 22nd, 23rd, 24th and 25th. It appears that they have captured Douaumont and Vaux, the two chief forts of Verdun. We can hear a terrific cannonade but can see nothing of the battle. My commanding officer tells me that we have won a great victory.

It seems that all the French are demanding peace. Poincaré has written to the Kaiser to ask for mercy, but the Kaiser wishes to end the war by a military success. When we have carried Verdun by storm there will be an armistice.

February 26th, 27th and 28th. The battle is raging, but we are still held in reserve. I am rather disappointed. I thought we were going to enter Verdun on the 25th at latest! We should have put such tremendous enthusiasm into the final assault!

March 1st. I have emerged from my hole to take up the duties of *agent de liaison* in the division. I have seen some awful sights. Our losses are terrible, but I am told that those of the French are greater. They have lost 200,000 killed. They cannot continue the fighting. Our dead are being sent away by train. We are going into the first line tonight.

March 2nd. It appears that our losses are more terrible than I understood. I have just met Ludwig Heller, my comrade in the 29th. He is in charge of the burial parties and gives me terrible news of the scenes of carnage which took place in front of Vaux and Douaumont.

March 12th. All I have told you, dear mother, is false. We have been badly informed by our officers. We are just maintaining our positions on the ground we have won after fearful losses and we must give up all hope of taking Verdun. The war will continue for an indefinite period, and in the end there will be neither victors nor vanquished.

March 13th. Yes, dear mother, we are well fed. I received your letter of February 28th. It makes me sad to think of the privations you have to endure. Please don't send me any more parcels. When will it all end?

The 'terrible news' passed to Gartner of 'scenes of carnage' in the vicinity of Douaumont and Vaux was not just a soldiers' rumour. For almost a week up to 4 March the Germans tried in attempt after attempt to seize Douaumont village, with a view to consolidating their achievement in taking the fort. But whereas the fort had fallen easily, the village was won only at huge cost. Supported by machine-gun fire from the fort's turrets, the 24th Brandenburgers were sent into the attack, this time to suffer heavily. A Saxon regiment was thrown forward to find itself shot up by its own supporting artillery. Meanwhile nests of French machine-gunners held out in the village as it disintegrated about them, raking the German infantry as it attacked until they themselves were finally silenced. Some notable French regiments also suffered badly, Pétain's own regiment, the 33rd, prominent among them. An account in the regimental journal subsequently recorded the brutal nature of the fighting on the day its troops were most heavily involved, 2 March – an account featuring a young company commander whose future remarkable career would be greatly influenced by his experiences at Verdun:

From six-thirty in the morning, terrible shelling by heavy artillery over the whole breadth of the sector and to a depth of three kilometres. The earth trembled without a pause; the noise was unbelievable. No liaison, either forward or to the rear, was possible; all telephone-wires had been cut and any messenger sent out was a dead man. . . . At about one-fifteen in the afternoon, after a bombardment that had cut the lines to pieces, the Germans launched their attack to encircle the 3rd Battalion. It was the 12th company, on the left of the 10th, that bore the brunt of their attack. The first who were seen were Germans rushing down from the fort *wearing French helmets*. Major Cordonnier, who was behind the centre of the 11th company, cried 'Do not fire: they are French!' and almost as once he fell wounded or killed by a bullet in the throat, while Sergeant-Major Bacro shouted 'Fire away; they are Germans', himself shooting furiously. Soon the Germans were in the rear of the 10th company.

It was then that the magnificent feat was performed. The 10th company was seen to charge straight forward at the massed enemy reaching the village, engaging them in a terrible hand-to-hand struggle in which these brave men received blows from rifle-butts and bayonets from every side until they were overpowered. Seeing itself completely surrounded, the 10th company launched itself into a furious attack led by its commanding officer, Captain de Gaulle, charging close-packed bodies of men, selling its life dearly and falling gloriously.

At first the future General de Gaulle was assumed to have died in the attack. Pétain would even include a brief obituary in one of his own despatches, calling him 'an incomparable officer in all respects'. In fact he had been taken prisoner. Badly wounded and suffering from the effects of poison gas, he would spend the rest of the war in Germany.

Two days after de Gaulle's capture, on the 4th, Douaumont village was finally taken, The local commander planned an instant counter-attack, but Pétain intervened and forbade it. Losing Douaumont might be a defeat but it was one that had severely shaken the Germans, and the prospect of a rout had now distinctly receded. In any case what the Germans had gained was the mere husk of a village, destined to join the unhappy ranks of such as Haumont, Beaumont and Bezonvaux as one of the lost communities of Verdun.

9 The battle: second phase

Two days after the fall of the village of Douaumont the Germans extended their attack to the left bank of the Meuse. In the light of the forthright lobbying of General von Zwehl and the Crown Prince, and the latter's Chief of Staff, General Schmidt von Knobelsdorf, Falkenhayn had no other option. This new phase of the battle would also produce its crop of notorious landmarks: such as the Mort-Homme — perhaps most aptly translated as 'Dead Man's Hill' — or Côte 304, both of which would become almost as central to the story of Verdun 1916 as Fort Douaumont and Fort Vaux.

For Pétain the surprise was not so much in the attack as in that it had not been launched earlier. Despite being struck down on the morning after his arrival at Souilly by a bout of pneumonia, he had been swift and vigorous in making his new dispositions. He had recognized at once that this was going to be a gunners' battle and had reacted accordingly. But having taken the immediate precaution of packing the left bank with French guns he could not understand why the Germans were so slow to make the obvious response. Daily he enquired from his sick-bed what news there was of the left bank. 'They don't know their business' he is reported to have growled when the answer came that there was none. Nevertheless he ordered the urgent strengthening of defences in preparation for the moment which he knew would come.

Despite being expected the German attack shook even Pétain with the impact of its opening bombardment and with the speed with which the infantry subsequently went in. On 6 March there was no cautious probing as there had been on 21 February. At the far north of the battlefield from the vicinity of Brabant and Champneuville the Germans launched two parallel attacks across the Meuse outflanking the left bank village of Regneville. They pinched out the salient thus created within hours. By the end of the day they had also taken another village, Forges, as well as much of the valuable high ground of the Côte de l'Oie (Goose Ridge), and were already pushing into the fringes of the Bois des Corbeaux, which occupied on the left bank a position roughly equivalent to that of Driant's Bois des Caures on the right.

There are distinct topographical differences between the two sides of the river at this point. The heaved up, much-ravined territory of the right bank was suitable for German infiltration tactics, at which they were adept. Much of the left bank, by contrast, with its great sweep of undulating ground and its minimal scatter of villages and woods, was too open for such techniques. But the Bois des Corbeaux, effectively a northern outcrop of the Mort-Homme, was a target to their liking. If they could seize it with the determination and efficiency with which they had taken the Bois des Caures, the Mort-Homme itself would soon be under serious threat.

31. *German shock troops training for the attack. German Stormtroopers were first used in the Verdun battle (Q 47997)*

The hour brought forth the man, another hero to join Colonel Driant in Verdun's already burgeoning Pantheon. The officer instructed to lead the required counter-attack, planned for the 8th, was Lieutenant-Colonel Macker, a soldier of traditional mode. He affected the studied nonchalance typical of the officer class of most of the European armies of this period; there would be many of similar kidney in evidence wearing British uniforms on the Somme just a few weeks later. Macker strolled into action monocled, smoking a cigar and brandishing nothing more lethal than a cane. German machine-guns hacked into the ranks of his men as they crossed the open ground in front of the wood, but the remainder held firm and then charged with fixed bayonets. They swept the enemy from the Bois and German plans to move on against the Mort-Homme rapidly had to be put on hold.

Sadly the magic failed to work the second time. A further counter-attack on the 10th promised equal success but the valiant colonel was killed by a German machine-gunner at what seemed the moment of victory. The French faltered, the Germans struck back and the Bois des Corbeaux was theirs.

The focus thus moved to the Mort-Homme, and subsequently to its fellow left-bank hill, Côte 304. These would be the setting for sustained and sacrificial fighting over the next two months. The Germans would slowly gain the upper hand and eventually hold both these strong points. But the cost would be high on both sides and the Germans would gain little advantage. Summing up the results of this second phase of the battle, Winston Churchill would comment:

32.   Côte 304, after the battle; no trees, relics of trenches, crosses (HU 82718)

The Germans achieved no success comparable to that of their opening. The conditions of the conflict had become more equal. Closely locked and battling in the huge crater-fields and under the same steel storm, German and French infantry fell by scores of thousands. By the end of April nearly a quarter of a million French and Germans had been killed or wounded in the fatal area, though influencing in no decisive way the balance of the World War.

This, in effect, was attrition in its purest, or rather its most evil, form; the brutal cancelling out of opponents unit for unit and man for man.

One notable participant who came to this area in the latter stages of the spring campaign was the 35-year-old Jesuit theologian and palaeontologist Pierre Teilhard de Chardin, serving as a stretcher-bearer with an African division. In a letter of the time he described the appearance of the landscape after the weeks of hard fighting, as seen from outside his aid-post — 'a dark shelter hollowed out of the plateau' — at a point between Avocourt Wood and Côte 304, almost at the extreme western end of the battlefield:

> From up there, there was a magnificent and entrancing view stretching from the Argonne to Vaux, but inexpressibly mournful. The ridges that are fought over are completely torn up and as though pock-marked by some disease: between the green and richly wooded banks of the winding Meuse you'd think the hillsides had been ravaged by fire.

The two principal hills, as seen today, clearly bear the marks of their terrible history. Both are thick with young woodland and from a distance an observer might assume that the scars of war have gone, but closer inspection reveals a mass of trenches and shell-holes stretching far out beneath the trees. Who knows what detritus, what fragments of metal or of broken humanity lie underneath this distorted ground? It would be tempting to claim that these are the kind of places, like Belsen, where reputedly no birds sing. That is not the case, but the knowledge of what happened there does not invite one to linger, and the stark marble memorials on both hills are grim and chilling.

Mort-Homme had acquired its name from the discovery of one dead body there years before, who thus became the anonymous forerunner of thousands of others. Côte 304 — Hill 304 — a name derived merely from its height above sea-level, also collected its massive crop of casualties and an almost equally sinister reputation. Descriptions by those who fought there do not make comfortable reading, though they can still surprise. The following, from an account by a French machine-gun sergeant of the 26th Infantry Regiment defending Côte 304, shows the desperation induced by the drumfire bombardments so typical of Verdun, but also the almost incomprehensible resilience of men fighting for their own ground:

> The pounding was continuous and terrifying. We had never experienced its like during the whole campaign. The earth around us quaked, and we were lifted and tossed about. Shells of all calibres kept raining on our sector. The trench no longer existed, it had been filled with earth. We were crouching in shell-holes, where the mud thrown up by each new explosion covered us more and more. The air was unbreathable. Our blinded, wounded, crawling and shouting soldiers kept falling on top of us and died while splashing us with their blood. It really was a living hell. How could one ever survive such moments? We were deafened, dizzy, and sick at heart. It is hard to imagine the torture we endured: our parched throats burned, we were thirsty, and the bombardment seemed endless . . . .
>
> Suddenly, the enemy artillery lengthened its fire, and almost at once someone shouted: 'The Boches are coming!' As if by magic, all of us, still exhausted only a moment ago, immediately faced the enemy, rifles in hand, for a true infantryman never drops his weapon. The redan's machine gun had been buried by shellfire, and all of its crew killed. The second machine-gun was lying nearby, its legs in the air, but nothing was broken. We cleaned it hurriedly, and were able to start firing at the very moment the Germans appeared.

One of Verdun's most celebrated and frequently quoted chroniclers is Raymond Jubert, a lawyer from nearby Reims and in 1916 a twenty-six year-old second lieutenant in the 151st Infantry Regiment. He would survive the 1916 battle, would be wounded in April 1917 in the Aisne offensive, would recover to return to Verdun, and would be killed in an attack there in August. His account of three months at the heart of the Verdun fighting was published in instalments in the magazine *Revue des Deux Mondes* in June and July1916. It would subsequently appear in book form in November 1918, under the title *Verdun (Mars-Avril-Mai 1916)*. Reading at times more like a novel than a memoir, it would become a classic of its kind.

The following is from his account of a counter-attack in early April, ordered after the Germans had temporarily gained advantage in what was increasingly becoming a ding-dong battle, with key points being frequently lost and gained:

We had just lost the Mort-Homme Ridge, and were ordered to recapture it at once. I have rarely seen less hesitation, more calm. We assembled without a word. Having put down our knapsacks, we took an ample supply of cartridges, as well as additional rations for one day.

To gain time, my company, disregarding the communication trench, moved ahead over open terrain in single line. Passing the first crest, we descended toward the ravine where, as in a crucible, the deadly explosions and fumes were concentrating in a hellish racket. Another hundred feet and we were in the danger zone.

The German shells were raining around us, and the men were silent. They kept marching on, grim-faced and in good order, toward the barrier of fire and steel that rose before us.

As I glanced back to make sure that my men were following me, the explosion of a shell threw a soldier high up in the air. He fell on the edge of a fresh crater, dead. Half a section had been thrown to the ground, but the men soon got up; after a brief moment of anxiety and fear, they quickly and instinctively formed line again. The man killed was our only casualty, and the danger was over. Death had entered our ranks, but without breaking their alignment.

Our sections, each led by an officer, kept marching on.

'We'll give them hell !' a man shouted at me, smiling. 'Darn' bastards, they won't be spared!'

More voices rang out, a sign of growing confidence. Smiling at my men, I calmed them with a gesture.

We'll sing, up there. Keep going, my boys! It was deeply gratifying to lead such an assault, and to defy death in such perfect order.

Beyond the crest, however, there was another crest, and we could still see no enemy trenches. The men were laughing: 'Another hundred yards gained, Lieutenant!' some of them shouted at me. 'Think we'll get at them?'

Our alignment was admirable. We advanced with slow steps, rifles in hand. I wondered whether my men realized the beauty of their movement as they kept advancing, looking for the enemy.

Some people enjoy defying death. When, about five hundred yards to our left, a machine gun suddenly opened fire against us, one of my men began singing a café-concert hit. He was soon joined by the whole company. Unfortunately, other machine guns entered the fray and made our situation most uncomfortable. I heard cries, but began charging ahead and shouted: 'Keep in line!'

'Forward!' men shouted behind me. We are winning! Our line rushed onward, reached the crest and jumped into the trench which, to our great surprise, was empty — but full of corpses.

At nightfall, and for the next thirty hours, we sustained a violent bombardment. By regaining the lost crest, we had restored the momentarily broken continuity of our front line. When, after a rest period, we returned to the Mort-Homme on May 20th, the lines were still unchanged.

Jubert's style in that extract is almost filmic; there is a sense of a dramatic bravado in his description. One feels he was clearly writing for publication, to promote — and why not in such circumstances? — his own, his comrades' and the nation's cause. Yet elsewhere in his account he shows an earthiness, a sense of realism that ensures that no reader could be allowed to see the fighting at Verdun simply in terms of Beau Geste dash and *élan*. Ask the ordinary *poilu*, he writes, what his thoughts are during and after action and you will receive the following replies:

'What sublime sentiment stirred you as you went up into the attack?'
'I only thought of how I could get my feet out of the mud in which they were sinking.'
'What heroic cry did you utter when you regained the crest?'
'We tried to resuscitate a comrade who thought he was done for.'
'What sensation of power did you experience after having mastered the enemy?'
'We groaned because the food wagon wouldn't come up and we would have to go several days without our wine.'
'Was your first gesture to embrace each other while giving thanks to God?'
'Each one of us went off on his own to satisfy the call of nature.'

The word for wine in this context is not *vin*, but *pinard,* the rough ordinary wine favoured by the *poilus,* sometimes translated as plonk, and drunk with the kind of relish with which the Tommies drank beer.

Among a race of generals known for their flamboyance, Pétain stands apart as a commander whose hallmarks were his thoroughness, solidity and balance. But even he could have his gestures and the story of Verdun 1916 could not be told without reference to his historic order of the day of 10 April. This was issued shortly after the counter-attack on the Mort-Homme described by Lieutenant Jubert, while on the right bank determined German attacks against the Côte de Poivre north-west of Douaumont had been successfully repulsed. His message read:

April 9th was a glorious day for our armies. The furious attacks of the soldiers of the Crown Prince broke down everywhere. The infantry, artillery, sappers

33. 'On les aura!': 'We will get them'. The poster, by Jules Abel Faivre, which immortalised Pétain's order of the day of 10 April 1916. It was much imitated; there was an Italian version in 1918 and an American one in the Second World War, using the words 'We have only just started to fight', a variant of the famous words of John Paul Jones, American naval officer, in 1779. (Imperial War Museum Department of Art)

and aviators of the 2nd Army vied with each other in valour. Honour to all. No doubt the Germans will attack again. Let all work and watch that yesterday's success be continued. Courage! We shall beat them!

'We shall beat them!' *'On les aura!'* is the ringing French original of this rallying cry from the crucible of Verdun. It has become one of the great slogans of that battle and of the war; and was soon to inspire a celebrated and much imitated poster [see above]. It has latterly been attributed to Pétain's aide Captain Serrigny, who it appears might have got it from a soldiers' newspaper, but it was the general who gave it currency and it seems uncharitable to deny him his one Churchillian-style utterance. Especially so, perhaps, because he backed the rhetoric of his *'on les aura!'* claim with the kind of preparation and planning that would make such claims possible.

He also showed care for his troops. The two countries involved adopted radically different systems in the matter of deploying their men. As he himself described them:

> We kept replacing our units rapidly and frequently, so as not to have them remain too long on the battlefield, where both their morale and their manpower were dwindling fast. Our divisions went to Verdun to contribute

their heavy share of blood and fatigue, and then were sent to the rear or into quiet sectors, where they could regain their strength and get ready for further tasks.

The Germans, on the contrary, maintained most of their units on the spot and kept replenishing them with men and material. As a result, most of their officers were eventually wiped out. . . .

The French system became known as the 'Noria'; a word which occurs both in French and English, and of which a fair dictionary definition is 'an endless chain of buckets on a wheel for water-raising'. Its implication is clear; perpetual movement, in and out. In practice this meant that by 1 May forty French divisions had served at Verdun but only twenty-six German. Pétain saw that morale was much more difficult to sustain when men knew that their regiments would be there indefinitely. At least the French could hope that if they survived their time at the front they would soon be moved elsewhere.

The 'Noria' system was one of Pétain's key successes at Verdun. More vital still was his success in ensuring that the defence of Verdun should never lack for food, guns and ammunition. To achieve this it was vital to establish a constant, assured method of supply, not easy in the case of a city in a salient and with inadequate connections with the rest of France.

10 The Sacred Way

On his way to Souilly on 25 February, travelling north from Bar-le-Duc, Pétain had found his progress impeded by a congested mass of men and vehicles struggling in clumsy, disorganized fashion up the narrow, twisting road towards Verdun. He saw at once that this would not do.

Strictly, the road from Bar-le-Duc to Verdun, well-metalled today, engineered to take at least the lesser gradients in its stride, and very fast, is part of Route Nationale 35, but between those two places it has been given a different nomenclature; it is simply called 'NVS': *Nationale Voie Sacrée* — i.e. 'The Sacred Way'.

The name, the invention of a highly patriotic Paris-based news columnist called Maurice Barrès, took some time to appear and take hold; the concept — of a road organized to the last possible degree to provide an effective umbilical cord between the rest of France and her exposed salient in Lorraine — was put into practice with astonishing speed. Indeed, it had begun its operation, if not with the sophistication Pétain would bring to it, before the German attack, for in this respect the French High Command had acted with foresight. They had also begun the re-development of a narrow-gauge railway called *'Le Petit Meusien'*, which roughly paralleled the course of the road and would also play a key part in sustaining Verdun. Under the new commander the system was rapidly developed which would make the supplying of Verdun one of the success-stories of the Western Front war.

The world's press responded at once and with admiration to the new phenomenon. Remarkably, the most famous image of it, a painting by the popular French artist Georges Scott, was reproduced, if in black and white, in the prestigious pictorial weekly *L'Illustration* as early as 11 March and in its cross-channel equivalent, the *Illustrated London News,* as early as the 18th. Two great snakes of lorries, one going one way, one the other, wind across an immense nocturnal landscape, headlights blazing, each vehicle, shown up by the lights of the one behind it, crammed with men, a wrecked car upturned at the roadside with its wheels in the air like the hooves of a fallen horse, a menacing winter sky brooding over all. The *ILN*'s sub-editors devised a striking caption for their double-page spread: 'As though whole streets of towns were on the move'. (See page 82-3)

On 23 March, *The Times* gave the subject its attention, under the title 'A Picture of the Road to Verdun/An Endless Chain of Lorries'. The report consisted of a translation of a letter to his family by a Frenchman described as 'serving on the lines of communication near Verdun'. A member of a motor section, he had begun his work of transporting shells — as he put it, 'into the region which you can well guess' — as early as 22 February; his account was written three weeks later, on 15 March:

34. *The road to Verdun as famously portrayed by the French soldier artist Georges Scott. Reproduced in the* Illustrated London News, *18 March 1916 (Courtesy* Illustrated London News *Picture Library)*

THE T.M. AND THE T.P.: "AS THOUG

HOW THE FIRE-TRENCHES AT VERDUN WERE STRENGTHENED WITH MEN. M

The extraordinary tenacity shown by the heroic troops holding the fire-trenches at Verdun, matchless and magnificent in itself, was made possible very lar causes of a kind to which proper praise is perhaps not always given. Never for an hour did the stream of reinforcements or of food-supplies from the lines slacken. The convoys of motor-transport vehicles, describes a French correspondent, covered every yard to the front by night and day, supplemen

OLE STREETS OF TOWNS WERE ON THE MOVE."

AND PROVISIONS: CONVOYS OF THE TRANSPORT DE MATÉRIEL AND TRANSPORT DE PERSONNEL.

-of-fact ... carrying wagon-loads of soldiers, convoys of munitions, convoys carrying wagon-loads of provisions. At night the lines of convoys speeding along at regular intervals made the of the ... countryside, with the lights on the vehicles, look "as though whole streets of towns were on the move." There were two drivers to each vehicle—one as relief. The Transport de onvoys ... Matériel and the Transport de Personnel are known as the T.M. and the T.P.—[*Drawing Copyrighted in the United States and Canada.*]

On arriving here we did the journey twice almost without stopping: that is to say, 48 hours without sleep and almost without eating.

I do not know if you can imagine what it means to drive one of these lorries weighing five tons and carrying an equal weight in shells, either during a descent of 12 or 14 per cent and with a lorry just in front and one just behind, or driving during a frosty night, or without lights for short intervals when nearing the front.

Can you see a driver alone in his lorry, whose eyes are shutting when a shock wakes him suddenly, who is obliged to sing, to sit very upright, to swear at himself, so as not to sleep, not to throw his lorry into a ravine, not to get it stuck in the mud, not to knock to pieces the one in front? And then the hundreds and hundreds of cars coming in the contrary direction whose lights blind him! If you can imagine all this, be happy that you can spend your nights comfortably asleep in a bed.

Yet he was far from downhearted; on the contrary he was exhilarated by what had been and was being achieved. His account concluded:

The snow has disappeared. The day before yesterday I left at 5 o'clock in the afternoon and returned yesterday morning at 10. I slept yesterday from 1 to 7 and from 10 till 8 a.m. Today there is a radiant sun, it is the spring which makes all things joyous. Life is good.

Thus the raw experience of an anonymous French driver. The Sacred Way was also a natural subject for the journalist. Hence this account, by an American correspondent, writing from the standpoint at this stage of a benevolent neutral, the USA not becoming an active belligerent until April 1917:

35.   *Lorries on the 'Sacred Way', the road between Bar-le-Duc and Verdun which was Verdun's lifeline throughout the battle. (Q 78038)*

The one sight of the battle at Verdun that will always live in my memory is that of the snow-covered and ice-coated road north of Bar-le-Duc constantly filled with two columns of trucks. Some were moving north, the others south, and their swaying and lurching progression was comparable to that of young elephants. It was well nigh impossible to drive on that icy road. As a result, many trucks skidded and turned over, while others caught fire, and still others were abandoned by their drivers, without apparent damage, in the midst of the never-ending flow. One had the impression of a remarkable organization, depending entirely and based upon the initiative of each and every one of its members. . . . A driver's momentary negligence could throw the whole column into confusion. His one and only way of staying out of trouble was a swift and accurate appraisal of the best means of solving each difficulty as it occurred: holes and the ice, his skidding truck, the vehicles passing him, either in the same direction or the other way, the truck ahead of him and the one behind him, and broken-down vehicles on both sides of the road. For long hours at night, I have watched the dim lights of all these trucks, winding their way from north to south, like the coils of some gigantic and luminous snake which had no end to it.

'A remarkable organization': it was Pétain's special genius, or rather his sheer instinct for common sense, that made the feeding and sustaining of Verdun a practical proposition. The area between Bar-le-Duc and Verdun was immediately divided into seven sectors, or cantons, each one under separate control, with Territorial units assigned to carry out all appropriate work. Precise codes of practice were established; thus vehicles which broke down were not to be allowed to stop the flow, but were unceremoniously pushed aside. Workshops were established to provide vehicles as necessary with replacement tyres, a precaution which became not merely useful but crucial when following a period of snow and rain the road had to be sustained with gravel from nearby quarries, without which it would soon have deteriorated into a ribbon of impassable mud. If, as could happen, the gravel ripped the solid rubber tyres, rapid replacement was vital. None of these arrangements would have been effective had there not been a steady supply of appropriate vehicles. At a time when most military transport was horse-drawn, it was a truly remarkable achievement that France was successfully scoured for the product of the internal combustion engine, so that at no time did the stream of lorries, cars and ambulances cease. The general had a valiant ally in the officer who made this possible, Major Richard, between whom and Pétain there occurred a significant and memorable exchange. Question: 'Will the road hold?' Answer: 'The road will hold'.

However, drivers and correspondents, as so far quoted, were accessories to the fact only; they were not heading towards the destination to which the road gave access, to what was becoming increasingly known as 'the hell of Verdun'. René Arnaud was, though his description was different; he saw the journey there as 'an ascent to Mount Calvary'. For him as for countless others this was not so much *voie sacrée* as *via dolorosa*. He and his fellow infantrymen of the 337th Regiment, awaiting their turn, observed the road during a two-

36. *One of the helmeted kilometre stones which now mark the Sacred Way between Bar-le-Duc and Verdun (Author)*

day pause at what he called the 'miserable village' of Erize-la-Grande, half way between Bar-le-Duc and Souilly. They were particularly aware of the condition of survivors coming out

their faces grey as their greatcoats and covered in ten days' beard. Some of them were wearing trophies taken from the Germans — filthy grey helmets and forage caps. With their legs dangling over the tailboards, they seemed to regard us with hostility, as if to say 'It's your turn now'. . . .

More lorries filed past, loaded with spent shell-cases, the copper of which sparkled in the sunlight, and sometimes with the remains of aeroplanes, pale yellow wings with the tricolour markings still fresh. Going up in the other directions were lorries full of recent recruits, with dejected or bantering looks on their faces, and others loaded with long slender 75mm shells, fat 220s with brass cases, or thin gas cylinders for the observation balloons. . . .

Sometimes a touring car insinuated itself between the heavy lorries, and one could make out the caps decorated with gold braid or oak leaves and the red, blue or tricolour arm-bands. These were the gentlemen of the General Staff who were masters of our fate, who pushed us about the battlefield like pawns on a chess-board, and for whom we felt at once hatred, scorn and envy. Whenever there was a lull in the procession of the lorries we heard the everlasting rumbling of the guns, which had become an obsession for us, like the Trappist's saying, 'Brother, we must die.'

Raymond Jubert was another who recorded what he saw when travelling on the Sacred Way, especially noting the difference between the men going north and those going south:

> The first crowd are young, their uniforms brand new; their faces and hands are clean; they look as though they were decked out for a celebration, but their aspect is sad, their eyes dream, they are silent like men who they have been abandoned to their fate. The second lot are dirty, scruffy; they have black hands and faces; compared with the others they look like outcasts. But their faces are cheerful; they sing; they wouldn't change their situation for anything, yet they have a kind of pity for the men in those fine uniforms whose paths they are crossing. Were they not like them yesterday? . . . There is a distinct contrast between the gaiety of those with the unclean faces, finally delivered from too long an ordeal, and the serious, silent faces of those who have not yet had their date with destiny.

Coming out from Verdun not only took men away from the private zone of the actual battle; it returned men to the public world of the rest of France. There could be tension in such a confrontation, as those who had been fighting for their very existence came face to face with those whose lives, in many cases, had continued as though no war were taking place. Such a moment was memorably caught in the diary account of the soldier-priest Paul Dubrulle. The setting was the railway station at Bar-le-Duc, where by chance a trainload of soldiers found itself next to a civilian express:

> At first sight its enormous coaches filled us with respectful dread. Was it not civilisation itself that suddenly loomed up before our eyes in the prestige of its superiority, before us poor savages who were being transported, like parcels, in cattle-wagons? Quite naturally the comparison between the two trains imposed itself. It was unmissable. On one side were vigorous men, the treasure of France, courageous men who had given up everything, even themselves, for the others. And opposite? . . . Who were these people who, throughout the length of the train, leaning on the doorways, were staring at us curiously?
>
> We studied them for some time in a frosty silence. Wasn't this the fine flower of that 'other-world', so much detested? The freight on that train, of what was it made up? Playboys, perhaps, who were profiting, to give themselves a good time, from our afflictions and our blood. These gross bourgeois? Weren't they those very tradesmen with no conscience who were fattening themselves at our expense? These gilded bellies? Weren't they those shameless financiers who speculated on our lives? And above all, these faces of important insignificance, were they not those of the politicians, enemies of the soldier, and of the cabinet strategists, six hundred replicas of Gambetta, who held up timely movements and decided on disastrous offensives?
>
> Under the influence of these thoughts, a veiled hostility rose up in us. The silence was menacing, the tension extreme: the least incident could have unleashed a storm. The incident ended in the opposite direction: as if under

37. *A symbol of solidarity between French soldiers and civilians. An Official French photograph entitled: 'The Peasants always welcome the soldiers to their warm firesides.' (Q 69865)*

the effect of a lightning conductor, the cloud suddenly evaporated. A soldier had crossed the platform. He stopped in front of a carriage door and, raising his head, with a timid air, asked: 'You haven't got a newspaper, have you, sir?' The traveller quickly turned back into his compartment and, a moment later, reappeared with the most gracious smile, holding an armful of paper. Then it was like a powder-train. Right along the length of the express, figures disappeared behind the glitter of the windows and immediately at all the doors newspapers appeared. The effect was magical. From our train, from all the wagons, men leaped upon the platform, with one bound crossed the lines and thronged round the doors. The newspapers were shared out. In succession, conversations started up: 'You've come from Verdun? What did you do? Where were you? Was it terrible?'

The passengers demonstrated an insatiable thirst for news. This thirst, however, eased little by little and, in proportion to the calm descending, the unity of hearts asserted itself. The general distribution was resumed afresh. Through the doors passed, in orderly fashion, provisions for the journey, cakes, fruit, cigars, cigarettes. The train was quickly despoiled and, their hands empty, these good folk had nothing more to offer but their hearts and their smiles.

The success of the Sacred Way raises an important question. Why did the Germans let it happen? Those long lines of lorries pounding endlessly north and south, clearly visible by day and with headlights blazing at night: surely if it were possible to bomb London or Paris it should also have been possible to disrupt, even totally close down, the Sacred Way.

To answer that question it is necessary first to ask another: how was air power used in the Verdun battle?

On 21 February, the sky was full of the aircraft of both nations, if with far more German than French. The honour undoubtedly lay with the attacker at this stage in both numbers and technology. But the French came back strongly that spring, especially when the Nieuport fighter became available. Even before that French hearts had been stirred by the deeds of their aces, especially when Jean Navarre achieved a minor revenge for the fall of Fort Douaumont by shooting down two German aircraft over it the next day. The French supreme ace Georges Guynemer also won fame here; he would continue to dazzle his admirers until, after fifty-four victories, he disappeared into a cloud above the Ypres Salient in 1917, never to be heard of again. No sign of him or his plane was ever found. All this was the stuff of legend and indeed in relation to Verdun it is the aces, the gladiators of the sky, who catch the eye, as they caught the eyes of the soldiers in (to use Churchill's phrase) the 'crater-fields' below. Many envied their freedom from the squalor of the battlefield, as they flaunted their gleaming aircraft among the clouds, but they did not envy their deaths. In a war that barred parachutes to its pilots, the airman's options if his plane was shot down were those of being burnt alive or of dropping like a stone.

The Germans had their aces too. Oswald Boelcke was one who went beyond the concept of the one-to-one fight and developed the *Jagdstaffel*, or hunting squadron. Another was Max Immelmans, but when he was killed in June the Kaiser intervened and ordered Boelcke not to fly, since he felt that Germany could not risk a second lost hero after the shock caused by the death of the first.

As against all this aerial glamour, any strategic use of air power appears to have taken second place. It was of course at a very early stage of development; a whole new means of waging war, whereas aerial dogfights were basically just a modern variation of mediaeval jousting or of the 'pistols at dawn' duel. Alistair Horne quotes 'the remarkable admission' of the Chief of the Luftwaffe himself, General Hoeppner; that at Verdun, 'We did not exactly know what should be required of aviation'. The Germans had three squadrons of suitable machines for bombing, each capable of dropping a 200-pound bomb. But they used them with little imagination. Thus, for example, they bombed railway junctions that were under artillery fire already. It was June before they attacked Bar-le-Duc. Curiously, since the battle's first shell was aimed at a Meuse bridge, not one of the thirty-four bridges in the area was destroyed by enemy bombing; the French wrecked one when demolition charges were exploded in error. And they never troubled the 'Sacred Way'.

It would have been so easy. A German critic, writing soon after the war about his own side's failure to grasp so obvious an opportunity, painted a picture of a road blocked by burning vehicles and cut in many places by bomb craters. He added: 'A chaos that could not be disentangled must have arisen. . .'

Was there perhaps another explanation? Was the policy of restraint deliberate? If France was to be bled white by the Verdun offensive, what would be the point of cutting the aorta, the artery by which France's youth was drawn to the bloodletting? But that must remain speculation. All through the long months of fighting the vehicles rumbled up and down between Bar and Verdun, as if whole streets of towns were on the move.

Air aces of Verdun:

38. *(left) German: Oswald Boelcke, killed in a collision with one of his own pilots, October 1916 (Q 63147)*

39. *(right) French: Captain Georges Guynemer; frail in physique but heroic in reputation, he was credited with 54 victories before his disappearance in September 1917 (Q 64213)*

11 The helping hand

Among the aces flying over Verdun and winning golden opinions for their contribution to the battle were pilots who spoke English with American accents. Their presence is most easily understood by referring back to what the British call the War of American Independence but which the Americans see as the American Revolution. It is a proud name, its dates (1775-1781) substantially predating the French, which began in 1789. In 1777 a French aristocrat from the Auvergne, Marie Joseph Paul Yves Roch Gilbert Motier, Marquis de Lafayette, born in 1757, sailed for America to aid the colonists. He became a close ally of George Washington, fought at Brandywine in 1777, in the defence of Virginia in 1781, and at Yorktown (where the British conceded defeat) in the same year. Among other notable Frenchmen who espoused the colonists' cause was the Comte de Rochambeau, commander of a 4000-man French expeditionary force in 1781.

The American presence on the French front in the First World War was an act of gratitude for such services rendered. By late 1915 there was a Franco-American aviation corps in France, its purpose being to help France and to train Americans in air warfare for possible service in the American army should the need arise. It produced a pamphlet to explain its motivation:

> What is the spirit that moves these young American citizens to cross the ocean and volunteer as French aviators? As one of them said, 'We wished to return the compliment which Lafayette and Rochambeau paid to us; we wanted to belong to that fine and sportsmanlike institution, the French aviation corps, and we feel that Americans ought to help a Republic that is in a conflict in which the liberty of all nations is at stake.'

Initially this would lead to the formation of the *Escadrille Americaine*: the 'American Squadron'. Later it would be re-named *Escadrille Lafayette*: the 'Squadron Lafayette'.

One of its aces, the first to be killed, was Victor Chapman. Gilded youth is a phrase often used about some of the best and brightest of the British who went to war in 1914, but if any American deserved the description it was Chapman. The son of an affluent family, he had graduated at Harvard and had then studied architecture and painting in Paris. When war broke out he joined the French Foreign Legion, spent a hundred consecutive days in the front-line trenches and saw half his comrades killed. But ground fighting was not his forte; when the chance came to join the camaraderie of the air, he went for it.

He became a kind of air genius, the one whom all admired. There was a grim inevitability about being seen in such a light. Like Guynemer, like Immelmans, he would

40.   *The French Nieuport biplane, one of France's most successful fighter aircraft, as flown at Verdun by the American ace Victor Chapman (Q 58033)*

become, literally, a fallen hero. In fact his death predated that of those two aerial immortals.

He died, not when seeking a fight with the enemy, but on a mercy mission to bring comfort to a comrade. Badly wounded in an air battle, Clyde Balsley was taken to hospital, where he developed a raging thirst that could only be satisfied by sucking oranges. Chapman decided to take a bag of oranges to ease his friend's distress, using his Nieuport as means of transport. In the air he saw ahead of him two fellow flyers, Norman Prince and Raoul Lufbery, under attack by a squadron of German Fokkers.   Chapman flew to help them and a desperate air-battle ensued. Prince and Lufbery got away and hurried back to base to tell how Chapman's diversion had saved them. They made ready to welcome his return. The hours passed by. Then a telephone call came from another squadron. One of its flyers had seen a Nieuport crash to earth. Its pilot could not have survived. A second call confirmed his identity. Another member of the American squadron, James McConnell, described the reaction:

> We talked in lowered voices after that; we could read the pain in one another's eyes. . . . To lose Victor was not an irreparable loss to us merely, but to France and the world as well. I kept thinking of him lying over there, and of the oranges he was taking to Balsley. As I left the field I caught sight of Victor's mechanician leaning against the end of our hangar. He was looking northward into the sky where his *patron* had vanished, and his face was very sad.

Interviewed later by an American correspondent, the French CO of the *Escadrille Americaine*, Captain Thenault stated:

41. *Raoul Lufbery, known as 'Luf',
saved by his friend Victor Chapman
in the latter's final flight. Lufbery had
flown with the French Air Force before
transferring to the American squadron.
Asked what he would do after the war,
he remarked 'There won't be any
"after the war" for a fighter pilot.' He
fell to his death during a duel between
his Nieuport fighter and a German
Albatross on 19 May 1918.
(Q 60572)*

Our grief was extreme, for we loved him dearly. At the moments of greatest
danger in the air we could always discover the silhouette of his machine, that
machine which he managed with such ease. One of my *pilotes* has just said to
me, 'Would that I had fallen instead of him'. With the army at Verdun his
bravery was legendary, and hardly a day passed without some exploit from
which he returned with his machine pierced by bullets and sometimes slightly
wounded himself. He was to have received the *Medaille Militaire.* when death
took him. . . .

Charles Hartley was aged fifty and a tea-planter in Ceylon when war broke out in 1914.
The now largely forgotten 'Native Rebellion' in that island detained him well into 1915,
his contribution being the modest one of driving troops to the affected areas. When the
crisis was over he sailed for England by way of China and Canada, reaching London after
an erratic voyage (his ship, the *Adriatic* was carrying munitions and there were German
U-boats about), reaching Liverpool on 10 November. He travelled south to London the
same evening and on the following day applied for a post of motor ambulance driver in
France.

42. *Advertisement in British newspapers following the opening of the Verdun battle, March 1916*

Several possible openings were explored and several promises made, but after some weeks the situation stalled. On 14 February he was informed that the Army Service Corps had taken over the ambulance convoys working at the front, and that all he could be offered was a job at a base. 'As this was hardly what I was out for,' he wrote in the meticulous diary account he would keep describing his adventures, 'and as I found I could get what I wanted through the *Croix Rouge Française,* I declined the offer and transferred my name to the French organization.' The onset of the Verdun battle produced a spate of advertisements in British newspapers and magazines asking for help for the French Red Cross. Acknowledging that there would be fierce and prolonged fighting and therefore heavy casualties, they stressed the urgent need for motor ambulances, clothing, food, surgical stores, money – and voluntary drivers. This was exactly what Hartley was hoping for. Thus it came about that a middle-aged expatriate Englishman became one of that honoured band of men who made their contribution to the war and to history by becoming drivers of the Sacred Way.

He did so as a member of *Section Sanitaire Anglaise (SSA) 10.* As the title suggests Hartley's unit was not the first in the field; some of its predecessors had been serving in France for months; members wore British uniform but worked to French orders.

To the new recruit's regret further delays followed his enlistment and he was not able

43. Section
    Sanitaire
    Anglaise 10;
    *the section's
    two
    ambulance
    mechanics,
    Lambert and
    Clarke,
    photographed
    by Charles
    Hartley
    (HU 66818)*

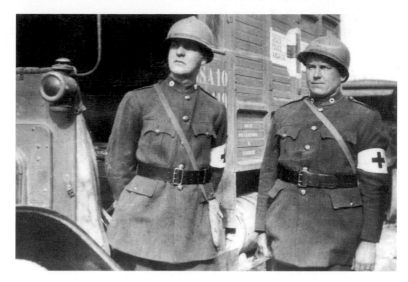

to leave for France until early June. Thereafter he served in the Verdun area until December, and subsequently for several months in 1917 in the Argonne.

Once the new unit arrived the work began at once and was intensive. Hartley had hoped they would be stationed close to the line but instead they were assigned to the task of evacuating wounded from behind the battle lines to hospitals in the area of Bar-le-Duc. Hence his swift acquaintance with the Sacred Way, though interestingly he never described it as such in his diary. His account's special value is that it offers, in addition to his own observations, a detailed description of the codes of practice on that route as carried out by the ambulance convoys. This from his diary under the date 25 June:

> The cars are now working very hard and one convoy carried over 200 wounded. We are up at 6.50 a.m.; have coffee and bread and jam — attend to our cars and push out at 9 a.m. and go backwards and forwards all day till late in the evening — getting our meals when we can.
>
> We are all longing for a move up [nearer the battle], but it is a satisfaction to feel we are putting in a lot of very useful work where we are. The roads have been very dusty of late. Everyone and everything is covered with the flour-like dust. As our cars proceed to and from Bar-le-Duc they take their place in the endless stream. Convoys of every description are on the road — artillery, huge buses laden with soldiers, lorries, ammunition wagons, trolleys with aeroplanes and supplies.
>
> This road — Bar-le-Duc to Verdun — is by far the most important connection with the Verdun Army. 'Convoys' may be anything from half a dozen to 50 or more military conveyances — usually, though not always, motor. A convoy is usually divided up in sub-sections of 5, the last wagon having a red disc at the back. When a convoy takes the road it is usually headed by an officer in a small car, whose duty is to see that his convoy keeps its proper formation. Out in the country the convoy can spread itself out, concertina

fashion, to a distance of fifty yards one from the other. The leading car maintains a fixed pace and it is the duty of each 'aide', who accompanies the driver, to look back from time to time to see if the car or vehicle immediately behind is keeping its distance. Taking a convoy of, say, 20 cars, should No. 5 break down, the 'aide' immediately puts out his hand to stop No. 6 (and, consequently, all the way back to No.20), while No.4, car, seeing that the convoy behind has stopped, comes to a halt and this works on up to No.1 and finally to the convoy officer who goes back to the cause of the stop and then decides whether to leave 'No.5' to work out its own salvation or leave a repairing car by it.

If it is but a temporary stoppage, the rest of the convoy wait.

In passing through villages the convoy draws in closer one to the other, to avoid risk of taking a wrong turning: some judgment has to be used by individual cars (not in convoy formation) in overtaking these long convoys. If such a car is travelling faster, the driver watches his chance to overtake and pass as many of the convoy cars as he has time to before he meets another convoy coming in the opposite direction. As a rule it is impossible to do this all at once. He dare not 'cut' in — i.e. slip in between two of the cars he is overtaking, but can only make room for the oncoming traffic by slipping in behind a subsection of the convoy, that is, behind a car with a red disc. Having at last succeeded in passing a convoy going in the same direction one finds another long convoy has to be dealt with and this may go on for 10 or 20 miles. When carrying wounded it is usually a simple matter, as a driver 'carries on' and leaves convoys to overtake him.

The Verdun road is well kept up considering the continuous heavy traffic, night and day. It is broad enough to permit of three streams of convoys – one going, one coming or one overtaking, but if the road narrows in places or there is overtaking on one's opposite side one has to slip in temporarily, behind a sub-section. Motor goggles are of course absolutely necessary as the dust is awful. This impressive never-ending stream goes on night and day and one feels that great happenings are in progress and history at this very moment is being made.

There were other pressures on drivers, as well as those of keeping one's distance and staying in line. Not all roads were subject to the stringent conditions that applied to the Sacred Way and then there was considerable latitude in the matter of speed. It was vital to drive at the most congenial pace for the often severely distressed men in his care:

Our cars can each carry five lying-down wounded, and anything from eight to twelve 'sitters'. The speed of the cars is governed generally by the nature of the wounds and also the surface of the roads. I have made it a rule that once I have formed my opinion as to these two important conditions, to drive accordingly. Although one cannot write highly enough of the almost superb courage of the French soldier and his fortitude in the most intense suffering, I have noticed

44. A stretcher case being unloaded from one of the section's ambulances; photograph by Charles Hartley (HU 668822)

that here and there it would be impossible to get to a destination at all if I went by what I might hear from some poor fellow inside. Under certain conditions a speed of barely 4 miles an hour might be too fast, whereas certain wounds and roads of a particular class of surface, could permit of a speed of 15 or 20 miles an hour without discomfort. I often consult the Surgeon when doubtful. In certain cases of gassing etc, it is often necessary to go as fast as possible. This speed question is one calling for a good deal of judgment at times, and a driver, if he possesses any feelings, cannot but be affected by the sufferings of his unfortunate passengers. I notice that the French ambulances go much faster than the British, and I have heard more than once the wounded speak of their preference for the cars we drive.

Towards the end of the month, under the date 29 June, Hartley wrote with some pride:

Our section has moved nearly 1,000 wounded during the last few days. When time permits the French officer holds lectures of a technical kind on Motors generally. He told us the other day that the Authorities are satisfied with No.10 and that he hopes it won't be long before we go up a bit.

There were many hospitals clustered around the southern end of the Sacred Way. One that gave honourable service throughout the battle and gained an excellent reputation was the British Urgency Cases Hospital at Revigny. It was the only British hospital in the Meuse area. The idea of creating such a unit had been mooted shortly after the outbreak of war, when the British Union of Trained Nurses offered to raise for the French Government 'an English mobile surgical ambulance, complete in all its details, with personnel, equipment and automobiles'. The offer was accepted, recruitment began in January 1915 and by early March the unit was ready. The French War Office assigned it to Bar-le-Duc, where a 'pavilion' of the Central Hospital was allocated to it. By 21 March the staff was ready to receive their first wounded. The *Médecin Inspecteur,* M. Mignon, visited the building the next day. As the unit's medical director, Mr J.A. Cairns Forsyth, wrote in a contemporary account:

> He spent a long time studying our equipment and inquiring about our methods. After tea in the dining room, he made a fine speech and congratulated us on getting the Hospital together in such a short time. He informed us that we were to be an individual unit, subject to the regulations of the French Army, but permitted to pursue our own lines in the matter of treatment of the wounded.

The staff, of over fifty British and some twenty French, including an interpreter, set to work with a will. But after six months the French authorities decided they wanted their premises back, so the unit was moved to a new site some kilometres to the west near the small town of Revigny: a château intriguingly named '*Le Faux Miroir*': 'The False Mirror', presumably due to its being next to a small lake capable of offering vivid reflections. Sadly the château no longer exists, having been destroyed by fire some forty years ago.

Among the staff was twenty-four year old Winifred Kenyon, the third daughter of a Major General, serving as a VAD: i.e. a 'Voluntary Aid Detachment'; a curious formula which frequently signified a well connected, unpaid volunteer. VADs could be assigned to a number of tasks; as ward-maids, laundresses, cooks, even motor drivers, though the majority, as in the present case, served as nurses.

Winifred Kenyon kept a detailed diary throughout most of her time in France, recording an assignment in which humanity and good humour had to be maintained in the presence of much suffering and tragedy. There was drama too, for just before the battle began many of its staff saw the shooting down by French gunners of a German Zeppelin, an event that turned Revigny briefly into a household name. Nurse Kenyon was among those who hurried to the crash site, fascinated but also frightened at the thought of what she might see:

> On we went, first along a cart track, then over a field of young wheat. You could see it well now, blazing on the ground, and dark forms of people showing up against it. We arrived. A huge pile of aluminium frame work, like a gigantic scrap heap. You could see dead figures amongst it too — thank goodness I didn't. It was most eerie — the night, the flames, the people talking and moving — and the mud. We got stuck in it. Some got their shoes pulled off, fortunately no one lost them. But it felt like a nightmare, and there we were trying to get free of the awful mud.
>
> I longed to get off, and the thought that I might get de Waru [the hospital's

45. *Wreckage of Zeppelin LZ 77, shot down near Revigny, 21 February 1916 (Nurse Kenyon Collection, Imperial War Department of Documents)*

interpreter, who had made overtures to Miss Kenyon but had been firmly if kindly rejected] to walk back with us was the last straw. Then Dr Harvey came up. 'Do you want to go home?' 'Yes' said I. So we started, leaving everyone and everything. Oh the relief of it. We went back along a track almost the whole way, it was a little rough, but it took us past the guns — the two of them out in a field about a kilometre from the Zepp. How proud they must be, those gunners!

We got to the château soon after 11, to find Marshall and de Waru already arrived. They had seen a dead German lying in the field as they returned and an unexploded bomb.

One amusing thing that happened in the afternoon. Old Deschamps, the owner of the château, arrived to say he was going to try and get a gun put here to protect it, and wanted to know if any of the French orderlies could work it!

Such events were of course exceptional. For the most part Winifred Kenyon's account focused on the surges and troughs of hospital life, against the background of a crisis of which she and her colleagues closely followed every turn. The following extracts give something of its flavour:

Tuesday Feb 29th
The biggest battle ever known is going on now. We guessed that an attack on Verdun was planned, as the fact that the Germans tried to cut the railway all pointed to it. Now we know. There has been the most tremendous attack conceivable, huge guns first, blowing everything to pieces, and men beyond all

46. *Le Faux Miroir Château, Revigny, home of the British Urgency Cases Hospital during the Verdun Battle, photographed c.1916 (HU 82711)*

count. At first it seemed that the Germans were getting the best of it, the French had to fall back a bit, all trenches on both sides were blown to pieces, the losses in men were enormous, the Germans of course suffering most, and they say that their bodies are lying in heaps.

Men, guns etc etc pouring along all the roads, no traffic other than military allowed. And though we felt certain that the Germans couldn't break through, we know now and guessed then, that they very nearly did.

Now the tide seems to have turned. The Germans have already been driven back a bit, and the roads are still packed with French troops going up. They say they are the spring reinforcement and the Great Offensive is to start now instead of waiting. Oh if it is!

Friday March 10

For ten days we have been up to our eyes in work, at least 20 *blessés* [wounded] arriving most days and as many going out most days. We in the theatre are practically never finished, nine and more ops a day, the other evening when we thought we'd finished early, we had three at 9 o'clock, so were working until 11.30. As we also did on Tuesday 29th, the day the rush began.

The Zepps had another try for Revigny station last Monday. We were woken at 1.30 by tremendous crashes, which made the whole house shake, and we all, obedient to orders, put on coats and trooped down to the cellar. Most people were frightened I think. Personally I wasn't a little bit, chiefly I daresay because I was so tired and sleepy, having had 12 ops the day before. They hit an ammunition train between Bar and Revigny, but fortunately it was on a siding, and didn't hurt the line at all and as a railway man went and uncoupled most

47. *Nurse Winifred Kenyon, left, with two other members of the nursing staff, Mrs Hill and Helen Somerville, photographed at Le Faux Miroir Château. (Q 111873)*

of the trucks, much ammunition wasn't wasted. Of course it went off in explosions for ever so long, and kept most people awake, but I was asleep as soon as ever I was in bed.

The work here is terrible. Such wounds and a great many cases of gas gangrene and in spite of amputations, we have had a lot of deaths. It is simply awful, for the number of wounded is impossible to cope with and they lie unattended to for days and there are no hospitals nearer than Bar, as Clermont has been shelled.

They say they are expecting even harder fighting. The French soldiers who come in are all extraordinarily cheerful, more so than they have ever been before, in spite of the fearful time they have been having. They all say it's Germany's last effort. Never has there been such an exciting time, and never has the end of the war seemed nearer. Oh that it might end, for these last ten days have made us realize the ghastliness of it as we never did before.

Saturday March 18

Still hard at it, though not quite so hard. The battle of Verdun is still going on, but people are now pretty confident that it will never be taken. The Germans have been simply throwing their men away, while the French haven't called up their reserves at all. The German credit is rapidly going down, while the French has gone up.

We've had over 100 ops this month already — endless amputations, there's so much gas gangrene. We were called up for an op the other morning, but the boy died before they got him to the theatre.

The most glorious weather this week, and we've been having tea on the verandah almost every day. The woods are lovely, FULL of anemones and sort of oxlips. I went for a lovely walk through them yesterday after tea with Dr Harvey, a glorious evening, and the moon almost full, had already risen. It was nearly 7 when we got back and found there was an op in 5 minutes — a secondary haemorrhage.

March 24 Friday

Work has been harder than ever for us in the theatre this week. 19 ops on Monday and I found I had a temp of 101, but of course didn't say so, and anyhow I haven't felt feverish since. But what with hard work and not sleeping, I was feeling absolutely done and on Wed. eve, I was told to stay in bed next day.

I slept almost all day, but am still in bed now, really very thankful, but hating it all the same when everyone is so busy. It IS rotten breaking down like this, but I think I shall be allowed on duty tomorrow all right.

April 3rd Monday

Such perfectly heavenly weather, only rather too hot when there are ops in the afternoon. However we've not been so busy lately, though there's by no means nothing doing. April 1st was a real slack day, with just one operation in the X-ray room. We sat outside all the morning, I mending stockings. Sister Marshall went off as soon as the op was over, it being her birthday and I was off after tea, and went for a lovely walk with Dr Harvey, along the cart track to the right of the Revigny Road, down on to the canal and along it to the left for some way, then back through the woods via Petit Swiss.

So the work continued, with the hospital never other than full, occasional minor troubles affecting the personnel — the interpreter de Waru again winning disapproval for 'playing fast and loose' with some of the staff: 'I'm terribly disgusted with him and don't intend to try and be nice to him ever again' — and morale-raising moments when their efforts were given official approval in a way which heartened everybody concerned. Thus under the date 19 June:

The hospital is feeling very bucked with itself, and we as individuals very pleased because firstly, Mr Forsyth was at Nettincourt the other day (Headquarters) and General Humbert sent for him into his room, all full of maps etc, and told him that the hospital was doing and had done excellent work, often showing the way to other hospitals, and so on for some time!

Then yesterday who should pay us a visit but General Pétain himself, the famous Pétain. There's an honour for a little English hospital.

12 'The mill on the Meuse'

Looking back on the Verdun battle, Crown Prince Wilhelm would state, in a remark that has become much quoted: 'The mill on the Meuse ground to powder the hearts as well as the bodies of our troops.'

His comment was as true for the French as they were for his own men. Moreover, the pressure increased as the weeks went by. A key reason for this was that at the end of April Pétain was replaced as commander at Verdun by the thrusting, volatile General Robert Nivelle, a master of publicity and a general brimming with persuasive self-confidence. Pétain had steadied French nerves superbly, and had achieved enough to become permanently established as the saviour of Verdun. But he had irritated Joffre by showing evidence of tunnel vision in relation to Verdun, implying that France's main effort for 1916 should be concentrated on the Meuse, while Joffre was eager to open up his long-dreamed of Anglo-French offensive on the Somme. There was also an element of caution, even pessimism, about Pétain. Joffre saw him as too ready to give ground and not eager enough to reclaim it. In Nivelle, by contrast, Joffre saw a commander who would go for the enemy hip and thigh, and if his achievements equalled his ambitions might effectively turn a likely draw into a glamorous victory. This would clearly redound to the credit of

48. *General Robert Nivelle, advocate of war* à outrance, *commander under Pétain of French forces at Verdun from May to December 1916 (Hulton-Getty Collection)*

the C-in-C, whose reputation had been somewhat damaged when it became known that it was he who had been largely responsible for leaving Verdun so vulnerable to attack.

But Pétain could not be sacked. Ignominiously to dismiss France's current idol would have shocked the nation and done Joffre no good at all. So he had to be, if not kicked, at least propelled courteously but firmly upstairs. The incumbent of the more senior post of Army Group Centre, General Langle de Cary, was rapidly *limogé* — i.e. removed, Limoges being a well-known resort for the military retired — and Pétain appointed in his place. This left him in indirect control of the Verdun battle, but at Bar-le-Duc rather than Souilly. It also left him with more time on his hands, so that, for example, he could cheer the hearts of such as the staff of the Urgency Cases Hospital at Revigny by making the visit so much appreciated by Nurse Kenyon.

Pétain showed no pique at being moved to his new post. He composed a gracious message, welcoming to his successor and encouraging to the men of the Army which he had commanded for many months. A prime souvenir of 1916, a framed copy still hangs in Souilly town hall:

30 April 1916
GENERAL ORDER No. 136

One of the greatest battles which History has placed on record has been joined, in the last two months, around Verdun.

Thanks to everyone, commanders and soldiers, thanks to the devotion and self-sacrifice of men from various services, a formidable blow has been struck at the German military power.

Your task is not ended; it remains to regain several important points which the enemy has managed to seize. This task, you will accomplish under the orders of General NIVELLE, to whom I hand over the destinies of the IInd Army.

For myself, called to the Command of the Group of Armies of the Centre, of which the Army of Verdun is part, I will not cease to be in the midst of you, to take part in your labours, to encourage your efforts and applaud your success.

(Signed) Pétain.

So Nivelle took over the conduct of the battle, signalling the new era on the steps of the Souilly town hall by stating, apparently to his Chief of Staff but in tones that were clearly meant for wider consumption: 'We have the formula!' Events would show that he had not. The price for his grandiosity was paid by the soldiers of both sides. Despite this, Nivelle would have one year of meteoric glory, until his bluff was called on the Aisne, at the Chemin des Dames, in 1917, after which he would become a subject of derision and contempt — in effect would be *limogé* for good in the eyes of his country and of history.

Nivelle, however, did not come alone; he had two outriders who shared his attitude and were equally eager to strike soon and hard at the enemy. His Chief of Staff, Major d'Alenson, was one: brilliant, cadaverous, menacing, slowly succumbing to consumption, and all the more bellicose because he was determined to see the war won before he lost his own private war with ill health. The other was General Charles Mangin, a First World War thrusting commander par excellence; a soldier honed in colonial wars which left him with scant concern about casualties.

In a passage in his post war volume *Comment Finir la Guerre* (*How to Finish the War*) — in which he always referred to himself in the third person and frequently used the present tense — Mangin described how the decisions were made that governed his and his superior's conduct of the fighting at Verdun. Strictly, it refers to a later stage of the battle, the end of June, but it clearly and succinctly expresses their military philosophy:

> General Nivelle, commanding the army, confers with General Mangin. They are both in agreement that it is necessary to counter-attack *à outrance*; the threatened front is in an unstable condition and can only be secured by a movement forward. General Nivelle approves the orders given in consequence.

49. *General Charles Mangin, similar in military philosophy to Nivelle, but more fortunate in his ultimate fate (Q 34781)*

Attack '*à outrance*' — outright attack, sometimes translated as 'war to the death' — had had its heyday back in 1914 and had failed. It was now to have a second season. In defence it is perhaps fair to quote a key sentence by Mangin in a volume of his war letters, *Lettres de Guerre*: '*Quoi qu'on fasse, on perd beaucoup de monde.*' 'Whatever you do, you lose a lot of men.'

Pierre Rouquet was one who was nearly 'lost' at this time, but just managed to survive. He had joined the 151st Infantry Regiment at Quimper, Brittany, in 1915. He was to be wounded three times and would fight on the Somme as well as at Verdun. Describing at the age of ninety-three experiences undergone when he was a young *fantassin* — i.e. infantryman — of nineteen, he recalled the grim conditions on the left bank of the Meuse in the vicinity of the Mort-Homme in early May 1916. His principal memory was of the unceasing savagery of the German bombardment:

50. Pierre Rouquet, infantryman at Verdun; photographed before being sent to 'the mill on the Meuse'. (Mme Françoise Eyraud)

You couldn't describe the deluge of fire that swept down on us. I was conscious of being in danger of death every second. I had the luck to come through those first fifteen days. But I ended up stupefied. I got the impression that my brain was jumping about in my skull because of the guns. I was completely KOd by the severity of the noise. At the end of fifteen days we came back down, seven to eight kilometres from the front to Jouy-sous-Lomballe. And that we thought was the end of that spell at Verdun as far as we were concerned. We had one quiet night's sleep; just one, that's all, then the next day the battalion that had relieved us was wiped out. They had lost as many killed as were taken prisoner. There were five or six left out of a whole battalion. No more.

We were sent up again with all speed to face another bombardment, one worse than ever. The shells of the 210s were coming over four at a time and we were being buried with every volley. Men were being completely entombed. The others dug them out. This lasted all day during preparations for a German attack. My moment came on the stroke of seven o'clock. It was my turn to be buried and you must understand I suffered greatly because being unable to move I could do absolutely nothing. I remember saying 'Well, that's it at last!' ['*Enfin*'] and I lost consciousness. I was dead. And then I was being disinterred with picks and shovels and they pulled me out, totally exhausted. My captain said, 'Lie down there', then later he sent me to a first-aid post two kilometres back.

Night fell and I could see the red flashes of shells passing in front of me.

At the first-aid post there was a major engaged in looking after a German whose leg had been badly smashed. The major put a dressing on him, and the German begged him, 'Finish me off'. ['*Finis-moi.*']

The major said to me, 'I haven't got time to see to you; go over there.' I went over there. I hadn't been there five minutes when a shell landed on the Major and the German. That's destiny. You're marked by fate. [*On est marqué.*]

After we'd been sent down to the field-kitchens, I was evacuated. I gather I stayed four days in a corner, exhausted, in total shock.'

On 21 May, almost opposite the sector that had been held by Rouquet and his comrades, Lieutenant Christian Bordeching, German Army, a student of architecture from Bremen, wrote a letter describing ten days in the line. He was at a point where the Mort-Homme rose to the left, while just to the right could be seen what he called 'the hell that was Côte 304'. He added that the word 'hell' was not wrongly used in relation to the area under the domination of the 'kingdom of the guns':

> The stench of unburied corpses rises from the ravaged former French trenches. Valuable equipment has been discarded everywhere along the road, weapons, munitions, food supplies, gas masks, barbed wire, grenades and other instruments of war. The last patches of grass are already well behind us and all we can see is a wilderness totally and violently created by explosives. The shell holes merging one into the other testify to the horror of the German artillery fire that preceded our advance and the answering fire of the French guns.
>
> It will take a miracle to cross this broken landscape, but we will soon have to do it for it is the only way to reach our positions in the rear, the lifeline to our victory at the front.
>
> News arrives through relays of runners for no telephone line stays intact for more than an hour, the cables are destroyed as soon as they are laid. If you pass the most dangerous zone of the hill at a run, you can cross the slightly less bombarded north flank of the hill and reach our position without being seen. The summit itself is at the moment neutral ground, it is a plateau a hundred metres long. Chancing their arm, some of our pioneers have crept out and dug trenches and set up barbed wire entanglements. Thus we can hold our own on the slope without too many losses for the French shells cannot reach this flank, it is only random shots that get here. Up here we are always on alert so as to be ready to defend ourselves or to attack. As regards sleeping or eating, it is not worth thinking about. We just have to put up with our hardships.
>
> The hill itself was originally partly wooded but now no more than a few blackened trunks are left visible, and there isn't a green leaf or a blade of grass, but in spite of this and amidst all the horror we have a daily miracle: every morning a lark sings and a multitude of maybugs buzz around us and remind us that beyond this war, which we have to endure, there is still a marvellous spring in progress, which, once we've taken our punishment, will delight us again.

Bordeching would survive Verdun, but would be killed on 20 April 1917, aged twenty-four.

As Bordeching's unit moved down from Côte 304. Reserve Lieutenant W. Weingartner's 38th Minethrower Company, 38th Jaeger Division, XI Corps, moved up; they might almost have passed each other on the road. It was his first experience of Verdun; long anticipated as inevitable, it had at last become reality. The following laconic, at times almost staccato notes from his diary make it evident that though the Germans were hitting the French hard, the French were not laggard in hitting back:

> During the night 20th and 21st we took two light *Minenwerfer* up to Côte 304. We fired and did a good deal of damage.

Grenade after grenade — a great many killed — many terribly injured — blown all over the place. The firing sounds like drums — it goes on and on.

There is wonderful visibility from Côte 304 and we can see across No Man's Land to Malancourt and Béthincourt.

May 22nd. Our trenches were absolutely smashed. 15,000 shells exploded and 4,000 of them were 21cm grenades. Everything in the munition depot, the station, line and road [sic] was blown to bits.

From 26th to 30th May we were at Côte 304 and built in a medium *Werfer* and then a second one.

Will F.R. 94 [Field Regiment 94] be in the next attack on the French?

The whole thing is put off until tomorrow.

Punctually at 5.15 in the afternoon the infantry troops went in and I was ordered to the front line. At 2.30 the heavy artillery started. The French replied with their well known quick-firers.

We had some men wounded — one next to me. They tried to get under cover. Lieut Spesshenz had an attack of shell-shock. I was just pulling myself together when another shell came over and burst about a yard behind me — a splinter got me in the face. Spesshenz was badly wounded in the right arm.

The fighting then finished and we went back to our dugouts and I had to sit down to recover myself. There were 70 men killed in my Company and in the 3rd Company 150, also Lieuts Jakob and Pezinna. It is remarkable what little damage was done to our trenches. I think it is our good work.

I wonder what will happen at the next attack.

The French are held up at the moment.

The French trenches were wired which we didn't expect.

I wondered should we be able to hold on.

May 31st. At 12 noon Lieut Pohl took my place. Thank God. Rested.

Lieutenant Alfred (Fred) Joubaire, of the French 124th Infantry Regiment, was an ardent young officer who went into the line on the right bank, in the vicinity of Douaumont, in late May. Although aware in advance that conditions at the front would be extreme and that the challenge would be severe, Joubaire seems to have found them much worse than he anticipated. He had kept a diary throughout his service with many optimistic and patriotic entries. What he wrote on 22 May after a long day of gallant but sacrificial fighting, however, showed a remarkable heightening of tone. In part it was a lament for those of his soldiers who had fallen, in part a paean of admiration for their amazing courage and gallantry under fire; it culminated, however, in what was in effect a denunciation of the whole situation and of the collective insanity which had put sentient human beings in such terrible conflict with each other:

> All of them were heroes. The 124th behaved magnificently. Led forward by their officers the men advanced to the attack with an irresistible élan. I confess I did not think they would behave so well. I had had my doubts. They were above all praise, and all those decent, perfectly peaceful peasants brought up to

the plough proved themselves as fierce as lions, splendid warriors, heroes. . . . It seemed as if their energy had become irresistible and was exalted in battle, that their strength had become formidable, had increased tenfold. You cannot help loving these ordinary soldiers, these anonymous heroes, who have been sacrificing themselves daily for nearly two years, without counting the cost, without hope of glory. How I love them!

But for how long is it going to carry on? You wonder with anguish when and how this unprecedented struggle will end. There is no solution in sight. I wonder if it will end simply for lack of fighting men. It is no longer a case of one nation struggling with another. It is two blocks of nations which are fighting, two civilisations which are in conflict with each other. People are suffering from the madness of death and destruction. Yes, humanity has gone mad. We must be mad to do what we are doing. What massacres! What scenes of horror and carnage! I cannot find words to express my feelings. Hell cannot be so terrible. Mankind has gone mad.

ALFRED JOUBAIRE

Mort au Champ d'honneur.

51. *Lieutenant Alfred Joubaire, 'fallen on the field of honour' Verdun, 2 June 1916*
(Frontispiece of his posthumously published diary, Pour la France, *1917)*

Other briefer entries went into his diary over the following days. Relieved on the 24th, the battalion went into reserve at Belrupt, a safe area to the south east of Verdun. It was a time to rest and recuperate, but also a time to mourn his comrades, among them his closest friend, Second Lieutenant Jacques de Lagerie:

Poor Jacques! At this moment you are an inert mass in horizon blue out on the plain. You were one of the first to fall, struck by a bullet. Where I do not know. But your men, whom you led so bravely, saw you fall, your face to the earth, without a cry or a gesture. You died as you have lived, heroically.

I didn't even have the consolation of seeing you for the last time, of paying honourable tribute to you in your hour of death. We didn't even say good-bye. But for us you are not dead, and in the new fighting that we shall have to face, your glorious shade will rise in front of us, will show us the road of honour and of victory, where you have found so beautiful a death.

Recognizing the very real possibility of his own extinction, Joubaire, before going into the line, had followed the by now time-honoured ritual of composing a 'last letter' to his parents to be sent in the event of his death. It was dated Sunday 21 May:

My dear Father and Mother

May you never receive this letter, for the day you read it, your Fred who loved you so much will have died for France. It is with joy that I will have given my life, and offered my suffering and my sacrifice for the wonderful cause which so exalts my heart. However, I leave with one great regret, that of leaving behind such a good and tender father and mother who are the objects of all my thoughts and affection. I realize also as I leave you that you will be overwhelmed by the weight of your grief, because I know that the affection I have for you you return to me a hundredfold.

But I know also that you are wonderful Christians and true French people. They are the finest titles to have. So I rely on you, on your patriotism and on your unswerving devotion to the sacred cause.

Do not weep! Your Fred is happy. He has died for his country. From heaven above where he is enjoying eternal and blessed life he is watching over you, he is taking care of you, he is loving you forever. It is there that one day we will meet again in blessed eternity.

Thank you, my dear Father and my darling Mother, for all the goodness you have shown to me. Thank you for the strong Christian education you gave me and which has enabled me to bear the harshest trials and overcome the most appalling suffering. Thank you! Thank you!

If sometimes I have hurt you or caused you sorrow, forgive me; let it be forgotten!

Au revoir, my dear Father and Mother. Au revoir, my dear little sisters, my beloved brothers. You, Jean, who have the honour of being a soldier, avenge me some day.

I cover you with kisses. Till we meet again in the World Beyond. Goodbye for now.

Your Fred

Having survived his baptism of fire, Joubaire's letter had remained unsent. But that would not be the case for long. After six days of rest, his battalion was once more ordered to the front. He wrote what would prove to be the final entry in his diary:

Wednesday 31 May. At 7.30 we go back up to the trenches. . . without enthusiasm. Three shells fall on us in the vicinity of Belrupt, without doing any harm.

At 7 a.m. on 2 June Joubaire's company was ordered to occupy a trench at Bois-Fumin which was under furious German bombardment. About 9 a.m. he was badly wounded in both legs by a German shell; the wound to the right leg was light, that to the left would later be described as *'affreuse'* — 'terrible', the bone at the knee being completely exposed. He died several hours later in a moment of calm remission after several hours of great pain. It was reported that his men were in tears. Despite the hints of disillusion in its final pages, Joubaire's diary was considered of such quality that it was published virtually in its entirety in Paris in 1917, under the title *Pour la France: Carnet de route d'un Fantassin* ('For France: An Infantryman's Note-Book'). He thus in death became an honoured part of France's continuing war-effort. He was a fitting hero, his story being all the more moving because of his youth; he had died — 'gloriously at his post of combat', according to an official citation reproduced on the book's final page — at the age of twenty-one.

13 The heroic defence of Fort Vaux

One quiet revolution carried out by Pétain was the restoration to use of some of the forts, which had been out of favour since the summer of 1915. They might have lost much of their defensive capacity, but they could offer safety and sanctuary to considerable numbers of troops who would otherwise be at the mercy of the enemy artillery. They could also function as aid posts to the wounded. This applied to both sides. Douaumont had now a far larger complement of Germans than there had been French when it was taken, while Vaux, from 15 March, was once more substantially garrisoned.

But being safe from shells under thick layers of concrete and earth did not always mean safe from danger. On 8 May disaster struck in the one of the lower galleries of Fort Douaumont. The Douaumont sector had been subjected to an intense French bombardment on the previous day, so the fort was full of wounded men as well as a battalion on rest from the fighting. At 6 a.m. there was a violent explosion in the grenade depot, which ignited a nearby depot containing flame-throwers. As well as the massive blast of an internal explosion, there was the added horror of flame rushing through the fort desperately seeking exit; not unlike the kind of effect that could result when a torpedo struck a ship at sea —

52. *The German 'war-grave' at Fort Douaumont, commemorating the loss of 679 victims of the explosion of a grenade store, 8 May 1916 (Cliché Editions MAGE)*

understandably so, because forts were in essence very much like battleships becalmed. Just as a stricken vessel would give out plumes of fire and smoke, so on that May morning a pillar of fire rose over Douaumont. The death toll was enormous; the estimated tally running to almost 700, though even higher figures have been quoted. Those in charge at first tried to solve the massive problem of disposing of the bodies by burying them outside the fort, but faced with so large a number it was decided to wall them up and turn the area where the disaster struck into a mass war grave.

So it has remained and the approach to it has been converted into a small sanctuary which is now known as the German chapel. Flags lean from the sidewalls on which permanent wreaths hang; a tall wooden cross against the back wall is fronted by a small white one, bearing the message: *'Den Toten Kamaraden'* — 'To the Dead Comrades'. It is as honoured within the fort as is its equivalent, the French chapel, where the keynote message is the somewhat different one: *'À la Mémoire des Disparus/en l'Honneur des Survivants/Pour que Soit Recueilli Le Haut Example d'Une Génération'* — perhaps most usefully translated as 'To the Memory of the Missing and in Honour of the Survivors, that the High Example of a Generation be Recognized'. Both shrines speak poignantly of the massive sacrifices endured on both sides at Verdun.

A German Medical Officer, Stephen Westman, a Berliner, saw the German shrine within weeks of its being set up. He had been in reserve but suddenly received an order to report for duty to a forward field-artillery regiment. Soon after he was summoned to an assignment not without considerable risk, for, as he put it in his memoir *Surgeon with the Kaiser's Army*, 'the artillery duel was at its height and the air was filled with smoke and dust and the whining of shells'. He described the circumstances:

> At Regimental headquarters a telephone message had been received that at an observation post on top of Fort Douaumont one of the telegraphists had been taken ill. He was complaining of severe abdominal pain and was vomiting. There was nothing else for me to do but go there, taking my steel helmet and one of the new contraptions, a gas-mask, because the French artillery had started firing shells with poisonous gases into the German positions. This most primitive gas-mask was like a surgeon's mask, and inside it we laid a pad of cotton wool, soaked in a fluid which was supposed to filter the air one breathed and protect the lungs from the poison. The eyes were left uncovered.
>
> The German sappers had dug two deep communication trenches, leading up to the hill on top of which the fort was situated. It did not take long before the French gunners had found the exact range, and they kept these lines of communication under constant fire. The earth right and left of the trenches was ploughed up by shells. The trenches themselves were hit time and again.
>
> I took with me two stretcher-bearers, one of whom knew how to find the observation post. When we arrived I found the man in agony, obviously suffering from acute appendicitis. We carried him into the fort and down one flight of stairs after another. Deep in the middle of the fort, protected by many feet of reinforced concrete, the French had built in one of the casemates an operating theatre, of which the Germans made good use. There were always two German

surgeons on duty, one of them from Berlin. They confirmed my diagnosis and immediately started to operate.

During the operation I could feel how the whole fort shook when a particularly heavy shell, most probably with a delayed action fuse, landed and exploded. However, we were safe, and only flakes of whitewash fell from the ceiling.

It was at this point that he saw the German shrine, though his figure of the dead differs markedly from that already given:

Afterwards I strolled through the fort, with its many dugouts and casemates. The entrance to one of them was bricked up and someone had fixed a plaque, with the inscription, 'Here rest 1052 German soldiers' — a whole battalion, who were sleeping in the casemate. Apparently one of them had smoked, and barrels of fuel for flame-throwers, which were stored there, had exploded, and not a single soul had survived.

Other theories suggest a less conventional explanation; that some Bavarian troops decided to brew coffee on upturned cordite cases, rashly using explosive taken from grenades as fuel. Clearly those responsible were unlikely to have survived to tell the tale, so the precise cause is beyond being established. Not only did the resultant explosion kill many Germans, however, it indirectly led to the deaths of many Frenchmen too. For the pillar in the sky was noticed on the French side and the correct conclusion drawn. It was also inferred that whatever disaster had struck the fort, it was now almost certainly highly vulnerable and was possibly ripe for the French to retake it. With Mangin in local command backed by Nivelle at Souilly, the situation was seen as one calling for a forceful response. Pétain counselled caution, but the new leadership could not resist the opportunity thus presented. Mangin had already made one bid to retake the fort on 22 April; his men had reached the superstructure but had then been repulsed by the enemy's machine-guns. Now he would try again with greater force and after a massive preliminary bombardment.

One of Nivelle's besetting weaknesses was a cavalier unconcern about security. His confidence was such that he had no compunction in letting the enemy know that he was about to attack. His battle plan, circulated too soon, was in enemy hands within forty-eight hours. When zero hour came on 22 May the Germans knew what to expect and their guns had the French trenches fully registered. They were thus able to exact a high price from the outset. Nevertheless within eleven minutes of the infantry going over they were in the fort. Panic struck the Germans; it was their time to question whether the cry of 25 February would be repeated — 'Douaumont ist gefangen' — this time to German dismay. Mangin assumed as much and turned up at Nivelle's headquarters with the cry 'Douaumont is ours!' It was a claim too soon. The German reply was swift and furious. By the morning of the 24th the fort was back in their hands. The French had not seized the whole of it, allowing the Germans to inject reinforcements through an underground tunnel; the Germans also imported a heavy mine-thrower which was able to lob aerial torpedoes at the French points of resistance. A thousand prisoners fell into German hands, and though the fort's defenders had suffered heavily, the French losses had been much higher. Mangin's star was suddenly in eclipse, though not for long; he would be back. But the forces under his command had undergone a fearsome ordeal. It was after the hard fighting of the 22nd that Lieutenant Alfred Joubaire was moved to make his comment that mankind had gone mad.

With regard to Douaumont the situation following Mangin's failure was a case of 'no change'. The most important outcome in relation to the winning of the war was a substantial addition on both sides to the body count — something which ultimately would benefit the Allies though at this point it merely succeeded in making Verdun even more of a charnel house than it already was.

The more significant episode at this time was the struggle which shortly developed for Douaumont's companion outwork to the south east, Fort Vaux. In contrast to the dispiriting débâcle at Douaumont, the fight for Vaux became a saga, a moving story of heroism and suffering out of which both sides could be said to have emerged with honour. In particular the final phase of its investment caught the imagination; Henry Bordeaux devoted a whole book to it with the title *The Last Days of Fort Vaux*. The episode had echoes of a mediaeval siege, or, searching for British parallels, one might turn to such an episode as the siege of Khartoum. Such events usually require a central figure. In the case of Khartoum there was the eccentric Victorian hero General Gordon. In the case of Vaux there was the quietly impressive, unflamboyant, unflinchingly brave Commandant Sylvain-Eugénie Raynal.

It was sensed in advance as the Germans probed towards Vaux that whoever commanded the fort would be a hostage to fortune. The French resorted to the unusual device of asking for volunteers among officers who had been incapacitated. Raynal, a forty-nine-year-old major recovering from his third wound, stepped forward and was accepted. Hobbling along on his stick, he took over command of the fort on the night of 30-31 May. He got there just in time. The next night, following a massive bombardment, the Germans seized the outworks of the fort and established themselves on the roof. The sensible outcome would have been immediate surrender, but Raynal and his men of the 142nd Regiment of Infantry were not there tamely to give in. They were to hold out and defy the enemy as long as they could, and, if the best came to the best, persuade the enemy to leave Vaux to its rightful owners. The fort was reasonably well victualled with preserved food and it had what was assumed to be an adequate supply of water. Unfortunately the depth of the cistern had been inadequately calculated so that the garrison had far less of that vital element than was thought. The struggle went on for seven days, with the Germans trying by every means at their disposal including gas to force the garrison to give in. Raynal created a series of defence points in the galleries so that if one was taken the next was ready to continue the fight. The wounded suffered terribly, bodies lay unburied, the atmosphere in the fort turned foul; but for the hard-pressed garrison the principal problem was not so much the enemy without as the appalling thirst within.

Commandant Raynal, who unlike Gordon survived to tell the tale, subsequently wrote a classic account of the defence of Fort Vaux. The following extract records a crucial moment on 4 June:

> It was in the course of that afternoon that the sapper sergeant in charge of the stores came and asked to speak to me in private, and said in a hoarse voice: '*Mon commandant*, there is practically no water left in the cistern.' I started, I made him

53. One of the galleries of Fort Vaux, with members of the garrison (Q 78064)

repeat what he had said, I shook him.

'There has been dirty work here.'

'No, sir, we have only served out the ration you laid down. It is the marks on the register which have been wrong.'

Then our agony began. I gave orders to hold back the little that remained and to make no further allowance today . . . .

There were those for whom already the agony was too much. Some men were so dehydrated that they were literally dying of thirst. Their only hope was to leave the fort at once. That same day a small group of such 'surplus personnel' was ordered by Raynal to attempt a break-out. Among them was a Corporal Guillantou, who later described what happened:

The moment of departure arrived. It was 1.30. Officer-cadet Buffet set out at the head. I followed him, and from then on, I went in front. The machine-guns were crackling, the rockets lit our way; a violent gunnery barrage accompanied us, from 305s down to 77s; it was a deluge of shells.

No matter! Our group of nine (several comrades had joined us on the way) didn't get disheartened and continued its advance.

The distance, however difficult and long to cross, was soon covered.

We reached a quarry that was part of the French lines. The cry 'Halt! Who goes there?' pulled us up sharp. Immediately several voices responded: *'France!'* Our task was almost ended; the break-out had been successful.

'*France!*' This was more than merely a means of identification. It was the assertion of a remarkable patriotic ideal.

Among the heroes of the story of Fort Vaux are the four pigeons which Major Raynal had at his disposal, especially the last pigeon which he released on that same day, 4 June; the soldiers gave it the name Valiant and it was to become a symbol of Fort Vaux. The message it carried to its homing point in the Verdun Citadel explained the garrison's desperate situation, and asked for attempts to be made to establish visual signal contact from the next fort south at Souville. The pigeon reached Verdun though mortally wounded; it was later honoured by a plaque to its memory placed at Vaux in 1929 by the French Society of Pigeon-Fanciers. Its epitaph was that which is common to all the graves of the French who fell in that war: '*Mort pour la France*'. There could be no higher tribute.

Raynal was eventually able to make contact with Fort Souville, though to little avail. Such attempts as were made to come to his aid achieved little progress in the face of the German artillery. To add to its difficulties Vaux was effectively in a salient and thus open to attack on three sides; in a sense a Verdun in microcosm. The end of the garrison's resistance could not be long deferred. Raynal's narrative graphically described the final hours before the surrender:

> During this day, 6th June, the Boche became more active against our barricades. It was as if he guessed the drama which was being played out within, and in actual fact the sufferings of my men, above all of the wounded, increased terribly. Thirst, that horrible thirst raged.
>
> I was in my command post with Sous-Lieutenant Roy, and my devoted sapper could find in his resourceful spirit no further remedy. Sounds of groans reached us. Mingled with the groans another noise struck our ear, that of a hesitant footstep and of hands rustling against the wall.
>
> The door suddenly opened. There stood a terrifying apparition. It was a wounded man, his naked chest swathed in bloody bandages. He leant with one hand against the door frame, and thrusting out a leg, went down on one knee. He held out to me his other hand in a supplicating gesture, and in a whisper, muttered: '*Mon commandant*, something to drink.'
>
> I went over to him and raised him up. 'I have no water, my brave fellow. Do as I do — hope. They are coming to our rescue.'
>
> Still groaning, my wounded man dragged himself back to the aid post. I looked at Roy. Like my own, his eyes were clouded . . . .
>
> It was the end. Unless a miracle happened, this would be the last night of our resistance. My men, who drank no more, ate no more, slept no longer, only held themselves upright by a prodigy of will.
>
> I summoned my officers to my command post. Every one of these brave men now despaired. They saw no salvation for their men, who must be preserved for the sake of the country, except by immediate surrender. But suddenly the guns outside began to bark, and the barking grew to a tempest. They were French guns. The fort was not being touched, but the vicinity was being violently barraged. The flame of hope once more sprang up.

'Listen, comrades. That is the French artillery. It has never fired so strongly. It is the preparation for an attack. Go to your positions. To-morrow morning, if we have not been delivered, I promise to submit to cruel necessity.'

Warmed by my words, the officers returned to their posts. About 11 p.m. our gunfire abruptly ceased, and the night passed away in complete calm, more nerve-racking for me than the storm of battle. Not a sound, not a hint of movement. I thought of the promise I had made. Had I the right to prolong resistance beyond human strength and to compromise uselessly the life of these brave men who had done their duty so heroically? I took a turn in the corridors. What I saw was frightening. Men were overcome with vomiting due to urine in the stomach, for so wretched were they that they had reached the point of drinking their own urine. Some lost consciousness. In the main gallery, a man was licking a little wet streak on the wall . . . .

7th June! Day broke, and we scarcely noticed it. For us it was still night, a night in which all hope was extinguished. Aid from outside, if it came, would come too late. I sent off my last message, the last salute of the fort and its defenders to their country. Then I turned to my men:

'It is all over, my friends. You have done your duty, the whole of your duty. Thank you.'

They understood, and together in one shout we repeated the last message which my instrument had just sent off: *Vive la France!*

In the minutes which followed a silence as of death fell upon the fort.

It is good to record that the Germans recognized the gallantry of the defence, the Crown Prince himself personally returning Raynal his sword. The Commandant was also decorated with the Legion of Honour. Meanwhile Henry Bordeaux was moved to heights of patriotic eloquence:

Hapless fort of Vaux, a stronghold reduced to ashes, a marvel of endurance, you who pulsated like a human heart, the whole world had its eyes riveted on you for the space of a few days. The whole world was not in error when it ascribed to you that significance which your courage enhanced. You were minister to plans whose full tenor you did not know, and today you play your part in the operations that are unfolding themselves and will continue to unfold themselves.

Land that has been overrun by the lava of volcanoes shows an unparalleled fertility when the lava has passed. Upon your tortured soil a harvest of victories will spring up, and from your defence will gush forth a fresh and inexhaustible fount of French heroism

As well as the lament, there was also the message. Henry Bordeaux's was simply stated: 'VAUX is lost, for the time being, but VAUX will be regained.' Thus Vaux joined Douaumont as an icon of France which would have to be reclaimed no matter how high the cost.

It is interesting to note Pétain's reactions to these two episodes, as recorded in his book on Verdun. Concluding a brief account of the attempt on Fort Douaumont with a reference

54. *General Joffre decorating a hero of Fort Vaux (Q 70069)*

to the events of 24 May he stated: 'The measures taken by General Mangin to retrieve the situation were not successful and during the evening he was forced to see his division relieved and that of General Lestoquoi substituted for it.' There was no hint of pique or anger at the failure of a scheme undertaken against his better judgement and certainly no crowing over Mangin's abrupt departure. He thus showed, in Alistair Horne's words, 'a magnanimity rare among the *ex post facto* writings of war leaders'. If there was any blame it perhaps lay in the brevity with which the subject was discussed, for his account of the defence of Fort Vaux is extended, detailed and, for someone only rarely given to outspoken prose, almost emotional. He retold at length the story of the fort's last stand, repeating verbatim Raynal's messages to Fort Souville and giving full honour to Vaux's last pigeon, while in his references to the attempts to save the Commandant and his 'heroic comrades in arms' he offered generously high praise to his successor at Souilly:

> The French High Command had never for a moment been deaf to [Raynal's] appeals. Counter attacks, prepared in advance or attempted on the spur of the moment, were launched almost without interruption, but none of them was able to break through the ring of fire that cut off the fort. As late as June 7th, when the German communiqué reporting the capture of the fort had already been issued, after Major Raynal and his soldiers had already fallen, crushed by shells, suffocated by gas, exhausted by thirst, General Nivelle was despatching to their aid the mixed brigade commanded by Colonel Savy, 'on the noblest mission that can be entrusted to French troops, that of succouring comrades in arms who are gallantly doing their duty under tragic conditions.' But it was too late! Fort Vaux had fallen, and must wait with Fort Douaumont for better days, before it could resume its place proudly within the French lines.

14 The martyr city

What meanwhile of the city at the heart of this long struggle?

The more hard-headed on the German side soon realized that it would never be theirs. Hence the cynical comment of General von Gallwitz, commander of Meuse Group West, whose forces advanced just over two miles in four months at a cost of 69,000 men; given the present rate of progress, he quipped, 'we will be in Verdun at the earliest in 1920'.

On the Allied side, however, from the moment the battle began there was a huge and inevitable curiosity surrounding Verdun. What were conditions like in this place with the resounding name and the long history that was now in the world's headlines, and on the successful defence of which so much seemed to depend?

Fortunately Mr H. Warner Allen, Special Correspondent of the British Press with the French Armies, was soon able to answer some at least of the questions in people's minds. His report, which appeared in *The Times* on 8 March under the heading DESERTED VERDUN, and was widely circulated elsewhere, is all the more interesting in that during his visit he met Georges Scott, the artist who so rapidly offered to the world his evocative interpretation of the Sacred Way. He found a city 'not crowded', with not a shop open, and with a muster of only three civilians 'all three of them rightly proud of their courage' in staying there:

> I have just been walking down the main street. Everywhere there is silence except for the crashing of the big shells and the sound of splinters falling on the roofs. . . .
>
> It was in the Rue Mazel that I met one of the three civilians of Verdun. He was contemplating the view from his door with a contented smile and looked at me with supreme contempt when I scuttled for cover at a particularly loud explosion. 'You are taking refuge on the wrong side of the road,' he remarked mildly. 'The left is the side to escape from splinters, since that is the side from which the Boches are firing. Anyway it is no use ducking, since by the time you have heard the shell the danger is over.'
>
> The first objective of visitors to a bombarded town is invariably the Cathedral — since the Germans have made a habit of the destruction of these sacred edifices. In Verdun, however, they cannot see their target and, consequently, so far, beyond an insignificant hole in the roof and the breaking of all its glass, the Cathedral is intact.
>
> As we went up the steep lonely streets towards the Cathedral our attention was suddenly attracted by a strange piping sound that contrasted quaintly with

55. *'Verdun' by Walter E. Spradbery, watercolour, showing a Croix Rouge ambulance amidst the city ruins (Imperial War Museum Department of Art)*

the continuing roar of exploding shells. It was a kitten mewing plaintively in the first storey of a house. It had obviously been forgotten in the haste of evacuation. The owner of the house had closed up the shutters and had never given a thought to the poor beast that was slowly starving to death.

A rescue party was at once formed. M. Georges Scott, the well-known artist, who is mobilized as a Chasseur Alpin, mounted on my shoulders and endeavoured to prise open the shutter with a stick. But his efforts were unavailing, and eventually the kitten's life was saved by the firemen of Verdun, who broke into the house.

Several large shells had fallen near the Cathedral. One of them had gutted a girls' school and another had landed fair and square on a shop that sold religious ornaments and emblems. For some unexplained reason there was a curé's hat lying pathetically on top of the *débris,* and at the back against a wall that had miraculously escaped destruction stood a stucco statue of Joan of Arc which had passed through the storm of fire unscathed.

Mr Warner Allen clearly saw a portent in this, though it is fascinating as well as curious that the preservation of a statue of a heroine of France burnt to death by the English should now be seen by an Englishman as implying that the hand of God was with the French in their present struggle with the Germans. New friendships, of course, make nonsense of old enmities; indeed, in Falkenhayn's view, France, far from being England's enemy, was now England's best sword. St Joan was thus an icon whose survival of the fire of 1916 could give hope and comfort to English and French alike. But the Special Correspondent had one other image to offer his readers, a *Mary Celeste* scene suggesting that even in their time of great trial the citizens of Verdun had maintained their honour:

> There is no pillage and the refugees who in their hurry left their windows open and doors unlocked can sleep easy as to the contents of their houses, except in so far as an enemy projectile may reduce them to powder. Just near one of the gates there is a house of which the shutters have not been closed and the window is still open. It seems that just before the evacuation the owner of that house had some special occasion to celebrate. Looking through the window one can see the table laid for 16 persons and everything prepared for an excellent meal. There was a beautiful clean tablecloth with napkins folded mitre-shaped for every guest. Decanters of wine, red and white, were standing beside each plate. On the sideboard piles of oranges and apples were waiting for the party that was never to eat them.

His report ends with a paragraph remarkably modern in tone, in that it makes clear that this was not just a privileged excursion for him alone, but was a fully accredited visit by the then media:

> We are at the present moment waiting for the Germans to allow us to leave Verdun. In the meantime the cinematographers have been taking everything they can find in Verdun, and their only grief is that so far no shell has burst near enough to their apparatus to be photographed.

Another Englishman who was eager to satisfy his curiosity in regard to Verdun was Charles Hartley, of *Section Sanitaire Anglaise No 10*. After several weeks of hard driving on the Sacred Way and a brief period of service in the Argonne, the opportunity finally came. He seized it with alacrity. He had declared his ambition soon after his arrival:

> *July 5.* I have a very strong desire to see the section sent to Verdun, but until we are permanently attached to a division there does not appear to be much chance of this. Those older members of the convoy who were there when the first German onslaught was made in February, tell me they have no desire to go back after their trying experiences, and this I can understand to a great extent. Nevertheless, that Sector has a particular attraction to me and I am glad to find that Turner has the same feeling about it and is keen to get up there.

He was finally able to 'get up there' a little over four weeks later, his unit having been formally attached to a French division, the 31st. He was fully aware that this would be no joyride, the city's crisis being far from over. As he expressed it: 'Although their first great attack in February has somewhat spent itself the enemy has never lost its grip on the Verdun Sector, and although the French say Verdun will never fall, these are anxious days.' But this was no deterrent; he noted under the date 2 August:

I heard this evening that one of our cars is taking in an Officer to the town of Verdun so I went to our O/C and asked and obtained permission to accompany Partridge who was driving. Although I knew that the convoy was going to the Verdun Sector no one could tell whether we would ever get into the town itself but it was, as the O/C said to me, a chance in a lifetime.

Aug. 5. We started at 6 a.m. having got the password and the run of about 35 miles was very interesting. We fetched up at the Cathedral in the upper part of the town and we got leave to 'park' the car there while we had some food which we brought with us, and had a look round. The town was full of soldiers and whole streets were in a complete state of ruins. The Cathedral itself was practically intact. The bridge across the Meuse, the entrance to which is through a Norman Gateway, has escaped the bombardment.

This being my first visit to a town under bombardment I was greatly impressed with everything I saw around me. Partridge and I went into a number of shattered houses and shops, in which furniture and valuables were lying about in confused heaps everywhere. Looting is of course '*défendu*' [forbidden] and the French soldier, at any rate, knows what to expect if he is caught. Sympathetic soldiers passing along nodded to us and asked us if we had found any little 'souvenir'.

I managed to secure some good snapshots with my camera which I always carefully carried with me and produce guardedly on suitable occasions. If one goes about it in a right way and does not show a camera under the very nose of the military police, one can do a great deal, and I have often succeeded in getting French officers to tactfully look away when photographing something of interest. After spending several hours in the town, where everything on this occasion was quiet, but for the distant booming of guns down the valley of the Meuse, Partridge and I made our way to Nixéville where the convoy had just turned up.

Sentiments of a somewhat different kind engaged the minds of those who were sent to Verdun whether they wished to go or not — the soldiers of the French army.

Lieutenant Henri Desagneaux came to Verdun in mid-June. For most of the spring he and his 106th Infantry Regiment had enjoyed the relative tranquillity of the Vosges but they were aware that under the Noria system their summons to the mill on the Meuse would be bound to come. On 26 May he noted in his diary:

Yet again, there is talk of our being relieved and going to Verdun. They have been fighting there for over three months now, all divisions are going there in turn.

The next entry was dated 10 June:

At one in the morning, order for departure at 4 a.m. We are to march in the direction of Verdun. That gives us an extra day of life! We are billeted at Rosières near Bar.

Photographs taken by Charles Hartley during his visit to Verdun:

56.   *(above) Street scene with the eighteenth century Chapelle du Collège in the background (HU 66833)*

57.   *(opposite) General view across the River Meuse with the Cathedral dominating the skyline (HU 66834)*

They footslogged approximately a third of the Sacred Way. He noted on the 12th:

> Issoncourt, last stage before Verdun. There is not much room as car-load upon car-load of supplies and munitions speed past us.

Thereafter they changed from boots to wheels. Their progress was less tiring but it got them more speedily to the focus of action:

> *13 June, Tuesday*
> Reveille at 2 a.m. At 5, we travel by car and are put down at Nixéville, 6 kilometres from Verdun. We bivouac in a wood in a lake of mud. The guns fire angrily, it's pouring down. At 3 p.m. we are ordered to stand by to leave. We don't, however. We spend the night and the day of the 14th waiting, in torrential rain with mud up to our ankles. Our teeth chatter with cold, we are very uncomfortable. Although the troops have been stopping here for the last four months to go to and from Verdun, there is not one single hut or shelter. We camp in individual tents in thick mud. You should hear what the men say about it!

At 5 p.m., order for departure at 6.30. We are going to be quartered in the Citadel of Verdun. Faces are grave. The guns are thundering over there. It's a real furnace, everyone realizes that perhaps tomorrow death will come. Numerous rumours are circulating; we are going to 'Mort-Homme' which has been captured by the Boches; or to the Fort at Vaux . . . . What is certain, nothing good lies in store for us.

We arrive at the Citadel at 10 p.m. after a difficult march through the mud.

15 June, Thursday
We spend the day in the Citadel waiting. The guns fire ceaselessly. Huge shells (380s-420s) crash down on Verdun causing serious damage. I walk as far as the town; it's in ruins and deserted. One can't stay outside for long as shells are dropping everywhere.

The Citadel is a real underground town, with narrow-gauge railway, dormitories, and rooms of every type; it's safe here, but very gloomy.

For many soldiers the Verdun Citadel — one of Vauban's most formidable creations now put to the uses of a twentieth century war — was their introduction to the Verdun battle. It was so for René Arnaud, who had noted the 'it's your turn now' look of the soldiers coming out of the battle as he and his comrades journeyed up the Sacred Way. For him as for Desagneux the Citadel was the last staging post, the last refuge, before the real thing. But first there was the matter of arriving in Verdun itself, by night:

> Soon the cool dampness of the Meuse reached us. Beyond the river mist one
> could just make out the dark, silent, dead town of Verdun. We crossed a road
> at a point where a dull lantern shone on a notice board: 'Danger Point. Pass

Quickly.' A man in a dark greatcoat watched us cross over from the depths of his sandbagged shelter. The furtive light from the lamp revealed the emblem of the white grenade on his helmet — a gendarme. I remembered the joke which had gone the rounds of the army: 'The real front begins with the last gendarme.' Was this the last one?

A bridge over a railway line, a road running between mist-laden meadows, zigzagging alongside the river. Suddenly an enormous dark wall, flights of steps, muffled shouts, and the warm odour of cabbage, mouldy bread and creosol. I went down a long vaulted gallery through which passed tip-up trucks drawn by mules, making a deafening din. Doors opened on to typists' offices, engine-rooms and bakeries smelling of warm bread. Then, in the weak electric light, I passed through hall after hall filled with soldiers, some of them changing their clothes after the march for fear of catching a cold — for great danger did not make them forget the little ones — others eating ravenously from their mess-tins and drinking out of their flasks. All these casemates with their tiny windows like portholes and the thick pillars supporting the low ceiling reminded one of the between-decks in a boat full of immigrants.

I at last reached the room which I was to share with six or seven other officers from the battalion. The only decoration on the whitewashed walls was the inscription: 'Max. weight 600 Kg per sq. metre' — doubtless meant before the war for the quartermasters who must have used this for storing their stocks of biscuit and tins of bully-beef. I thought to myself, 'As cannon fodder we weigh less'. The heat was suffocating. Through the window, which looked on to a gloomy courtyard, there came the filthy stench of soil-tubs. In front the eye was struck by a dark wall which rose like a counterscarp above the well of the courtyard. Shell-bursts, probably from a 380, had made fresh yellow scars on it. One could hear the sound of guns, a heavy metallic boom on three notes, like the bass stops of a cathedral organ: probably a French armoured train firing in the neighbourhood. On the other side the barrage continued as always.

15 The turning-point

Forts inevitably dominate the story of Verdun. Forts constructed at huge cost under the dictates of one military philosophy; forts abruptly demoted at the impact of the next. A supreme fort almost casually lost to the enemy; a lesser fort held to the last despite extremes of suffering.

The Battle of Verdun reached its crisis in the last week of June, with an important codicil in the first two weeks of July. A fort would provide the focus for this stage also.

Almost midway between Fort Douaumont and Verdun, at the Chapelle Sainte-Fine crossroads (so called after a small ruined shrine that was a minor place of pilgrimage before 1914), stands a monument that is all too easy for present-day visitors to overlook as they hurry past to greater and more famous memorials. It consists of the figure of a wounded lion, lying as though collapsed on a sturdy stone plinth. Strictly it is the monument to the French 130th Division, though the plinth also bears the names of all the other divisions that fought in this sector. But it has a second significance in that it marks the extreme point of the German advance in 1916. In fact the high watermark is even nearer to the city, in the deep woods that cloak the final ridge before the ground falls away steeply to the Meuse Valley. Fort Souville, however, is not easily accessible today; mainly it is an undergrowth-covered ruin of which the most significant element that survives is the Pamard casemate, an outwork built to house two machine-guns, impressive enough in its own right as it lurks menacingly among the thickly encroaching trees.

Souville was always a second-line construction, never being made up to the specifications of its more famous neighbours. But it was not spared the attention of the enemy artillery which struck it with an estimated 38,000 shells between April and June 1916, many arriving during the days when it was the last point of visual contact with the heavily besieged Fort Vaux. Now the Germans saw it as a key target. The only defence works between it and Verdun was the minor Fort St Michel on the lower edge of Meuse Heights and the Fort de Belleville which was virtually in the city's outskirts. Seize Souville and who knew what might happen. General Schmidt von Knobelsdorf devised a plan to take it, against the better judgement of a now extremely reluctant Crown Prince, who increasingly saw no virtue in further carnage.

The attack, which was also meant to overrun other important sites such as Thiaumont and Fleury, was launched with great optimism on the night of 22-23 June. The optimism sprang from the fact that this was seen as the most promising assault since 21 February, the Germans having assembled a force of 30,000 men to launch against a relatively small area. Among them as a spearhead force was the Alpine Corps, one of the best units in the German Army with the extra advantage of just having arrived at Verdun. They were therefore fresh and at the peak of their form. The Germans also had a formidable new weapon to deploy: a more sophisticated form of poison gas. This was phosgene, alias carbonyl chloride: 'Green

58. *French gas-masks, December 1915 style: to be put under severe trial during the German phosgene gas attack in June 1916 (Q 79011)*

Cross Gas' as it was known to the Germans because of the distinctive marking on the shells containing it. Vicious, asphyxiating, a killer that attacked vegetation and which, if briefly, even cleared the battle area of flies, it produced shock as well as horror. Von Knobelsdorf hoped it would cause extreme panic among the French who would therefore leave open the road to Verdun, at that point a mere two and a half miles off.

In the evening of 22 June, the French were aware that the more or less continuous German bombardment had ceased. This was a battle in which sudden silences were distinctly disturbing. There was good reason to be concerned.

Then a strange low noise was heard, almost as of a massed flight of birds; in fact it was the sound of shells flying over which did not explode. Some Frenchmen thought the Germans had sent over a mass of duds. And then they became aware of a hideous, putrefying smell that sent men reeling back and groping for gas-masks which failed to have the expected effect. It was the nightmare experience of the Second Battle of Ypres back in April 1915 in an enhanced form.

The effect was devastating. Horses ran wild then collapsed, foaming at the mouth. Abandoned ambulances and soup-kitchens littered the roads. The French gun-crews took the brunt, as was intended; for the first time in the long artillery duel one side had the advantage of the other. By the following dawn only a handful of French guns were firing. Then, abruptly, the quiet inferno of gas-shells ceased and the standard high-explosive barrage was resumed. Everybody in the French trenches knew what this meant. The German infantry would soon be at their throats.

What happened next was graphically described by Henry Bordeaux:

> Masked, blinded, half-suffocated and half-buried in the earth thrown up by the incessant shell-fire, the troops in the line of the Garbit, Toulorge, Giraudun Divisions knew perfectly well that, when the tornado lifted, that moment would

be the signal for the attack. They waited (and what a waiting that was!) on ground churned up by fire, listening to the pitiful cries of the wounded, and with the dead to keep them company. They waited, controlling their nerves, all on edge but strung towards one object, one idea, never to give ground but to fight and hold on. The sentries wiped with their benumbed fingers the glasses of their periscopes and peered into the smoking horizon. The barrage lifts, the enemy are leaving their trenches. 'Ah! Here they come!'

At 7 a.m. the storm battalions advanced, marching in mass formation, preceded by an extended line of bombers armed with hand-grenades. Bavarian units of the Alpine Corps swarmed towards the Thiaumont redoubt on Froideterre hill, which capitulated after fierce fighting, the chasseurs of the 121st Battalion being outnumbered ten to one. Only sixty of them escaped with their lives. Through this breach in the line four Bavarian companies burst through as far as the Froideterre redoubt. But the hard fight at Thiaumont had allowed time for the 114th Battalion of Chasseurs to come up. They deployed as if on parade and using the grenade and the bayonet to devastating effect threw back the Bavarians from the redoubt. Meanwhile, the village of Fleury had been outflanked by two Alpine Corps units, the Bavarian Leib Regiment and the Second Prussian Jaegers, who managed an advance of a mile in just three hours. Twenty-four German field guns were rushed forward to support the attack. The French artillery, recovering from its earlier shocks, pounded the Germans in reply. But by the end of the day Fleury was firmly in the Alpine Corps' hands.

In front of Souville the French fared better, the main attack being stemmed by the 307th Brigade. But to the north east, where the 407th Regiment were dug in on the wooded slopes of the Bois de Vaux-Chapitre, the Germans broke through on the regiment's left and threatened the defenders from the rear. Its Colonel managed to slow down the Germans with machine-guns and then so surprised them with an attack mounted by an improvised force of reserves, including telephonists, stretcher bearers, pioneers, orderlies and cooks, that they were forced to fall back.

The situation, however, remained extremely severe. The first impact, especially when information came through about the enemy's secret weapon, had been enormous, with increasingly depressing reports reaching Pétain at Bar-le-Duc. In Verdun the garrison began hurriedly to prepare for a possible siege. A senior medical officer of the 129th Infantry Division noted: 'This is a tragic hour. The Governor has put both the city's immediate environs and the city itself into a state of defence. From my hospital window I watch the digging of a trench on the terrace below.' The city seemed seriously under threat and for a time the old spectre arose of having to withdraw from the right bank.

However, the German attack did not achieve the hoped-for miracle. Von Knobelsdorf arguably called off the gas attack too soon. The gas itself tended to settle in any available lower ground thus leaving much of the higher ground in contention clear. The French gas masks proved to be not so ineffective as had originally been assumed. More, the Germans had not enough reserves to press home their initial advantage. And then there was the weather. 23 June was a day of fearsome midsummer heat which, as if in revenge for the sufferings of Fort Vaux, inflicted the attackers with a raging thirst. If to defend with dry

59. *Kaiser Wilhelm II, centre, with General Paul von Hindenburg left, and General Erich Ludendorff right, the team that took over German strategy after the dismissal of General Falkenhayn in August 1916 (Q 23746)*

and parched throats was agonizing, to maintain a bitterly contested offensive was even worse. One unit signalled: 'If no water can be brought up, the battalion will have to be taken out of the line.'

If that was a keynote statement on the German side, the day produced a more lasting one on the French. The circumstances were later described by Pétain:

> General Nivelle, even while he was sending urgent appeals for reinforcements, attempted to play upon all the responsive chords in the hearts of his troops by assuring them that their isolated rôle in the battle would soon cease: 'This is the decisive moment. The Germans feel that they are being hunted down on all sides and are launching violent and desperate attacks against our front, in the hopes of reaching the gates of Verdun before they are themselves attacked by the reunited forces of the Allied armies. Comrades, you must not let them pass.'

Thus the authorized translation of Pétain's account. The original French reads: '*Vous ne les laisserez passer, mes camarades.*' This would be transmuted in due time into the more famous form: '*Ils ne passeront pas!*'; 'They shall not pass!' With '*On les aura!*' the phrase would become one of the great slogans of the Battle of Verdun. The fact that it assisted, if only in terms of morale and pride, in producing the response required would eventually be symbolized best of all in the inscription on the so-called 'Skeleton Memorial' erected after the war on the crest of the Mort-Homme. It reads, in sturdy stone capitals: '*Ils n'ont pas passé*' — 'They did not pass'.

60. *Fleury after the fighting; a member of* Section Sanitaire Anglaise 1, *which also served at* Verdun, *photographed on the site of the village's destroyed railway station* (HU 82709)

All this lay ahead. The Germans had struck hard and made gains, but the Souville road was still barred, and the fort was still in French hands. But General von Knobelsdorf was not yet ready to concede. He tried a repeat scenario on the night of 10-11 July, again starting the attack with gas and again achieving some initial success. It was on the morning of the 12th that the historic moment occurred which gave the Souville ruins a fame that make them an essential part of the epic of Verdun. Thirty men of the German 140th Regiment briefly held the top of the fort and, so it is said, glimpsed the city and the river far below. But they could not go further. The French swept them off the glacis, some being taken prisoner, the rest being either sent packing or killed.

In a telling comparison, Alistair Horne has written of the moment when the Germans stood on Souville and looked at the 'promised land' they would never enter: 'The spires of Moscow as seen in the grey distance of autumn 1941 cannot have seemed more enthralling — or more unobtainable — to German soldiers.' In another foreshadowing of events to come, the Regimental Adjutant of the Second Prussian Jaegers who fought at Fleury on 23 June was Oberleutnant Friedrich Paulus, who as General Paulus would be forced to surrender to the Russians in the Second World War's nearest equivalent to Verdun, Stalingrad.

The second German failure at Souville was effectively the end of the Verdun offensive, if not of the Verdun fighting, which would continue for some weeks — until the start of the return match, the revenge, which would inevitably follow.

Between the two Souville attacks, another event had taken place which would also contribute in a major way to the development of events at Verdun. Away to the west Joffre's cherished dream was now being turned into reality and the other great battle of 1916, that of the Somme, was under way. It had a distinctly unpromising start— producing for the British the costliest day in their military history — but at least it was up and running and would give the Germans something other to think about than the now almost stalled 'mill on the Meuse'.

16 The continuing battle

No Englishman watched events at Verdun with greater interest and a more sharply critical eye than Winston Churchill. Sometime in August he wrote an essay on the subject which would appear in the *London Magazine* in November. Discussing the French response to the German offensive he suggested that his allies had been far too inflexible:

> The French suffered more than the defence need suffer by their valiant and obstinate retention of particular positions. Meeting an artillery attack is like catching a cricket ball. Shock is dissipated by drawing back the hands. A little 'give', a little suppleness, and the violence of impact is vastly reduced.

Cricket, however, was not a Frenchman's game and certainly there was no thought of 'giving' in the late spring and summer weeks of 1916, even when the tide was moving France's way. If the Germans attacked, they countered. If the Germans did not attack, they attacked. Meanwhile, the Germans, still under the grip of Falkenhayn's hard philosophy, fought with equal determination and commitment. Indeed, they sometimes amazed the French opponents by continuing to launch attacks which had a huge expenditure in casualties and little or no positive outcome. Thus one French infantryman, a Corporal René Pigeard, wrote at this time:

> We are holding on, it's fantastic. But what is beyond understanding is the way the Boches keep on attacking. You have to admit that never again will anyone see such persistence in useless sacrifice: when by some chance they gain a patch of land, they know what it costs them and even then they often don't hold on to it.

'Useless sacrifice': *'sacrifice inutile'* in the original French. In this context the adjective could as easily be rendered as 'futile'. 'Futility' is a word frequently brought out in the context of the Western Front war, often without real justification, but it could well be used in relation to the fighting on both sides during the summer phase of the Verdun campaign.

Against this, of course, it could be said that although it is possible now, with hindsight, to describe the German failure at Souville as the battle's defining moment, this was not so evident at the time. No whistle blew. Neither side was ordered from the field. Indeed, an undismayed von Knobelsdorf began agitating for yet another attack towards Souville. At last the Crown Prince decided he could take no more; he appealed to his father, who for once felt the need to intervene. Von Knobelsdorf suddenly found himself *en route* for an appointment on the Russian front. There then followed an even greater coup. On 29

August Falkenhayn was dismissed. This was less to the Kaiser's liking but Hindenburg, seen by many as his obvious successor and with a reputation untouched by failure, was induced to threaten his own resignation unless Falkenhayn was removed. There was no answer to this, for Hindenburg after substantial victories on the Eastern Front had become, to quote the eminent British historian Cyril Falls, 'a hero-God; Wotan in human form'. He and his doppelganger Ludendorff took over the German war-machine which they would run to the edge of the defeat of 1918, when they would make their exits and leave others to take the consequences. Falkenhayn was sent to cope with the consequences of the recent enrolment of Roumania on the Allied side, a task which he did successfully, though this was not to redeem the reputation that he had forfeited at Verdun. As for Hindenburg he was now set on the course by which, to pursue Cyril Falls' Wagnerian theme, he would eventually introduce on to the stage his own version of the evil Hagen, Adolf Hitler, who would ultimately bring the drama to a dreadful end with the *Götterdämmerung* of 1945.

But all that was far in the future. In the summer of 1916 neither of the two new German supremos had any time for the mess that Falkenhayn had left behind him, but the battle could not be stopped overnight. It was like a train out of control, careering along the tracks, a thing with its own momentum. And whatever the Germans decided they knew the French were in no mood to let them return quietly to their trenches. France wanted *'revanche'* — revenge — the return match, no matter what the cost in human lives.

Remarkably, however much the battle was ratcheted up by the thrusting philosophies on both sides, some men still managed to maintain their link with the world outside by recording their experiences in vivid and often harrowing letters.

Pierre Prouteau was just 20 when he arrived to fight at Verdun; he would survive, but that was far from certain when he wrote to his parents on 10 June:

> For four days we have been in a forward position by night and by day in a sort of shelter which is really meant for four people whereas there are fifteen of us.
>
> We were relieved this evening to go into reserve for eight days where I can hopefully pick myself up.
>
> Today I am duty liaison with two others and as we are just about all right, though still unable to go out anywhere, I am writing you a few lines.
>
> You will never guess, no, not if I give you a thousand chances, where we are sheltering. So I had better tell you.
>
> Well, we are in a cellar, in a breech made by a shell which we are sharing with two skeletons. As a shelter it is strong enough but it's macabre at the same time. Perhaps we're in some old cemetery, though I couldn't vouch for that, given the state of the terrain.
>
> At night our post is in the ruins of a farm of which a few stones scattered here and there are all that remain. Here is a daisy that I picked there.
>
> After our eight days in reserve we will have a further eight days penance to do. During this time do send two or three parcels if you can.

61. *A symbol of attrition; a German infantryman fighting on in a damaged trench beside the corpse of a French soldier   (Q 23760)*

If the weather clears up as it seems to want to do, we would be better off but we haven't had any luck in our eight days. It has been awful weather, water above, water below, mud everywhere. You seem to think that it is a bad thing that I am not drinking my wine, but I have no stomach for it. My digestion is wrecked, poor thing. My legs feel a bit the same way, so altogether I am in a sorry state. . . .

Goodbye for now, with love.

A letter describing remarkably similar conditions was written from the German side on 17 July by Anton Steiger, a former student of philosophy aged nineteen who would be killed on the Somme just three months later. He described the dugout which he and his comrades had shared during their recent spell in the line:

Our dugout was an old, half blown-in, French casemate about 150 yards away from the fort of Thiaumont. From our side it had looked a mere hummock of earth. The entrance was like that of a fox's hole. At the end of a short passage some broken steps led down into the place we had occupied for four days. Dead bodies were lying under the soil, one of its legs protruding up to the knees. There were three separate chambers down there: one was full of rockets and detonators; another — as big as our kitchen at home – in which we were housed, also contained French ammunition; the third was full of French explosive. It was pitch dark the whole time, as we had only a few candlesticks.

There was a horrible smell down there too — the reek of decomposing bodies; I could hardly eat anything the whole four days.

On the third day the French artillery opened such an intense fire on the dugout with 28cm guns that we thought it would certainly be blown in altogether.

On the fourth day, Friday, the heavy artillery fire started again early in the morning and continued till 9.30 p.m. Just think what that means! Ten hours in a dugout under shell fire; ten hours in the expectation of being buried alive, or of being blown through the air if a shell should happen to fall where the explosive is stored. . . .

René Pigeard, aged 22, wrote to his parents on 27 August when out of the line recovering from a wound. His letter (quoted earlier for its incisive comments on the futility of many German attacks) catches the sense of almost intoxicating relief at leaving behind the rigours of the battlefield:

You can imagine that to rediscover life in this way seems almost like madness. To go for hours without hearing the whistle of a shell over one's head . . . To be able to stretch full length, and on straw . . . To have clean water to drink after we have been seen behaving like deer, ten or so around a shell-hole, arguing over a mugful of stagnant, muddy and filthy water; to have hot food to eat, enough of it and without earth in it, which was the case whenever we did have something to eat. . . To be able to wash your face, to take off your shoes, to be able to pass the time of day with those that are left. . .   Do you understand, all this happiness at a stroke, it is too much. I have been in a daze all day long.

Reliefs are all carried out at night, and so you can understand how I have this impression of having left an ancient little wood where no living tree remains, where no tree still has three branches, and then the following morning, after two or three hours' feverish rest, suddenly seeing a row of chestnut-trees in full leaf, full of life, full of sap, in short seeing something which is life-giving instead of something which destroys!

Imagine that on each side of the front lines, over an area of a kilometre, there is not a single blade of greenery left, just a land grey with dust, endlessly turned inside out by the shells: piles of broken stone, rubble, slashed tree trunks, fragments of masonry which make you think that in that place there had been a house, that there had been 'people' . . .   I thought I had seen it all at Neuville. But no, that was an illusion. Over there, it was still a war: one heard gun-shots, machine-guns, but here nothing but shells, shells, nothing else; then there are the trenches battered by both sides, shreds of flesh which fly through the air, the splattering blood. You are going to think that I exaggerate, but no. It is actually less than the full truth. You wonder how it has come about that we have allowed such things to happen. Perhaps I ought not to describe these atrocious things, but people need to know, for they are not aware of the too brutal truth. And to think that it is two thousand years since Jesus Christ

62. *More troops for the furnace. Senegalese soldiers entraining for the front, June 1916. France's colonial troops played an important part in the Verdun fighting (Q 78086)*

> preached of the goodness of men! That there are people who invoke the divine goodness! But let them understand his power and compare it with a German 380 or a French 270! . . . Poor creatures that we are!
>   P.P.N. *[Priez pour nous.]*

His letter's last sentence articulated the standard dream of home of any front-line soldier. 'I hope to see you again soon and then we will drink a hearty slug of wine to the health of your *poilu* who sends you all his love.'

Pigeard would be taken prisoner in 1917; he was electrocuted in October that year while trying to escape from his prison camp.

Fighting on the Western Front could often give way to moments of brief armistice, pauses in the action allowing the retrieval of wounded men from No Man's Land without the would-be rescuers running the risk of being shot down. It would appear that such events were rare at Verdun. This was certainly the view of the German Medical Officer, Stephen Westman:

> It was always a big problem how to bring the wounded or soldiers freshly operated on to the rear. We had observed that on those parts of the front line where we were opposed by British troops a white flag with a Red Cross was carried through the most advanced trench. Immediately our soldiers stopped firing and the guns were kept silent until the red-cross flag disappeared. The Germans acted similarly, and the British ceased firing.

We tried the same procedure here, at Verdun. A kind of convoy was formed, in front of which a man walked with the red-cross flag; another man was in the middle and a third at the rear. The French, however, reacted differently and intensified their artillery fire, with the result that quite a number of our stretcher-bearers and wounded were killed. There seemed to be a difference between a British gentleman and a French cavalier! In the end we decided to trust our luck and bring down our men, some of them strapped to the backs of their comrades, during the hours of darkness.

From the French side René Arnaud's evidence would seem to confirm Westman's view. One night a sentry sounded the alarm and there was a burst of rifle fire:

Was it a false alarm? The sentry was sure that he had seen shadows moving in front of him. Perhaps they were German stretcher-bearers come to collect their wounded. But we were no longer in the days of truces between battles. And often, or so we had been told, enemy soldiers would approach under the cover of the Red Cross, concealing a machine-gun in their stretcher.

Yet soldiers' truces of the kind described did take place. The German Lieutenant Bordeching, writing in May from his unit's exposed position between the Mort-Homme and Côte 304, mentioned one, if somewhat vaguely:

There is a truce, a rare event that allows us to see the beautiful view beyond the multitude of graves and the demolished villages of Malancourt and Béthincourt — and we look up at the aeroplanes in combat above our heads, which happens rarely — but the poetry is fleeting.

He was soon back to the description of the horrors of that much disputed area:

When the north wind come with its appalling smell of putrefaction or with the stench of sulphurous grenades and phosphorous and when the battery-fire takes up again, our nerves are again put severely to the test, which triggers off a state of despair. The tensest moments are at nightfall when one most dreads an attack.

A hauntingly memorable episode, located at Froideterre later in the battle (though no date is given), is recorded in the writings of one of Verdun's best-known German chroniclers, Werner Beumelburg — an incident which packs a powerful impact in spite of, or perhaps because of, the unusual style in which it is described. Two Germans are determined to reclaim a severely, perhaps fatally, wounded comrade:

Here and there a few corpses lie in a crater. Here are some Germans, here some Frenchmen. In one shell hole, two Germans and two Frenchmen lie together. The first German is lying breast to breast on top of a Frenchman. The Frenchman has a bayonet in his chest. The German's skull has been shattered by a blow from a rifle butt. The second Frenchman has been bayoneted in the neck; the second German has a rifle bullet in his forehead. The legs are intertwined.

Rat-a-tat, rat-a-tat. . . . can be heard in front of them. The bullets whistle right over their heads. Wammisch jumps into the nearest shellholes. Siewers follows him.

'Is it still far to go?' asks Wammisch.

'It's no more than fifty metres' says Siewers.

'Have you got a white handkerchief?'

'Yes'

Wammisch takes the handkerchief and fastens it to the muzzle of his rifle.

'How do you say in French "we're looking for a casualty"?'

'Nous cherchons un blessé.'

'Say it again.'

'Nous cherchons un blessé.'

Siewers says it again.

'Right, forward!'

Wammisch walks without crouching between the shell holes holding up high the rifle with the handkerchief attached. Siewers follows.

Rat-a-tat, rat-a-tat. . . . swish, swish – then it stops.

'They're over there', says Siewers. They can see a group of Frenchmen forty yards off.

'Scherchong blessé,' Wammisch shouts at the top of his voice and then stops.

'They're on the very spot', says Siewers. 'We can't go there.'

One of the Frenchmen also stands up and raises his arm.

'Over here!' he shouts.

Now the Frenchmen can be seen talking among themselves, and withdrawing to other shellholes.

Then they find Esser. Siewers starts trembling all over. Esser's eyes are still open. He has a glazed look, vacant, horribly distant. His face has grown smaller, almost doll-like.

Wammisch climbs down to Esser. He gently holds the head with its blond hair and raises it slightly. Then he lays it back on the ground. He takes his wrist and holds it for a moment. Then he releases it. He kneels beside Esser and, with his fingers, lowers the eyelids over the pupils. For a moment he rests his forefingers on the eyes. Then slowly he slips his hands under Esser's back. He stands up carefully and takes him on his shoulders. Esser's hands hang down Wammisch's back. His head rests against Wammisch's neck. His blond hair has fallen over his eyes.

'Let's go!' says Wammisch.

Siewers follows him.

As they stand upright on the edge of the shell-hole, Wammisch turns round once more.

'Merci!' he shouts to the Frenchmen, and then off they go.

The Frenchmen slowly return to their shell hole. No shot is fired.
Facing them, above the Côte de Froideterre, the sun shines on.

But such events were exceptions to the rule. And the general lack of charity to the wounded applied equally to the dead, as Dr Stephen Westman noted:

> It was almost impossible to bury the fallen soldiers, not to mention those lying in no-man's-land. In daytime, digging parties came immediately under artillery fire. The best thing to do was to make shallow trenches at night, into which the bodies were laid, as they were, with their uniforms and their boots. Later orders were issued to remove the boots, as leather got scarcer and scarcer in blockaded Germany. In the forward positions the dead were thrown into spare communication trenches, one on top of the other; the 'graves' were sealed off by a few sandbags. If the pits were too shallow, our friends, the rats, appeared from nowhere and burrowed tunnels till they reached the corpses. The rains washed the soil away, and quite often one could see a half-eaten hand or a foot sticking out of the ground.

The battle, in fact, was going sour. Men were not just noting the horrors around them, they were objecting to them. The ants in the anthill were beginning to seethe. There had been signs, minor portents, for many weeks. Descriptions of horrors by those undergoing them could often carry the implicit message that such things should not be. Thus Lieutenant Alfred Joubaire's statement that 'Mankind has gone mad' was not just a piece of fine writing by a soldier with a gift for words; it was a cry of protest from the heart on behalf of himself and his comrades. In other cases, however, criticisms were more overtly expressed. Lieutenant René Arnaud's account records a deviant viewpoint expressed by a fellow officer even before their regiment received its orders to proceed up the Sacred Way:

> We remained three days in Belval in boring idleness, which did nothing to improve our morale. We walked up and down, exchanged rumours, argued steadily. I can still see the senior medical officer, Truchet, stooping, his legs apart, and a shifty, worried look on his face, scratching his black beard with his left hand more nervously than usual:
> 'It's wicked! This butchery ought to cease! Why haven't they evacuated Verdun? Thousands of men are massacred in order to hold on to a group of obsolete forts. It's madness! Oh, what brilliant commanders we have!'

Arnaud himself might have endorsed such a reaction when later, in June, the regiment was enduring the usual rigours of the front. His soldiers passed him a message which his Captain had sent on to him:

> It was a bombastic order signed by General Nivelle, in which I read amongst other things: 'The storm is gathering along the British front, it is gathering

along the Russian front. . . . Stand firm, men!' I was about to shrug my shoulders, but restrained myself as the men were watching me. I refrained from reading out the text and limited myself to announcing the allied offensives. I knew better than the staff-officers what one could say to the men and particularly what one could not say. I could only imagine what their reactions would have been to that pompous message:

'The old bastard has only to come down here with his arse-lickers if he wants to stand firm. He'll find out what it's like far better than in his town hall at Souilly. If the son of a bitch sent some of his frigging staff-officers down here they wouldn't put so many fellows into the front line just to get them blasted to hell quicker.'

Arnaud would eventually become filled with such disgust at the appalling waste of human lives that he would admit to 'a sense of revolt against the folly of war'.

Captain Henri Desagneaux was another who noted signs of disaffection when his regiment took the full force of 'the hell of Verdun'. In his diary entry under 24 June he described his company's parlous situation in the vicinity of Fleury, then continued:

Now something worse: my men, who have been suffering all sorts of hardships for the last seven days, are becoming demoralized. The word 'prisoner' is being whispered. For many this would seem salvation. We must fight against this notion, raise morale. But how?

What of the German side? Why did they go on fighting? Raising this question in his analysis of the battle the historian Holger H. Herwig offers as a keynote testimony the thoughts of a private soldier wounded in the early weeks of the left bank fighting and therefore with time to question why a recent attack had gone so badly wrong. The statement which Herwig quotes appears at greater length in the recent major German work on the subject, German Werth's *Verdun, Die Schlacht und der Mythos*: *Verdun, the Battle and the Myth*. The relevant passage reads:

'The sense of the whole operation was never apparent to us. Should we not have advanced further, had the artillery failed in its groundwork? Or was the whole undertaking to divert the enemy?' Grenadier Rudolf Koch asked himself as he lay in hospital, reflecting on the failed attack on the Mort-Homme on Easter Saturday 1916. His answer: 'The soldier does his duty and does not question why. It was duty alone that held us upright and together the whole time. One cannot speak of enthusiasm in such a place; everyone wishes they were a thousand miles away, and the easy wound that will get them home is everyone's silent desire, from the company commander to the lowliest grenadier. But if we had to go in to attack again the next day, we would have clambered out of our trenches with a simple sense of duty just as quietly as before, most of us from force of habit. The order arrives and is carried out, some acting from fear of the shame and ridicule of the others if they remain behind. And even if a soldier brags that he has managed to dodge his duty, he will be harshly judged after his day of shirking, and all the others will be examined thoroughly to see if they were there, if they remained behind, and how they behaved.

Herwig also cites an Alsatian soldier, Dominik Richert, as providing 'another sober assessment': 'In truth, courage has nothing to do with it. The fear of death surpasses all other feelings and terrible compulsion alone drives the soldier forward'. Richert, writes Herwig, was motivated to go on fighting by 'the damned discipline' of the Prussian Army, the occasional threat of being shot by his commanding officer, and the simple feeling that 'the terrible must be done'. Had there been a choice, 'not a man would have remained voluntarily at the front'.

So the battle ground on.

17 The recapture of Fort Douaumont

The Michelin Battlefield Guide, published shortly after the war under the title *Verdun and the Battles for its Possession*, identified four periods in the 1916 battle. The first, from 21 February onwards, it named the 'surprise attack'; the second, when the left bank was drawn into the frame, the 'general attack'; the third phase, which it dated from mid-April to the first day of the Battle of the Somme, 1 July, was that of 'attrition'; the fourth phase, which it dated from 1 July 1916 to 1917, it named the period of 'retreat and stabilization' — the implication being that the retreat was by the Germans, the stabilization by the French. From the beginning of July, the Guide's editors were suggesting (though it might be argued the date chosen was too soon), the issue was in effect decided; all that was required was to bring the campaign to a satisfactory conclusion. However, stabilization in French eyes did not mean sealing the line at the farthest point of the German advance; it meant winning back the ground they had lost. In other words, the French wanted their *revanche*: their revenge.

Before the *revanche* began, the French suffered their own hideous minor tragedy, to match the German horror at Douaumont in May. It happened on 4 September and its setting was the Tavannes railway tunnel on the line — non-operational since the start of hostilities — between Verdun and Metz and close to the Fort de Tavannes. It was being used as a supplementary fort and was packed with weapons, explosives and troops. Again there was combustion of some kind that got out of hand — probably caused by a mishandling of grenades — which led to a series of explosions and an appalling fire which raged for three days and killed several hundred men. Those who tried to escape were caught by the enemy artillery, which had noted the tell-tale signs of disaster, as the French had done in May, and reacted accordingly. The tunnel was not turned into a shrine, however, as had been the case at Douaumont. Perhaps this unhappy event's best memorial is the fact that the tunnel was returned to the function for which it was constructed as soon as conditions allowed. Trains still run through it today.

An event of a very different kind took place at Verdun just nine days later on 13 September. At a ceremony in a casemate of the Citadel, temporarily transformed into a *salle de fêtes*, President Poincaré formally presented the municipal authorities with a range of decorations conferred on the city by the Chiefs of Staff of the Allied countries: the St George's Cross of Russia, the British Military Cross, the medal for military valour of Italy, the Cross of Leopold I of Belgium, the medal 'Ohilitch' of Montenegro, and the *Croix de Guerre* and *Croix de la Légion d'Honneur* of France. Present at the occasion were Generals Joffre, Pétain and Nivelle, the Military Governor of Verdun, General Dubois, plus the French War Minister and representatives of the Allies. Later the French Government would confer on the city a Sword of Honour. The drama of Verdun 1916 was not yet over but whatever might happen in the weeks ahead the city had clearly acquired a reputation that was considered to be unassailable.

The French were not in a mood to rush their new offensive. If the earlier attempt on Douaumont in May had been launched prematurely and under a divided command, with Pétain disapproving of the plans of his subordinates, this would not be the case in October (though, later, success would significantly shift the balance as between the ever-cautious Pétain and his more thrusting colleagues). Meanwhile among some Germans, there was the feeling of modest satisfaction, a sense that for once in the Verdun sector there were better prospects ahead. There were clearly going to be no more sacrificial attacks, while previous experience suggested that if the French moved against them they could cope. So much is evident from the diary of Lieutenant W. Weingartner of the 38th Minenwerfer Company. Writing in September while out on rest, he noted:

> Life is quiet at the moment and we lie in the sun and sleep.
> The French cannot reach us with their guns.
> We are not afraid of a French attack and we shall be able to beat them back because our *Werfers* are so much better than anything they have.

As it happened Weingartner would not be there to learn in person that his confidence was misplaced. On the night of 11-12 October his 38th Jaeger Division was despatched to the Somme, an indication that the Somme battle was fulfilling one of its principal functions, that of weakening the German commitment to the Verdun campaign.

There was no doubt as to the main ambition of the French as they made their preparations for the next and final phase: they wanted to reclaim Fort Douaumont.

Lack of suitable artillery had been central to the failure of the Nivelle/Mangin attack in May. This would now be remedied. Heavy guns were to be brought into action on the French side, including two super-heavies; monster 400 mm guns so formidable that they were at first kept under wraps — much as 'tanks' had been kept under concealment on the Somme, only a few weeks earlier. Great attention was given to preparing the infantry for the moment when they would go over the top. Near Bar-le-Duc a full-size model of the battleground was created, so that they could become familiar with their points of attack. They were also trained to advance behind a creeping barrage — a steadily advancing bombardment in the wake of which the infantry could move with some assurance of protection. There had been earlier instances of this technique (for example, on the front occupied by the British 18th Division on the first day of the Somme), but here it was to be applied on a much larger scale. Additionally, there would be a massive and sustained bombardment before the infantry attack went in — a barrage that would be 'warmed up' in stages so that the really big guns only struck towards the end.

Meanwhile, before that, a steady softening up process was begun, peppering the German lines with shells so that their inhabitants were never allowed to relax. For once the gods of the weather played on the French side by providing a period of almost incessant rain, which combined with the effects of artillery fire to turn the German trenches into all but uninhabitable lines of mud. The softening-up process also extended to the Fort itself; bit by bit the covering of earth was blown away, making it more vulnerable to the larger French shells when the moment came for them to make their crucial contribution.

So much rain did not mean available drinking water, so the French, mindful of the fate of Fort Vaux, hired an engineer who had worked on the Panama Canal to ensure that when their troops got into the fort a reliable water supply would get there soon after.

Ironically, when the French actually attacked Fort Douaumont on 24 October it was even emptier than it had been when the Germans seized it all those months before. The pre-battle French bombardment had worked better than the French commanders had dared hope. Pétain, writing over a decade later, following the release of information from the German side hitherto unknown, allowed himself almost a hint of contempt when he described what had happened:

> Five shots from our 400 calibre mortars during the day of October 23rd caused real disasters, demolishing in turn the sick bay and four of the most important casemates of the second storey. That evening other explosions destroyed the pioneer post, set fire to a depot of fuses and ammunition for machine-guns, and made most of the galleries uninhabitable by filling them with thick, suffocating smoke. Having no water to check the conflagration, the Germans threw on the flames bottles of charged water intended for the use of the wounded, which were thus wasted to no purpose. On the 24th, between five and seven in the morning, the garrison withdrew from the fort, leaving in it only a group of about thirty men commanded by Captain Prollius. One cannot say that the garrison 'abandoned its post' by this act, for the command gave its approval to the manoeuvre, and yet we have the right, it seems, to contrast in our minds this attitude with that of the little group of soldiers under Major Raynal who held Fort Vaux to the end of their strength . . . .

When the infantry attack went in on the 24th a dense autumnal mist threatened to cause confusion and delay but at the vital moment it was pierced by a ray of sunlight clearly indicating the outline of the fort on the crest ahead of the advancing troops. In a memorable description one infantry commander, a Lieutenant-Colonel Picard, described the fort as it suddenly loomed through the murk as having *'l'effet d'une baleine échouée'* — the aspect of a beached whale. It is tempting to extrapolate from that that Douaumont had effectively become a kind of Moby Dick for the French, to be seized whatever the effort involved. Certainly the commander of the one of the battalions of the Colonial Division from Morocco which took Douaumont, Major Nikolai, reported his success in the most glowing terms, hailing the recaptured fort as 'an emblem of determination and power marvellously recovered.' Describing the key moment when his battalion approached the actual structure of the fort, he wrote — like Mangin using the present tense and referring to himself in the third person (in a somewhat clumsy guide-book translation):

> The battalion commander, who has halted at the bottom of the moat to see that the movement has been correctly carried out, now rejoins the head of the column, and while paying homage to this sacred and unforgettable sight [sic],

he gives orders to attack the machine-guns which start to fire from the bottom of the casemates. The first resistance is overcome, and everyone reaches his objective (the operation having been fully rehearsed before the attack). All opposition from the turrets is likewise successively dealt with. . . .

Was it worth it? As has already been stated (*see* page 54), it has been estimated that, taking earlier efforts into consideration, Fort Douaumont was recaptured at the cost of 100,000 lives. To a later age it can seem an absurdity that so much blood was spilt to reclaim the moribund hulk that mighty Douaumont had now become. But the commitment to retake it had become fixed back in February. For the French it had to be reclaimed, more for the fact of its retaking than for any military advantage that might ensue. For the Germans too it had become a mighty token: Hindenburg wrote of it: 'The name DOUAUMONT blazes forth like a beacon of German heroism', and the grief at its loss would be felt across the German nation. Another commentator, a Frenchman, would admit to being more moved by Douaumont and Vaux than by the Coliseum of Rome or the Temple of Paestum. All this suggests that to dismiss the reconquest of Douaumont as an act of pointless pride is seriously to misjudge the spirit of the times. Even among the *poilus* who had to carry out the attack there was a feeling that it had to be done. Hence this description by an ordinary infantryman which he wrote shortly afterwards while recovering in hospital from a serious wound; his account begins at the moment of going into action:

The sublime moment has arrived. Then, with a single bound, we see the three attack divisions leaving their small trenches, yelling, *'On les aura!'* and launching themselves in serried columns on the enemy front lines, throwing them into confusion, not giving the Boches time to get on the defensive, taking them all prisoner.

How wonderful it is to see all these brave-hearts continue their advance with the same irresistible impetus through shells and machine gun fire. On every side we can see the Boches coming out of shell holes or out of their small trenches, their hands up, calling to you: 'Kamarade, *pardon,* don't shoot!' We advance all the time; in a ravine we come upon a Boche battalion which has arrived as reinforcement; they've no time to deploy, they are made prisoner. We surround the fort of Douaumont, and nearly encircle that of Vaux. One regiment mounts the first attack, the Boches retire, and in the blink of an eye, it's ours! We advance another 700 or 800 metres beyond the fort. We stop, the target is achieved. And that in the space of four hours. We begin to dig out a small trench in the shell holes with our entrenching-tools. But the stone is hard, and in digging we come upon the debris of tree trunks. We work like this all night to dig a hole to the depth of one metre so as to get a bit of shelter for the daytime. We wait for counter-attacks. The day of the 25th is quiet, but rain begins to fall and half fills our trench. All the same, we have to stay in the mud and the water. We're wet through to the bone, trembling with cold, we're suffering, too, and above all, with hunger and thirst, for we can't be revictualled. But at the same time, a noble sentiment fills our hearts and cheers us; we have

THE SPHERE

AN ILLUSTRATED NEWSPAPER FOR THE HOME

With which is incorporated "BLACK & WHITE"

Volume LXVII. No. 880. {REGISTERED AT THE GENERAL POST OFFICE AS A NEWSPAPER} London, December 2, 1916 Price Sixpence.

French official photographic record, 1916

A SOLDIER OF FRANCE—THE FIRST TO ENTER DOUAUMONT

Fortunate as he is brave, this French soldier is to-day the pride of his regiment. When in the recent heavy fighting on the Verdun front the French battalions swept up the hill to Douaumont, carrying all before them by their splendid dash and bravery, the soldier seen above was the first to enter the fort. There were no laggards that day, and it is no small honour to be the first Frenchman to set foot in Douaumont

63. *Saluting a proud French victory: 'The First Man to Enter Douaumont'. The admiring caption stated: 'There were no laggards that day, and it is no small honour to be the first Frenchman to set foot in Douaumont.' (Courtesy* Illustrated London News *Picture Library)*

chased the enemy from his positions, we are fighting for humanity, for civilisation. We are fighting with the sentiments of bravery, faith and generosity. And it's that which gives us new strength and courage.

This is from an unexpected but highly valuable source. As the battle drew to an end, the British staff of the Urgency Cases Hospital at Revigny decided to produce a commemorative one-off magazine to chronicle their contribution to the Verdun battle. It was finally got into print in January 1917 under the title — from the name of the château where they were based — of *Le Faux Miroir*. Among much that was light-hearted, there were serious accounts of aspects of the battle, including several by French soldiers wounded in the fight for Douaumont. The author of this account (known only by his initials, 'G.D') also described how he was wounded and how he came to be looked after by Winifred Kenyon and her fellow nurses:

Suddenly a shell of I don't know what calibre arrives without our hearing it, crashes down on our trench, tearing my comrade into shreds, wounding me on the left hip, and burying us both. What a stink of powder! — I thought I was poisoned! — What a din! — I was deafened by it! At that moment I felt a pain as if someone had given me a violent kick. I'd been wounded; a splinter had penetrated. I stayed like this for an hour in our trench, my legs jammed as in a vice between two tree trunks. When this violent cannonade stops, my sergeant with a volunteer rushes to get me out of my sorry plight.

For the moment my wound didn't make me feel too bad, I could still walk after a fashion. I dragged myself along like this across the battlefield ploughed by the shells, through the curtain-fire between holes full of water and mud into which I fell at every step, for night had fallen.

The First Aid Post was six kilometres away. The major put a dressing on for me and gave me an evacuation chit. I still had to make it another two kilometres to get to the lorries which were to take us behind the lines. But it was high time to get there because, exhausted with fatigue and above all with pain, I couldn't stand up any longer.

They laid me on a stretcher, and we were sent off to the rear in lorries. But what suffering on the way there; the lorry was bumping over the broken road so that it felt as if stilettos were being jabbed into my wound.

So we come to Dugny, where we're put into an ambulance, given an injection of cocaine, made ready for off. At last the lorries unload us at Souilly, where they change our dressings. It's at 8 a.m. on the 29th when we embark afresh on the train; this time everyone says, it's the lucky break, we're off to the Côte d'Azur, and a smile begins to light up our faces, we're bowling along now! Suddenly the train stops: Revigny. They put us in an ambulance, someone looks at my wound, and not being able to cope with it at the centre, the major says to me: 'You're off, my lad, to the English hospital; you'll be alright!' Then the English medical orderlies carry me with great care in a stretcher to their lorries, and off I go to the Faux Miroir Hospital.

64. French soldiers trying out a captured German machine gun, Fort Douaumont (Q 69971)

The following is from an account by another soldier, simply identified as 'M':

At last the time has come, and we set off to conquer the enemy positions, which don't offer any resistance, and the few men who are still alive come out of their holes crying, 'KAMARAD!'

The artillery lengthen their range, one hundred metres by one hundred metres, so we continue to advance behind the wall of fire and in this way we arrive at the first line; from there, after a short five-minute breathing space, we start off again for the assault on the second line, which is the goal indicated by the General of the Division.

There, as at the first line, the enemy don't put up any resistance.

Arriving in the line, we begin to dig some small holes to allow us at the same time to keep out of sight of the enemy, and to take cover from his artillery. The day passes like this, at night everyone works and keeps watch at the same time, and we carry on like this right up to the evening of the 25th, without being disturbed by the enemy.

Weariness begins to make itself felt, the water-bottles are empty, and the water fatigue parties don't arrive, but all the same we put up with it in the hope of being relieved next day in the evening.

Everything adds to our misery. At eight o'clock big drops of rain begin to fall, the earth gets slippery and fills our trench with mud; on the other hand, this water, collected so preciously in our mugs set up on the parapet, this water will serve to moisten our parched lips, and in this way the night passes right up to dawn on the 26th.

At dawn the clouds begin to break and the sun appears at several points; our planes take advantage of this in order to fly over the enemy lines; the German pilot doesn't stay inactive, and signals our new positions to his artillery. Besides this, towards 6 o'clock the shells from our guns of all calibres begin to fall around us.

At 2 o'clock, in spite of this terrible bombardment the losses are minimal, but at that very moment the missiles fall exactly in the trench; to the left of my section someone tells me that there are already several victims, but there's not even time to ask the names of his comrades before a large-calibre shell comes exploding in the midst of us.

I feel myself struck down, this time I realize that I'm seriously injured, a wound no doubt grave grips me as if in a vice in the abdomen, and I'm certain, too, that I've lost all use of my right arm.

Gathering my strength, I lift myself up and look around me; my two corporals who were there have been struck down dead.

The horror of the spectacle gives me back more strength. And without caring about the consequences I drag myself painfully to the First-Aid Post. where the medical orderly immediately gives me the first attention which my condition requires.

At 5 o'clock the difficult transport of the wounded begins; the work is hard for our stretcher-bearers who are carrying us away.

At last, here we are, arrived at the first halt, the battalion First-Aid Post; there, I'm going to pass the night.

Early the next day, other stretcher-bearers come to take us and transport us to a second Aid-Post, and in this way from Aid-Post to Aid-Post we are transported right to Marceau Barracks.

From there we are transported in lorries, only a short distance; at the end of ten minutes we've arrived at the field hospital at Dugny. Straight away they take me into the operating room; the doctor encourages me by saying that I've had a bit of luck, that the wound in my abdomen, which he himself thought serious, is very light.

The same evening, I'm selected to be transported to the rear.   I'm taken by lorry all the way to Souilly where I'm put on a hospital train, and from there I'm de-trained at Revigny, where I'm detailed for the English Hospital at Faux Miroir, where I am at the present time surrounded by the greatest care of the staff.

Both accounts have that closeness of vision of the fighting man caught up in the mêlée — the ants in the anthill. But the seizure of Douaumont could seem almost an experience on a mystic level for those not involved in the cut and thrust of action and thus able to understand the significance of what was taking place. Thus Lieutenant-Colonel Picard, rounding off his description of the fort's seizure, was moved to write:

> When victory, with her great luminous wings, touches the soul of a combatant, there is such an intoxication, so noble a pride that nothing, nothing, not even glorious death on the field of battle, could equal the happiness of living through such a time!

If the early phase of the battle had been observed by a distinguished British commentator in the person of H. Warner Allen, the later phase saw a visit by the well-known war correspondent of the *Daily Telegraph,* Ellis Ashmead-Bartlett, famous for his eye-witness reports from Gallipoli the previous year. Travelling with five other members of the British and American press, he reached the city on the day before the offensive against Douaumont. The party's first visit was to the Citadel, where they were shown 'every single detail of this wonderful underground fortress'; one detail which particularly impressed him was the fact that 30,000 loaves of bread were baked daily within the Citadel for its huge, constantly changing garrison. They were then entertained to a meal by the city's military governor, General Dubois: 'a really wonderful lunch beautifully cooked by a prize chef and washed down with some of the finest wines of France. This kind-hearted officer had actually sent all the way to Bar-le-Duc for luxuries such as cakes and pastry for which the town is famous.' There followed a guided tour of the city streets, to be shown, again 'in very great detail', the steps which had been taken for the door-to-door defence of Verdun should such a contingency have arisen: 'The scheme was to turn every single house — or rather cellar — in which the place abounds, into a separate fort, and each was to be defended *à outrance.*'

But the prime focus of their visit was the real fort they knew was about to be attacked and whose recapture would give them the story that would make their journey worthwhile. On the following afternoon, the 24th, having been taken to a suitable vantage-point at the Fort de la Chaume, on the left bank of the Meuse, they were able to observe, if from some distance, the actual moment of victory:

> At about 3 p.m. the weather lifted somewhat and the sun made a brave effort to come out. Thus we were able to witness the final stages of the advance against Douaumont. One could watch the tremendous curtain of artillery fire creeping slowly up towards it. Suddenly some red rockets flashed skywards through the gloom. This was the prearranged signal that the fort had been re-won.

The event moved Ashmead-Bartlett to remarkable heights of eloquence:

> Thus was accomplished the crowning moment of the war, perhaps of all history. The French army of Verdun — exhausted and useless, according to the enemy's reports — retook in seven hours, without withdrawing a man or a gun from the Somme, practically the whole ground which the Crown Prince's army was only able to gain and hold at a cost of roughly half a million of the

65. *General Pétain decorating the Colours of a Moroccan Regiment, presumably in honour of their key role in the retaking of Fort Douaumont (Q 79473)*

best German troops, and by the expenditure of an unprecedented quantity of material and ammunition.

But the most memorable event of their tour was yet to come: a visit under escort to the actual fort, before the fighting was entirely over and while the area was still under fire from German guns. German signs were still in evidence in the galleries but it was now fully garrisoned by the French — in fact with Chasseurs like the doughty soldiers who all those months before had fought with the late Colonel Driant. Ashmead-Bartlett noted the long vaulted chambers radiating from the galleries used as barracks, each containing double rows of wooden bunks: 'Inside you see hundreds of warriors off duty rolled in their blankets asleep.' But what he was most eager to see were the signs of the recent successful attack:

> Especially interesting was the spot in the upper galleries where 400 mm shells had entered. Dawn was breaking and the pale light was shining through this arch cut out of the solid concrete by these heavy shells. Sentries stood guarding the aperture which was rapidly being put in a state of repair. You look out and beyond on to a sea of huge shell craters. There are no luxuries or comforts of any sort for the garrison, for it has only been possible to carry up the bare necessities of life and a reserve supply of ammunition. I made my way through all these long

galleries, damp, cold and filthy and studied the heroic defenders. They are great fellows, these Chasseurs. They are cold and caked with mud and weary from the incessant labour of carrying up supplies, but ever determined and indomitable. They have got back the fort and will never give it up again.

Summing up his whole visit to the Verdun sector, Ashmead-Bartlett wrote, in terms that can only have been music to his French hosts:

The battlefield of Verdun has a different atmosphere from any other I was ever on. Its horrors are also greater. But withal there is a feeling of intense satisfaction. You recognize the completion of a great masterpiece. You feel, as you so seldom have the chance of feeling in this war, that something vital and decisive has been accomplished, and that the work can never be undone. . . . It was at Verdun that the French people found themselves again, and emerged from the clouds which have hung over them for forty-five years.

When the French took back Douaumont fort they also reclaimed Douaumont village. The regiment that seized it had among its members the soldier-priest Pierre Tailhard de Chardin, though his battalion was in reserve for the actual attack. 'The colonial troops of my brigade captured the strong-point.' he wrote to his cousin a few days later. 'You see that we had our share of the glory, and that almost without loss, at least during the attack itself.' The next morning, at dawn, they moved forward to a position on the ground gained: 'I must say that that was not the best moment. I spent a most unpleasant day with my C.O. in a shell-hole just by Thiaumont farm, under a long-drawn-out continual bombardment that seemed to want to kill us off piecemeal. Such hours are the other side of the glory of attack.'

He attempted to describe his impressions, acknowledging 'a sort of depression and inertia, partly due to the not very active part played by my unit. Fortunately this lack of activity, this lack of "go", were put right by the stimulus of having plenty to do. All the same I didn't feel that my spirit was really heroic.' So much for himself, but contemplating the surroundings and the circumstances produced a strangely exhilarating response, though the awareness of the underlying tragedy of it all was never far off:

From a more speculative, almost 'dilettante' angle, I profoundly enjoyed, in short bursts, the picturesque side of the country and the situation. If you forget that you have a body to drag over the mud like a snail, the Douaumont area is a fascinating sight. Imagine a vast expanse of grim, naked hillsides, wild as a desert, more churned up than a ploughed field.   All this we recaptured. I saw again the places where, in August, I huddled in holes that I can still distinguish — and in which my friends fell. Now one can make one's way over them without fear: the crest above, and two kilometres beyond it too, are now held by us. Hardly any traces of the Boche can be seen — except round certain shelters, some appalling sights that one looks at without turning a hair:

everything has been buried by the shells. To get back to the rear for rations you have (until some communication trenches have been contrived) to make your way for three-quarters of a kilometre across this chaos of enormous shell-holes and treacherous patches of mud, following a few makeshift tracks. . . .

A few concrete pillboxes were still standing, marking the painful route. You can't imagine how odd it was to see these shelters lost in the chaos of the battlefield, particularly at night. Just as in the inns along a main road or the mountaineers' huts among the glaciers, a whole motley population of wounded, stragglers, somnambulists of all sorts, piled in, in the hope of getting a few moments' sleep — until some unavoidable duty or the angry voice of an officer made a little room – soon to be occupied again by some new figure, dripping, wet and apprehensive, emerging from the black night. . . .

All these horrors, I should add, are to me no more than the memory of a dream. I think that you live so immersed in the immediate effort of the moment that little of them penetrates to your consciousness or memory. And on top of that the lack of proportion between existence on the battlefield and life in peacetime (or at any rate in rest billets) is such that the former, looked back on from the latter, is never anything but a fantasy and dream.

And yet the dead — they'll never wake from that dream. My battalion had relatively few casualties. Others, on our flank, were more unlucky. The little White Father who went to see you at the Institute last February, was killed. Pray for him. Now once more I'm the only priest in the regiment.

The Douaumont battle produced its huge crop of fatalities and, inevitably, its greater number of wounded. Among the staff at the British Urgency Cases Hospital at Revigny coping with its influx of casualties was a senior colleague of Nurse Winifred Kenyon, Sister S.M. Edwards. She wrote a description of her experiences at this time which would eventually appear in the *Faux Miroir* house magazine under the title 'Thoughts of a Night Sister'. Her account, which shows how many and varied and from what different backgrounds were the patients who came under the hospital's care, is perhaps all the more effective for being written in the third person, almost as though it were a scene from a novel. But though she wrote with style, she wrote with much compassion:

The Surgeon has done his last round, and with a cheery 'Goodnight,' is gone. Sister stands at the door of the ward till his footsteps have died away. One by one the lights of the château, gleaming through the trees, go out and, save only for the glimmer of light from the huts and the shining stars above, the place is wrapped in darkness. With a shiver, for the nights are cold, she turns and enters the ward. She passes from bed to bed, giving a drink here, smoothing a tossed pillow there, tucking up as she would a child some brave fellow who has just come through the horrors of those hideous slopes on which for nine months the battle of Verdun has raged. All then being quiet, she sits by the little iron stove, trying to keep warm this bitter winter night, and as she sits she listens, and she thinks.

She hears the muttered, half-broken sentences of the men as they toss and turn in their restless sleep, and she thinks of the sons of France lying there suffering *'pour la Patrie'*. She thinks of No. 20, from far-off Brittany, his face rugged like the rugged rocks of the coast on which he has weathered many a storm. Now he has weathered his last and most terrible storm, the storm of battle. She thinks of No. 12, who has come from the heights of Savoy. Frightfully crippled he lies there, for the deadly gas gangrene has done its fearful work, and never again will he climb his beautiful mountains. He stands on the threshold of life only. *'Oh! C'est triste la guerre'* — that is all they say, these men: 'It is so sad, this war.' A wonderful spirit, this spirit of France. Yes, it is many of her men who are gathered here; for here are men from the fields of Normandy; from the sunny skies and orange groves of the Côte d'Azur; from the vine-clad slopes of the Pyrenees; and from farther still have they come; for there lies Abdallah from far-away Tunis, and Bamboula from still farther Senegal. Again she listens, and she thinks.

She hears the cannon booming. How near it sounds in the stillness of the night. How it makes the hut rattle and shake. She thinks of the terrible destruction that is being wrought by the hand of man on God's beautiful earth. She thinks of the men who, away in the firing line, where terror and desolation reign, are veritably passing through hell. And she asks the unanswerable question, Why should such things be? . . .

She hears the rumble of heavily laden trains, as they pass without ceasing up to the front with their load of men and ammunition, to be hurled against the might of Germany. And she thinks of the indomitable heroism and endurance which have withstood that might all these long months, and her heart is filled with gratitude and admiration. Again she listens, and she thinks.

The wind is rising, and she hears it sighing in the pines, and it is as if it were the *Voix de Morts* – the voices of the dead — pleading for their sacrifice not to be forgotten, and she thinks of those brave men who have passed through those pines to their last resting-place. She thinks of the little wooden crosses she sees everywhere in this sad corner of France – in the fields, in the woods, in the gardens — and she asks, 'Is it in vain they have died?'

'Ma Soeur, ma Soeur!' 'Sister, sister!' Sister is roused from her reverie. It is No. 8 — Bébé he is called, because of his curly hair and youthful spirit. He has been dreaming. He had lost his regiment and was struggling to find it again. A reassuring word, a *'Quelque chose à boire'* — 'something to drink' and he is soothed to sleep once more.

The long night has passed. They are all awake now, and how bright and jolly they are. *'Bon jour, ma Soeur, bon jour,'* resounds from all sides, and *'Bon jour, tout le monde,'* replies Sister as she hurries round, getting them ready for their breakfast. Brave, cheerful fellows. It is the lasting memory of the *'blessés'*, with their child-like simplicity, their good humour and their patient endurance, that Sister will carry back to England with her from a hospital 'Somewhere in France'.

18 The closedown

Raymond Abescat took part in the offensive against Douaumont and was lucky to come out of it alive. Eighty years after, as one of the last of the Verdun veterans, he recorded his memories of 24 October 1916 and they were as vivid as if they had happened the day before. He recalled 'a particularly disturbing moment' quite unrelated to the military achievement of that day:

> There were a few of us in some shell holes. About four in each crater. In one of these hollows there were only three men, whereas the one that I was in held five along with the sergeant. As it was a bit of a squeeze the sergeant said to me: 'Look, get in with the other three!' I was about to do so when a comrade volunteered and went there in my place. A moment went by. Suddenly, a German plane flew over us. . . . 'A bad sign, that!' And in fact, a few minutes later a whole artillery discharge rained down on our heads and a shell landed right in the hole where I ought to have been. Of the four who were there three were killed and the fourth — the one who had taken my place — was buried under the earth. We got him out gravely wounded. Because of that I have always felt that survival depends on factors that are completely arbitrary.

He was in action again on 16 November:

> On that occasion I got a piece of shrapnel in my ankle. It was between nine and ten in the morning and there was no question of moving a muscle because everything that did move was shot down! I had to wait till night-time to get myself as best I could to the first-aid post. My war ended there. The time that had elapsed between being wounded and getting medical care had brought on the beginning of gangrene. I almost had to have my leg amputated. When I got over it, I wasn't sorry to have left that hell behind me without meeting a tragic end. . . .

Abescat's reference to the fighting of 16 November shows that the battle did not end with the reclaiming of Douaumont. Nivelle and Mangin were eager to inflict more defeats on the now discomfited Germans. Fort Vaux was added to the tally of success on 2 November, the Germans having abandoned it as being not worth defending; to the French this low-cost seizure helped to cancel out the easy taking of Douaumont that had rankled ever since February. But a more positive flourish was required before the fighting could be closed down. It came in mid-December with a three-day battle on a six-mile front, in which Mangin's troops advanced two miles beyond Douaumont and took 115 guns, a

66. Fort Vaux, south-west side, photographed shortly after its recapture (Q 58317)

mass of machine guns and mortars, and 11,000 prisoners. Though only a right-bank offensive it was seen as an unambiguous triumph, and was acknowledged as such by the German Crown Prince. He wrote in his memoirs:

> At dawn on December 15th our artillery positions and all the ravines north of the line Louvemont-Hill 378-Bezonvaux redoubt were heavily bombarded with gas shells. The French infantry advanced shortly before 11 a.m., after a two hours' drum-fire on the whole front from Vacherauville to Vaux. On our side the co-operation between infantry and artillery again left much to be desired, and our barrage came down too late.
>
> In the centre of our front in Chauffour and north of Douaumont part of the 10th Division and General von Versen's 14th held their positions with great stubbornness till late in the evening. In the sectors to the right and left of them, however, the enemy broke through on a wide front. On our right wing Vacherauville, part of Poivre Hill, Louvemont and Hill 378, and on our left the whole Hardaumont and Bezonvaux redoubt ridge were lost. During the latter part of the day the enemy extended his large initial gains, and enveloped the positions still held by our troops in the centre from either flank and in rear. Fighting went on till late in the evening, but all our struggles were in vain . . . This second defeat before Verdun was marked by a disproportionately high total of prisoners lost, exceeding even those taken on October 24th. The enemy's communiqué claimed 11,000 prisoners, mostly unwounded, from all five of our divisions engaged . . .

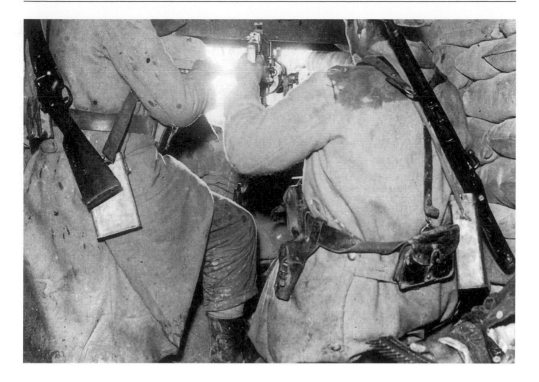

67. *Fort Vaux reclaimed; French machine gun in action, 22 November (Q 78041)*

The spirit of our troops had declined to a marked degree. . . to a considerable extent their morale and power of resistance was unequal to the demands placed on them by their onerous task . . . .

The mighty drive of the battles for Verdun in 1916 was now at an end! To the bold confident onslaught of the first February days had succeeded weeks and months of fierce, costly and slow advance; then the gradual diminution of our forces had led to the cessation of the offensive, and finally two regrettable setbacks had wrested back from us much of the blood-soaked ground we had so dearly won. Small wonder if this ill-starred end to our efforts wrung the hearts of the responsible commanders.

I knew now for the first time what it was to lose a battle. Doubt as to my own competence, self-commiseration, bitter feelings, unjust censures passed in quick succession through my mind and lay like a heavy burden on my soul, and I am not ashamed to confess that it was some time before I recovered my mental balance and my firm confidence in ultimate victory.

That confidence too, it is scarcely necessary to add, would also end in disillusion.

This final stage of the campaign, spectacularly conducted under new management, was bound to cause casualties in the structure of the French high command. Nivelle and

Mangin were so much in the ascendant that they had to be rewarded. Pétain slipped back somewhat into the shadows, to return in a vital role some months later, but the more significant victim was Joffre. On 13 December, two days before the final attack began, he was appointed technical adviser to the government and deprived of direct powers of command. On the 15th Nivelle was summoned to GQG to take over the post of Commander-in-Chief. On the 26th Joffre effectively fell on his sword by resigning. Some honour was retrieved when he was made Marshal of France on the following day, but the die was cast and he began his journey into an obscurity from which he would never emerge. An embarrassing scene took place at Chantilly in which Joffre, appealing for loyalty among the staff who had worked under him since August 1914, found only one officer prepared to stay with him as he relinquished his command; the fact that he had '*limogé*' numerous generals in his time did not make his own removal seem the less pathetic. He would still have duties to perform but they would be ceremonial only, such as heading a French military mission to the United States in 1917 or serving as figurehead president of the Supreme War Council in 1918.

Meanwhile Mangin celebrated the new regime with an Order of the Day that trumpeted greater glory to come: 'We know the method and we have the Chief. Success is certain.'   Future events — though not this time at Verdun — would show that his claim was as empty as Nivelle's 'We have the formula' assertion on the steps at Souilly all those months before. But for the moment Nivelle was the hero of the hour, and Verdun was his triumph. And if nothing else the long struggle was over.

What kind of a battle was it that had thus come to an end after 298 days? Where in its almost ten grim months had Verdun taken the concept of modern war?

The Germans seized the opportunity of a major campaign to try out certain technical innovations. Von Knobelsdorf's use of phosgene in his June offensive added another name to the burgeoning list of noxious gases; curiously, or perhaps not in view of the way the secretive Falkenhayn was running the campaign, the Kaiser only heard about it from the newspapers. Flamethrowers, initially tested in the region in 1915, were also employed on a major scale here for the first time. In July the flamethrower units were given the insignia of the death's head; this would later become the insignia of the Waffen SS. Steel helmets were first used en masse at Verdun; the British equivalent came into use roughly at about the same time. Additionally German *Sturmtruppen* — 'Stormtroopers', trained to break through at speed leaving other units to 'mop up' behind them — had their first trial runs at Verdun: they would wreak much havoc in the great German attacks of 1918.

Artillery dominated the battle, and was by far the greatest killer. It was used on a massive scale. In his book specifically devoted to 'the new warfare 1914-18', *White Heat*, John Terraine wrote about Verdun: 'The statistics of the artillery war. . . are staggering. For their initial attack the Germans brought up 2,500,000 shells, using for the purpose some 1,300 trains. By June the artillery on both sides had grown to about 2,000 guns, and it was calculated that in just over four months of battle 24 million shells had been pumped into this stretch of dedicated ground.' But the artillery on both sides was often massively inefficient and wasteful. The heavy guns were not always the super-weapons they were

68. German prisoners in the courtyard of the Bishop's Palace, Verdun (HU 22687)

thought to be; some had to be re-bored after firing 50 to 100 rounds; moving them meant rendering them ineffective for many hours at a time. There were innumerable instances, on both sides, of casualties by 'friendly fire'; thus the infantry could find themselves hating their own apparently careless or uncaring gunners rather more than the enemy. Communications were primitive and vulnerable; telephone wires were constantly being cut by shell fire; runners with vital messages often took hours to get through or never got through at all. Any assumption that one might have of cool Teutonic precision or brilliant Gallic inspiration and dash should be put to one side. This was for much of its time a monster of a battle in which gallantry had little meaning and glory was only in the eye of the distant beholder.

The cost in human terms was enormous. Estimates vary but one much quoted is that total French casualties, dead, wounded, missing, or taken prisoner, were around 377,000 while the Germans lost about 337,000, a very high proportion of these figures being fatalities.

The concept and conduct of the battle attracts few approving nods from military historians. Summing up the campaign Peter Simkins has written:

> The French Army had come through major crises in February and June and had saved Verdun, but nobody had gained any strategic advantage from the bloodletting, certainly not the Germans. Falkenhayn's fatal irresolution and failure to match the means to the end had merely resulted in the German Army being bled white along with the French. Neither side ever fully recovered from the hell of Verdun before the end of the war.

Adding together the casualty figures as given above, and noting some of the collateral consequences of the battle, Richard Holmes has commented:

700,000 and for 1916 alone: rather more than half the casualties suffered by Britain and her Empire in the Second World War. Nine villages, which had stood on those uplands for a thousand years, were destroyed and never rebuilt. Woods and fields were so polluted by metal, high explosive and bodies that they were beyond cultivation. Declared *zones rouges*, red zones, they were cloaked in conifers and left to the recuperative powers of nature.

A distinguished scholar of the German Army in the twentieth century, Michael Geyer, has written:

> More than any other battle, Verdun showed the military impasse of World War I, the complete disjuncture between strategy, battle design and tactics, and the inability to use the modern means of war. But most of all, it showed, at horrendous costs, the impasse of professional strategies.

Alistair Horne has been honourably referred to, and frequently quoted, in these pages, so that it is perhaps superfluous to include him in this brief gathering of opinions. But there is one passage towards the end of his book which sums up so much so pertinently that it virtually demands its place, if offered here in slightly abbreviated form:

> Who 'won' the Battle of Verdun? Few campaigns have had more written about them (not a little of it bombastic nonsense) and accounts vary widely. The volumes of the *Reich Archives* dealing with it are appropriately entitled 'The Tragedy of Verdun', while to a whole generation of French writers it represented the summit of *'La Gloire'* . . . .
> [I]t suffices to say that it was a desperate tragedy for both nations.

Among the century's great battles, Verdun has been bracketed with Stalingrad (no more tellingly so than by Hitler, as quoted in this book's first chapter.) However, Antony Beevor, in his book *Stalingrad*, gives that battle the palm, stating: 'In its way, the fighting in Stalingrad was even more terrifying than the impersonal slaughter at Verdun. The close-quarter combat in ruined buildings, bunkers, cellars and sewers was soon dubbed "Rattenkrieg" by German soldiers. It possessed a savage intimacy which appalled the generals, who felt that they were rapidly losing control over events.' (One might add that, in common with the whole Russo-German war of 1941–45, Stalingrad was conducted with a racial-cum-ideological viciousness which would have appalled both sides at Verdun.) But if there was no 'savage intimacy', there was at Verdun a kind of terrifying loneliness. As the French historian Marc Ferro has written, 'Each unit was on its own, often bombarded by its own guns, and told only to "hold on". . . The only certainty was death — for one, or other, or all.' It could be said that this was not so much a battle between victors and vanquished — such terms rapidly lost all meaning in so attritional an encounter — as between victims.

19 The experience

What was so special about the Battle of Verdun?

Verdun marked those who fought there. They would become '*Ceux de Verdun*' — 'The Men of Verdun': a race apart from the rest. Veterans who had fought and suffered even on the Somme would nevertheless think less of themselves because they had not fought at Verdun. For the French soldier of the twentieth century Verdun was the equivalent of St Crispin's Day for the English knights and bowmen of Agincourt.

Soldat J. Ayoun, of the 119th Regiment of Infantry, who went there in June, wrote:

> I wanted to see Verdun. I wanted to take part in the great battle. As soon as I saw the battlefield, in spite of my fourteen months of active service, I thought: 'He who has not seen Verdun has not seen the war'.

Many survivors would look back with pride. For others the imprint of Verdun would be far too painful. Hence Pierre Rouqet's comment on his experience at the Mort-Homme when he was nearly buried alive and then badly wounded: 'These were the most tragic moments of my life. They have marked me forever.'

One of the most quoted comments on Verdun is that by Maurice Genevoix: '*Nous avons connu l'incommunicable*': 'We have known that which cannot be told'. That sentence clearly claims a speciality for the experience of Verdun. Yet the importance of that experience made it impossible for those who survived not to make the attempt to describe it. The story *had* to be told, whether or not people understood. It also had to be told as a warning, so that people should not unthinkingly assume that those who had come through so harsh an experience would be content to go down the same road again.

This was the message of Raymond Jubert when he wrote what has been seen as a keynote expression of the participants' view of Verdun, a statement in which he spoke for all involved, German as well as French:

> They will not be able to make us do it again another day; that would be to misconstrue the price of our effort. They will have to resort to those who have not lived out these days.

There was, he was clearly implying, something unique as well as terrible about the experience undergone by those who fought at Verdun. Uniqueness is a quality difficult if not impossible to justify — not a few British, Australians, Canadians, New Zealanders, South Africans who fought at the Somme or at Passchendaele would see their own experience as unique — but certainly there were many at Verdun who saw what happened there as a kind of ultimate in suffering and fortitude. Thus Pierre Teilhard de Chardin

69. *A Verdun veteran, one of* 'Ceux de Verdun'; *'The Men of Verdun' (Cliché Editions MAGE)*

writing in August, after his division had been caught up in fierce fighting at Froideterre during which he had lost a number of his friends:

> I don't know what sort of monument the country will later put up on Froideterre hill to commemorate the great battle. There's only one that would be appropriate: a great figure of Christ. Only the image of the crucified can sum up, express and relieve all the horror, and beauty, all the hope and deep mystery in such an avalanche of conflict and sorrows. As I looked at this scene of bitter toil, I felt completely overcome by the thought that I had the honour of standing at one of the two or three spots on which, at this very moment, the whole life of the universe surges and ebbs — places of pain but it is there that a great future (this I *believe* more and more) is taking shape.
>
>   . . . Yesterday, after a fortnight of not being able to say mass, with so many friends to remember, with so many dangers safely avoided to thank for, and with the consciousness of the crying needs and bitter sorrows of the world, I said what was perhaps the most fervent mass of my life.

   Teilhard de Chardin, writing at the time, was mourning friends recently killed. It was the common experience of *'Ceux de Verdun'* to remember their fallen comrades for the rest of their lives. Thus Raymond Abescat, speaking eighty years afterwards, and

70. *Pierre Teilhard de Chardin, priest and stretcher-bearer at Verdun. His courage under fire and devotion to his men won him the Croix de Guerre, the Médaille Militaire, the Légion d'Honneur and three mentions in despatches (Editions Bernard Grasset)*

describing his relief at having 'left that hell behind me without meeting a tragic end', added: 'Other men, however, my friends — I have never stopped thinking about them — were there forever.'

There was, in effect, a Verdun brotherhood, an unbreakable tie with those who had been there. This was not just true of the French. Hence this comment by the German, Werner Beumelburg:

> It seemed to us then as if a quite exceptional bond linked us with those few who had been with us at the time. It was not the normal sensation of affinity that always binds together men who have endured common hardships. . . . It derived from the fact that Verdun transformed men's souls. Whoever floundered through this morass full of the shrieking and the dying, whoever shivered in those nights, had passed the last frontier of life, and henceforth bore deep within him the leaden memory of a place that lies between Life and Death, or perhaps beyond either.

One element that marked out Verdun as being exceptional was the sense of impotence felt by the soldiers out in the mud and squalor and under the endless fury of the guns. They could do nothing except wait to be wounded or killed, meanwhile desperately hoping to survive. A French soldier, Gaston Biron wrote to his mother after a brutal baptism of fire in early March:

> By whatever miracle I came out of this hell, I still keep asking myself time after time if it is true that I am still alive. 1200 of us went up, and 300 of us came back down; why I am one of these 300 who have had the luck to escape, I have no idea, and yet I ought to have been killed a hundred times, and every moment throughout those eight long days I believed my last hour had come. To the mental suffering of believing each moment that death was about to overtake us add the physical suffering of long sleepless nights: eight hours without drinking, and almost without eating, eight hours of living in a human charnel house, lying amidst corpses, treading on our comrades fallen the day before. We have all aged a lot, my dear Mother; above all, hair turned white will be the everlasting mark of sufferings endured; and I am one of those. No more laughter, no more gaiety in the battalion; we carry in our hearts the mourning for all our comrades fallen at Verdun from 5 to 8 March.

A German soldier, Karl Fritz, after being in the front line near Fleury in August, wrote in markedly similar terms to his family:

> You cannot have any idea what we saw there. We spent three days lying in shell holes seeing death at close quarters, waiting for it at every moment. And all without a single drop of water to drink and amidst the horrible stench of corpses. One shell blast would bury the bodies in the earth and the next would exhume them again. If we tried to dig out somewhere to shelter we would immediately come across dead bodies. I was one of a group of comrades yet each man prayed only for himself.

There was the permanent fear that if death came it would come horribly. Men who saw their comrades disintegrate under the impact of shellfire could not avoid anticipating the same fate for themselves. Thus the soldier-priest Paul Dubrulle spoke for countless soldiers on both sides when he wrote:

> To die from a bullet seems nothing; parts of our being remain intact; but to be dismembered, torn to pieces, reduced to pulp, this is a fear that the flesh cannot support and which is fundamentally the great suffering of the bombardment.

Life in such circumstances was also degrading. There was no means of preserving any personal dignity. Lieutenant René Arnaud, describing a particularly dispiriting period in the line when, as he graphically put it, 'one felt that the artillery on either side was firing blind into the mass', wrote:

> So the hours passed. From time to time one had to crawl behind the trench in order to satisfy a call of nature — a subject never mentioned in war novels.

There one risked an ignominious end (how many soldiers have been killed while they were in 'the bushes' — a euphemism to describe a place far from poetic!), an accident which a mention in despatches would happily transform into a glorious death.

There was also something uniquely awful about the actual battlefield of Verdun. After so much close fighting in such a limited area over so long a time, the ground became hideous. It was an appalling place in which to fight. Thus in the memory of Raymond Abescat:

> Verdun was a wasteland marked by death. Nature martyred, vegetation torn or obliterated, only a few remains of trees repeatedly shattered and burned, and everywhere the mud, the shell-holes. A landscape from the end of the world.

Airmen flying over Verdun were often stunned by what they saw beneath them. To the American flyer, James McConnell, the battlefield was

> that sinister brown belt, a strip of murdered nature. It seems to belong to another world. Every sign of humanity has been swept away. The woods and roads have vanished like chalk wiped from a blackboard; of the villages nothing remains but grey smears.

Others, not involved, but moved by their awareness of the nature of the battle, have offered their verdicts on Verdun, emphasizing its tragic nature and its uniqueness. One often quoted is that of the poet Paul Valéry:

> Verdun was a complete war inside the Great War. . . It was also a kind of duel before the Universe, a strange, almost symbolic struggle, fought in a confined field.

That Verdun had a special quality is still the accepted view among French historians; there seems to be no revisionist tendency to downgrade its impact on men, morale and landscape. Hence this powerful statement by Alain Denizot in his book *Verdun 1914-1918*, published in 1996:

> By its duration, its horror, the battle of Verdun became a myth, the symbol of the Great War, a thing on its own. Even if the Somme resulted in heavier losses, only the 'hell of Verdun' remains in the memory, no other battle asserts itself so powerfully.
>
> The fighting-man of Verdun is thus invested with an aura, a prestige of which he is proud, but also with disgust, for what he has seen, done, endured, touches the depths of misery that no beast could bear.
>
> To arrive on the battlefield of Verdun for the soldier is to know fear. Verdun already has become legendary, those who 'come out' are the living dead, they have no need to speak to express the horror they have lived through. The closer one approaches to the front lines, the more the ground appears desolate, lunar. The

stench grips one by the throat, the guns never cease their thunder. When the relief troops arrive, the company or battalion pulls out at night, with the risks of being sucked into the mud, or wandering about for hours, if the guide makes a mistake or the equipment is heavy. If a man has to flatten himself on the ground because of artillery fire, he might fall on a putrifying corpse. In the presence of asphyxiating shells, it is essential to put on his mask, and so the *Poilu* loses his beard at Verdun. A column of blinded men advances, holding on by hand to the hooded greatcoat of the man in front, so as not to get lost in the ravine. They stifle under their masks, and can see nothing, but to breathe fresh air is asking for death.

Each relief brings losses, often heavy, under the shelling.

Close to the 'Boches', more often than not, trenches and communication trenches no longer exist, they have been levelled out by the artillery fire, and the lines are nothing but craters, shell holes, with or without links between them. The foot-soldier squats in his hole with a few comrades. Verdun is a war of little groups, isolated in shell holes. The infantryman lives, or rather survives, in cold, heat, frost, snow, rain, with for his protection his ground-sheet, which also serves as his shroud. If it rains, this sheet allows him to drink, for his number one problem is water, a rare commodity. It reaches the point where soldiers drink the foul water from a shell hole, even their own urine. The fatigue parties are the only links which bind together the front and rear lines. They bring up coffee, wine ['*pinard*'], rum ['*gnole*'], soup, letters. Often the food is cold when the 'Boches' are shelling; sometimes it doesn't arrive at all. . . .

Attacks, counter-attacks, bombardments each day put men's lives in danger. To gain a few metres of ground, troops come under deluges of shells of all calibres (and sometimes their own artillery fires too short); they find themselves facing machine guns, flame-throwers, gas, uncut barbed wire.

Denizot also reminds his readers of one of the curious paradoxes of the campaign, true of other First World War battles but perhaps especially true of this one:

Many of the men who died at Verdun did not see a single German soldier. . .

Thus the powerful analysis of an eminent contemporary Verdun historian. This is perhaps as appropriate a place as any to ask the question: how does Verdun 'play' generally to French people today? During the course of research for this book, a number of French friends — none of them scholars of Verdun, but all with a considerable, sometimes even a professional, interest in twentieth-century history — were invited to set down their reflections. What follows is no gallup-poll; more a collage of comments which, it is hoped, might be of interest and value.

Philippe Braquet, aged 28 and, by his own declaration, 'passionately interested in the Great War', recently opened a small museum in the village of Villeroy, Seine-et-Marne, where the famous soldier-poet Charles Péguy, was killed in the Battle of the Marne in 1914:

The battlefield of Verdun is a museum open to the sky, with its forts, its tunnels, its trenches, its shell-holes, its traces of combat — shell splinters, bits of shovels, picks, water-bottles . . . . One cannot speak about Verdun; it is necessary to make your way there to understand what Verdun was: a few square kilometres of ravaged French soil, rendered barren forever; destroyed villages razed from the map; six months of the most formidable battle of all time, by day and by night; hundreds of thousands of dead, wounded and mutilated Frenchmen and Germans. Joffre had said to the defenders of Verdun in his order of 10 March 1916: 'You will be among those of whom it will be said: 'They barred the road to Verdun to the Germans!' Yes! — but at what a price! Never again! As the survivors of the Great War will always say.

Christophe Leclerc is a rising French historian in his thirties, a specialist in the Middle Eastern campaigns of the First World War:

What can Verdun signify for my generation? In the first place, a desperate struggle which cost the lives of some hundreds of thousands of fighting-men on one side or the other in barely six months. I think of the sufferings which these soldiers endured, in most cases with a stoicism which is beyond comprehension, up to the terrible feeling of finality (that clear awareness of the inescapable presence of death) which must so often have assailed them. Emerging alive out of the second great German attack on Verdun, in March 1916, the simple soldier Gaston Biron [quoted on p.164] does not understand why death has spared him: 'By whatever miracle I came out of this hell', he writes in a letter to his mother, 'I still keep asking myself time after time if it is true that I am still alive. . . . We didn't think that it would be possible to emerge out of such a fiery furnace.' Like his comrades, Gaston Biron marches to death, resolute or resigned. . . . But how could he accept the prospect of his sacrifice with such abnegation? That is beyond me, even if I take into account the ardent patriotism which inspired most of our forebears; had they no other concern beyond preserving their land, their homes?

Rather than these examples of heroism, I prefer to hold on to the poignant testimony of Roland Dorgeles *Les Croix de bois* (*The Wooden Crosses*), or of Erich Maria Remarque *À l'Ouest rien de nouveau* (*All Quiet on the Western Front*) which I read in my adolescence. They express well the absurdity of the fighting, in which advances and retreats for a slice of land followed one another with no result except the deaths of thousands of men and the greater glory of the generals. Can one forget the bloody defeats of Joffre in Champagne and Artois in 1915, or those of Nivelle on the Chemin des Dames, in April 1917? . . .

Verdun is therefore for me the expression of an immense squandering, the sacrifice of a generation which is illustrated with a morbid lyricism by the film of Abel Gance, *J'accuse*. For a long time after I had seen it, I cherished the memory of a sequence which created a sensation at the end, that of an army of phantoms on the march, the dead of Verdun who rise up to demonstrate their silent rage at a confrontation with the living, who are ready to refurbish their arms for a new war . . . .

Marie-Laure Blay-Gilbert is a young woman in her thirties with a good command of English, living in Lyons, thus far to the south of Verdun, a not insignificant factor in a country as large as France:

> When a schoolgirl, Verdun had vague meanings to me: it was a battle, an important one, cruel like any battle in any war. Where exactly was Verdun situated? As a real southerner, I answered: 'north-north'. Won or lost? Unsure. And there were those war veterans, very old, very trembling, a little bit ridiculous with their row of medals and dignified air, inevitably standing not very far from the President of the Republic on 11th November Armistice TV broadcasts. They seemed to beg for respect. As for the Poilu, I imagined him as a dirty unshaven poor old chap (remember *poilu* means 'hairy') whose main objective in life was to receive letters from some woman behind the lines, and who fought with a bayonet whenever he emerged from his trench.
>
> A few years had to pass before I more fully captured the essence of the event...
>
> Today I see in my shameless schoolgirl ignorance an indication of the injustice towards the Battle of Verdun. In history books, there is much emphasis on totalitarianism in relation to many subjects, French, History or Civics. And the Holocaust is always denounced as 'top' of the horror, of the unacceptable, of the 'never-that-again and be watchful about it, kids'. Of course, World War I, with its numerous consequences and the horror of the trenches, is studied as well. But it takes the inspiration of a good teacher to make a member of the young generation really understand that, to attain the rank of a symbol, a battle first has to HAPPEN. And the fact that General Pétain bungled, so to speak, the last part of his life, doesn't make things better.
>
> Perhaps to get to 'real History' you need 'little history' as a go-between, as a sort of 'rear entrance': the experience of someone you care about, an anecdote in a good book or a good programme.
>
> My first interest in World War I was in the campaigns in the East. Then I fell on this line: 'If I should die, think only this of me: that there's some corner of a foreign field that is for ever England'. Rupert Brooke died in the East, and I think he never experienced trenches. But his line moved me to tears. It is as if I suddenly 'felt' how it feels to die that way. The mud. The vermin. The stench. Death away from home, away from any love. Flesh and soil mixed together ALIVE, like those tramps whom one can't tell from the filthy pavement. This very person who was a father, a son, turned into a beast. Dying like a beast.
>
> This is what Verdun is for me: the human soul buried alive. Spirit humiliated by matter. Man as a material, unloaded in trenches for five months like shovelfuls of coal. Dying one day to win a few metres that will perhaps be lost the day after.
>
> Verdun is the antithesis of the Battle of Britain. A war without glory or heroes. Every day the same sky, the same trench. No strategy, no movement, no hope. How to transcend such an event, when no explanation, geostrategical or political, can soothe the mind, even in 1999?

71. *Verdun celebrates: the Victory Monument, Verdun, built on an ancient twelfth-century rampart; inaugurated on 23 June 1929 (Mr Neil Smith)*

Yet despite 500,000 visitors a year at the Museum of Verdun, I believe the memory of the battle fades in young generations. 500,000 visitors, 500,000 dead. What's the meaning of it? Verdun is the symbol battle of the French in World War I, like the Somme is the English one (at least in French eyes).

For those to whom the battle still means something, Verdun is the symbol of resistance and courage. Therefore a synonym both of suffering and victory. When all's said and done, though an event with which it is not easy to come to terms, at least it reflects the basic beliefs of our Christian code.

Maurice Larès is a Doctor of letters of the Sorbonne, a biographer of T.E. Lawrence and a scholar and translator of the Middle Eastern War.

Verdun. The name had perhaps better be touched with a barge pole. It is full of impact. In part it is the symbol of an awful, gory, meaningless, useless, unendurable mess, a never-ending struggle taken almost to the level of unacceptibility by the generals in charge. It is also the symbol of a tremendous French victory. And undeniably, it *was* a French victory.

The significance of strategic sites, not only at the time, but through the centuries should be taken into consideration. Verdun changed hands countless times, and never ceased to be the target of invaders. No one then should be surprised when Falkenhayn selected Verdun as a theoretically 'psychological' target in February 1916. For us French, keeping the 'salient' of Verdun became a matter of life or death, whatever the cost. It was thought (and it may not be untrue) that if the front collapsed at Verdun, France would go on her knees. Hence the enormous amount of reserves thrown

72. *Verdun mourns: the Ossuary at Douaumont, built on the Thiaumont crest. Its foundation stone was laid on 22 August 1920; it was officially opened on 7 April 1932. Some of the 15,000 graves of the vast Douaumont cemetery can be seen in the foreground (Author)*

into the '*enfer de Verdun*'. And the enormous cost, both to the French and the Germans.

Today, the visitor to the great Ossuary of Douaumont left unsatisfied by the sight of its facade may pass behind and examine its rear. It is made of big blocks of stone separated by thick-paned windows only partly tinted on the inside. This allows the grim visitor (I was one, at about the age of 12) to visualize the horror of hundreds of white skulls, tibias and whole sorts of bones piled up in an unbelievable mixture. And this applies to one single 'window'! The bones continue for more than 100 metres. The artillery did its work well. . . .

It is difficult not to endorse Dr Larès' singling out of Douaumont Ossuary as the supreme visual symbol of the suffering endured at Verdun. It preserves the bones of 130,000 of the missing of Verdun. Perhaps the one thing that can be said in its favour is that nationality has no meaning in the haunting catacomb of the fallen which spreads out, submarine-shaped, on either side of the tall Ossuary tower, for here there is no distinction between French and German. It is nevertheless a chilling place; the phrase charnel house came to many minds in the course of the battle, and that is exactly what this is, on the grand scale. Adding to the sense of desolation and loss is the huge, immaculately groomed cemetery spread out in front of it, with its 15,000 graves. The historian Richard Holmes has said of it: 'It is the saddest place I know', a sentiment with which it is hard to disagree.

20 The legacy

A major consequence of the Battle of Verdun for Germany was that it deprived her of so much of the commodity without which no country can fight: manpower. In that sense it was a milestone on the road to defeat just under two years later.

A major consequence for France — one that became evident within months — was that it brought her army to the brink of self-destruction.

By the end of the battle signs of disillusion of the kind noted by Arnaud and Desagneaux were widespread. There were reports of units bleating like sheep as they were ordered up to the front; though at this stage the orders were still obeyed. But morale was plummeting. In January 1917 a 'soldier's account' was published, of which the title was enough to suggest its mood — *L'Holocauste*. The author, Paul Husson, did not mince his words of protest:

> Lying prone, while the shells whistle overhead, I think. Die! Why should we die on this battlefield? . . . Die for civilization, for the freedom of the nations? Words, words, words. We are dying because men are wild beasts, killing one another. We are dying for bales of merchandise; we are dying for squabbles about money.

There was even evidence of sympathy with the invader, not because he was such, but because he was a human being caught in the same trap:

> Everyone was cursing the war, everyone hated it. Some were saying: 'Frenchmen or Germans, they are men like ourselves, they suffer as we do in body and in mind. Do not they, too, dream of the homecoming?'

The only development that would save the situation was a swift, miraculous victory. As it happened, the miracle worker par excellence was, or so he himself thought, to hand in the person of Verdun's last-stage hero, General Nivelle. He proved so seductive a propagandist for his own cause that he was entrusted with the next great move forward on the Western Front. He even succeeded in persuading the new British premier, Lloyd George, to put Haig's Army under his command. For the British the first half of 1917 is best known for the Battle of Arras, launched on Easter Monday in a snowstorm, with as its principal achievement the seizure of Vimy Ridge. But to Nivelle Arras was a sideshow, a diversionary overture to the mighty French offensive to be launched on the Aisne. More, that offensive was to be an attack *à outrance*. The battle was to be won with dash and *élan* and it would be all over in 48 hours; indeed the palms of victory were virtually being claimed before the first shot was fired. The location chosen was the so-called Chemin des

73. *An American howitzer battery at Samogneux, 2 November 1918. The battleground of Verdun was not fully reclaimed for France until the final days of the war, by which time Verdun was in the Western Front's American sector. (American Official Photograph 28532)*

Dames, a country of high ridges and steep valleys between Soissons and Reims. There was the usual unconcern about security, with the result that the Germans were primed and ready when the moment came. (Indeed, they had launched a successful spoiling attack on 4-5 April which brought back a document setting out the precise details and timetables of the French plan.) Unaware of this, the troops as they prepared for the zero hour to come were generally in high spirits. Nivelle's enthusiasm had proved so infectious that even veterans of Verdun believed it possible that one more thrust would end the war.

On 16 April the French infantry duly poured over the crest of the high ground of the Chemin and was duly massacred. The result was a humiliating French defeat, all the more shattering because of the extravagant hopes aroused.

Defeat was followed by sporadic outbreaks of mutiny, or, in the parlance of the time, 'collective indiscipline', of which 119 acts spread across 54 divisions were officially recorded over the following weeks. Nivelle was dismissed, as was his cheerleader Mangin. The latter would return to fight again, successfully, in 1918, but Nivelle was now beyond redemption, his career ending ignominiously with minor commands in north Africa. It is almost unnecessary to record that the steady hand that was called upon to restore the situation was that of the general who had arrived at Souilly on the day of the fall of Fort Douaumont, General Philippe Pétain. On 28 April he became Chief of Staff of the French Armies and he would shortly become Commander-in-Chief. He achieved what he was asked to do with a combination of stick and carrot — no mercy for the ringleaders, better and more humane conditions for the mass. The French Army pulled itself together, if slowly; it would not be back to anything approaching its best form until well into 1918.

A sympathetic witness of the disarray of Britain's French allies at this time was the ambulance driver Charles Hartley. Aware more of a general discontent than of the fact that some units were now in open mutiny — indeed the French kept their crisis under the closest of wraps in their anxiety that the Germans should not hear of it — he wrote in late May 1917:

> I am afraid the French are becoming very depressed about the way the war is dragging on and it is quite common to hear the *poilu* shouting out *'à bas la guerre'* — 'down with the war'. Many of them predict that trouble will show itself in the ranks if the war goes on much longer. However, beyond it being natural that the French should be very very tired I do not think for a moment that the gallant army will not carry on to the end.

His confidence was justified, in no small degree thanks to Pétain. And even in 1917 there were some achievements, notably in the Verdun sector. In August, during what has been titled the Second Battle of Verdun, the French recaptured Avocourt, Mort-Homme and Côte 304. In the final phase of the war, however, when the French were again an effective force in the field, and a Frenchman — Marshal Foch — was Supreme Commander of all the Allied armies, it was the Americans who reclaimed for France the last occupied sectors of the former battlefield. It was a further gesture of homage to the memory of Rochambeau and Lafayette.

But there was a later, more tragic consequence of all this, arguably the worst element of all in the mixed legacy of Verdun.

When France was in crisis yet once more, in 1940, to whom did her citizens turn but to the Saviour of Verdun and to the after-the-event Hero of the Chemin des Dames? And this time the outcome was disastrous. The pessimistic side of Pétain came to the fore, while hopes that in his eighties he might produce the kind of miracles he had achieved at sixty proved illusory. The days of *'Courage! On les aura!'* and *'Ils ne passeront pas!'* were far in the past. Instead it was a case of France defeated and suing for peace; subsequently France divided, between direct German rule in the north and the puppet government of Vichy in the south, with Pétain as figurehead leader and with Pierre Laval as Iago to Pétain's feeble Othello. If there was any Desdemona it was France herself, deeply wounded, indeed in the eyes of some at the time, almost terminally so.★ Thus it is possible to see a strong connecting line between the stalwart defence of Verdun in 1916 and the shaming collapse of France a generation later, while the nation's hero of 1916-17 would ultimately become the nation's arraigned traitor of 1945, to be found guilty of treason and condemned to death.

★ This comment is not entirely arbitrary. In 1999 I met a lady born in the Vichy area of France in 1942. Her grandfather had fought at Verdun. Her father, deeply distressed at the state of his country in the third year of a deep national humiliation, decided to give her, not the standard name Françoise, but the more obviously demonstrative name France. It was a gesture of confidence that *France la patrie* would survive her appalling crisis and rise again.

Fittingly, it was another veteran of Verdun, former Captain Charles de Gaulle, who came to the rescue of his country's reputation and honour in 1940, and commuted Pétain's death sentence five years later, while Laval was unceremoniously executed.

Dr Maurice Larès, quoted in the previous chapter, takes a similar view of the connection between Verdun and Vichy:

> One might wonder finally if the prestige even nowadays attached to the name of Pétain, and the ease with which in 1940 he substituted himself for the legal political authorities, were not made possible by his fame as *'Le héros de Verdun'*. A less well known character might not have given 'Collaboration' the tremendous impulse it received. Pétain's strictly military fame may thus have become the unfortunate prime mover of our desertion from the battlefield in 1940 and of our treason towards England in spite of the treaties we had signed. His fame, still indelibly intact in the minds of many French people, may be due as much to his collaboration with the Germans as to his generalship at Verdun.

It was Pétain's hope that, despite being arraigned for his role in the Second World War, his motives would be understood and that he would not be denied his wish to be buried at Verdun, or more specifically at Douaumont. At his trial in 1945, after he had been condemned to death but before his reprieve, he rose to plead his cause: 'The French people will not forget', he said. 'They know that I defended them as I did at Verdun'. In November that year he was transferred to the island of Yeu, some fifteen miles off the French coast between Nantes and La Rochelle. It was almost like being sent to a local St Helena, except that there would no equivalent, as in the case of Napoleon, of a triumphant reinterment in the Invalides. Pétain died on Yeu on 23 July 1951 aged 95, remembered (in the view of *The Times* in its magisterial obituary) 'not as the defender of Verdun but as the Marshal of Vichy', and was buried there. The 1960s saw a serious campaign to rehabilitate him, but it made no headway. De Gaulle had saved him from death but was a powerful voice against his being given an honourable return to Douaumont. At Yeu he remains.

Another, almost inevitable legacy of Verdun was that it provided both France and Germany with many of her military and political leaders in the Second World War. As well as de Gaulle, those fighting for France included the future President Lebrun, who served there as an ordinary *poilu*, the future Admiral Darlan, who was in charge of a naval gun, and the future Marshal de Lattre de Tassigny, who cannot have been unaware of Verdun overtones during the siege of Dien Bien Phu in Indo-China in the 1950s.

Those on the German side included: von Brauschitz, Guderian, Hess, Keitel, von Manstein, Paulus (of Stalingrad), and the man who for much of the second war was Governor of Paris, Karl-Heinrich von Stülpnagel, who would add a minor but macabre postscript to the 1916 battle. Implicated in the Hitler bomb plot of July 1944, he was arrested and ordered back to Germany. *En route* he asked the favour of being allowed to travel via Verdun, and in particular to visit the Mort-Homme, where he had served as a battalion commander. He stopped the car, walked into the woods and shot himself in the

74. *Part of the 'beatification' of Pétain, which would have such dire consequences a generation later. The photograph records the ceremony on 8 December 1918 at which he was presented with the Baton of a Marshal of France, in the presence of (in the row behind) Marshals Joffre and Foch, Field Marshal Sir Douglas Haig, and Generals Pershing (USA), Gillain (Belgium), Albricci (Italy) and Haller (Poland). (American Official Photograph, Q 46480)*

head, but succeeded only in putting out his eyes. A pathetic wreck, he was taken on to Berlin to be executed together with his fellow-conspirators.

Verdun's own legacy was to become a place of pilgrimage, as the focus of national pride and grief following a war which had been won but at an alarming cost. When, in 1920, it was decided that France would choose an unknown warrior — a *soldat inconnu* — for interment under the Arc de Triomphe in Paris, the place assigned for the selection ceremony was the Citadel of Verdun. In the presence of the Minister of War, himself a one-time Verdun *blessé* (though of 1914), M. André Maginot, the choice was duly made. It was entrusted to a young soldier who was the son of one of Verdun's countless missing; his task was to place a bunch of flowers on one of eight tricolour-draped coffins laid out in one of the Citadel's underground galleries — eight coffins representing France's eight Western Front battle zones. The selected body was duly taken to Paris in time for the second post-war Armistice Day and was formally buried under the Arc de Triomphe some weeks later. The others were given special burial at the heart of the largest war-cemetery within Verdun city, the cemetery of the Faubourg Pavé. This is a moving place, not least because if you stand opposite its geometric centre, you see not only the tall cross and tricolour above the graves of the unselected seven, but directly behind it in the distance the twin towers of Verdun Cathedral, first target, if not by intention, of the first shell of the battle of 1916.

75. *The Faubourg Pavé Cemetery, Verdun, where the seven unselected 'candidates' for the role of 'unknown soldier' lie buried, in graves around the central cross (Mrs Jenny Suddaby)*

76. *Contemporary postcard, showing two of the graves, each with its own cross*

Verdun's supreme legacy, however, was to create an enduring wound in the psychology of the French nation. Lieutenant Raymond Jubert's statement 'They will not be able to make us do it again another day' — the testimony not of a survivor but of one who had perished at Verdun — was not a piece of empty rhetoric, it was a word of warning, indeed in effect a prophecy. It chimed in precisely with a powerful attitude of revulsion against war that dominated political and military thinking in the years following the 1918 Armistice, and that was greatly reinforced by the poignant memorials which soon began to appear in every French village, town and city. Such memorials, a high proportion of the names on which were those of the fallen of Verdun, might give solace to the bereaved but they also helped to make people feel that the kind of ordeal which had produced them had to be avoided at all costs. Thus conventional military precautions and preparations came to be neglected while huge efforts were made to find alternative methods of keeping *la patrie* safe from danger. So it transpired that M. Maginot, whose modest role in the choosing of the unknown soldier is almost entirely forgotten, entered the European history books in a context which would give him permanent if dubious fame, by lending his energy and name to a system of defence which in essence was one further link in the chain reaching back to Seré de Rivières and Sebastian de Vauban.

The Maginot Line, built across northern France in the 1930s from the Ardennes to the Swiss frontier, consisted of a skein of forts and smaller works, which, though technically far more sophisticated than their predecessors, repeated the old familiar theme. Forts had emerged from the war with a mixed reputation, but they had represented both in their construction and the way they had been fought over a deep longing in the French soul to find some tangible, visible means of defence that would protect their country from would-be invaders. It is thus scarcely surprising that a similar need gave rise to a similar response. Having no moat, no English Channel, the French tried to create its equivalent in guns, steel and concrete: a 'Wall of France', as Pétain defined it, having campaigned for such a concept from as far back as 1922. The attempt failed, for in 1940 the Germans, instead of challenging the Maginot Line, virtually ignored it, brushing past it with an outflanking movement which briefly engaged two outworks on its western edge and then swept on to far greater success than was ever achieved in the previous war, while Verdun itself was rapidly pocketed after 24-hours' fighting and at the cost of fewer than 200 dead. Certain of the Maginot forts can be visited; and despite their more modern appearance and generally pristine condition, they seem distinctly familiar to anyone who has walked the grim galleries of Douaumont or Vaux. They are a powerful reminder of the state of fear and anxiety which for so long dominated this border territory between France and Germany, but which now at last — it is surely safe to say — dominates it no longer.

Personal postscript:
Verdun revisited

In his account of the preparations for the 1916 battle the French historian Georges Blond described Verdun as a 'dark lodestar' drawing men towards what soon became a consuming furnace. In his final chapter he quoted the evidence of a former café proprietor from the village of Lemmes, half way between Souilly and Verdun on the Sacred Way, whose experience in the 1930s showed that Verdun's lodestar attraction did not cease with the end of the fighting:

> The café wasn't anything very much, sir, but it gave us a living. Because of the visiting veterans. All sorts, who had come to see the places where they had fought. There were group visits, organized by tourist agencies, pilgrimages, and veterans' reunions, but also single individuals, you can't imagine how many. They came by train, or by car, and often by bicycle, loaded like donkeys. From every class of society, sir. I remember one fellow — he must have been very well off — in a car driven by his chauffeur; they had fought together. They sat down at the same table, and he ordered omelettes and a bottle of white wine. They both came back in the evening, after their visit, ate another meal together, and then they got back into the car, the chauffeur at the wheel, the other in the back seat, just as when they had arrived.
>
> Some fellows used to arrive virtually in uniform, wearing puttees and field-jackets — everything but the helmet and the insignia. All these men had come back to find their old trench or shelter or shell hole where their best friend had died beside them. Why, sir, some of them brought along camping equipment and cooking utensils, and spent the night in their old dugout, which they did up a bit, field-kitchen and all. Every now and then one or other of them would get his head blown off when their fire heated up an unexploded shell or hand grenade. But nobody seemed to bother. My wife and I used to listen to some of these chaps talking, of course. They would exchange tips about the location of a battery emplacement which they'd found or a communication trench or something else. Then would follow the discussions: 'I was in Death Ravine...' 'Which one do you mean?' There seem to have been at least a dozen by that name, as far as I could gather.
>
> And would you believe it, sir? Germans came too. As time went by, nobody called them *Boches* any more. They ate something in a hurry, without very much conversation. They didn't talk to the Frenchmen, but every now and

then they exchanged nods. Yes, there were some who came back like pilgrims every year, sir, every year without missing. They covered on foot as many as fifteen or twenty miles a day. Some of the campers stayed for several days or a week; it seemed as if they couldn't tear themselves away, sir. One would have said that they were happy to be there.

So it has continued. Verdun has been revisited by countless men who fought there (though the last have by now all but faded away), and it has attracted many thousands more who did not. Daily the cars and coaches keep coming, cruising at a sedate speed along the battlefield's roads, mainly to Douaumont, both the Fort and the Ossuary, or to Fort Vaux, less frequently along the narrower left-bank roads leading to the Mort-Homme or Côte 304. The Citadel also has its huge number of visitors, now even offering them a 'virtual reality' experience of life in that sombre many-galleried fortress as it was in 1916. The 'lodestar' metaphor still holds.

Anniversaries have offered especially attractive occasions for visitors. I myself first went there to film for an anniversary TV documentary in 1978, sixty years after the Armistice, and have been back there on a number of occasions since. But on re-visiting Verdun most recently I sense a change. Verdun may be indissolubly linked to its past but it is also consciously trying as one century ends and a new one begins to mould a different future. Though its visitors come to see a symbol of the worst aspects of modern war, it is no longer only that to its citizens. A fresh identity is being forged. It was in 1984 that there took place a much publicized act of reconciliation between France and Germany, at the seventieth anniversary of the outbreak of the First World War, with President Mitterand and Chancellor Kohl standing side by side in front of the Ossuary at Douaumont. This, one should add, was viewed with a kind of weary cynicism by many French people, in that, apart from the slightly absurd spectacle of the tall German and the short Frenchman holding hands, in reality the meeting only confirmed a relationship of which the prime creators were no longer present to claim the credit: Adenauer and De Gaulle. Nevertheless the gesture was made, was noted elsewhere and considered to be one of some importance. Three years later, in 1987, the United Nations christened the city 'World Capital of Peace, Freedom and Human Rights'. It might seem bizarre to strangers, or even naive, for so heavy a legacy from the past can hardly be sloughed off by a new label, but, on whatever terms, Verdun's acceptance of its new role should surely be respected, and indeed encouraged. Ironically, a lavish new Museum celebrating the city's new role has been opened in the Bishop's Palace, next to the very courtyard in which the first salvo of the great battle exploded in 1916.

A smaller but hardly less eloquent token of the changing times can be seen at, of all places, the summit of the Mort-Homme, where, near a tall marble memorial to the dead of the 40th Division of Infantry, a small wooden cross catches the eye, bearing the legend

1916-1984
Par dessus les tombes
l'amitié franco-allemande

77, *A new Verdun 'slogan' on the crest of the Mort-Homme; a cross planted seventy years after the outbreak of the Great War, in 1984, bearing a message of reconciliation between ancient enemies: 'Above the graves/Franco-German friendship'* (Mrs Jenny Suddaby)

literally: 'Above the graves/Franco-German friendship': a remarkable gloss on the savagery and venom of the fighting which once took place there — of which the nearby Skeleton Memorial serves as a powerful reminder, with its slogan: *'Ils n'ont pas passé'* — 'They did not pass'.

At the same time, perhaps healthily, Verdun's reputation as a city of heroism and defiance is, it would appear, losing its hold on the rest of France. The British still use the Somme as a useful comparison in any situation, whether military or political, where there is a prolonged and bitter confrontation (or even, when it comes to Glastonbury in a wet summer, in relation to the mud in the fields of that now famous festival!) but Verdun is not appealed to in the same way in France. Thus, as I have been informed by someone of the present generation who should know these things (I refer to Marie-Laure Blay-Gilbert, quoted in Chapter 19), Vietnam or Beirut come more swiftly to mind as standards of comparison than Verdun. *'C'est le Vietnam'* or *'c'est Beyrouth'* are phrases in popular currency, but, she writes, 'I know of no expression using Verdun'.

Nor does Verdun particularly attract as a place for the French to visit. Again my correspondent writes: 'Verdun and the Meuse are not exactly like Normandy, where French people allergic to the Riviera — or living in the North of France — naturally gather at summer-time: "and why not visit the landing beaches and the soul-searing cemeteries?" She continues: 'World War II sites are, I think, perceived as more "attractive", more close emotionally to members of the young generation. Perhaps Verdun smells "old and sad", whereas Normandy smells "heroic and lyrical".' Though she feels compelled to add: 'And that's unjust'.

78. *Ornes, as it was in 1918; destined to be one of the* villages détruits *of Verdun (German Official Photograph: Q 45664)*

79, *The Ornes memorial church, typical of the modern 'shrines' built on the sites of the nine lost villages (Author);*

80, (above) & 81. (opposite) The roof of Fort Douaumont today, with machine-gun cupola; the view across the former battleground from Fort Douaumont. (Both photographs, Author)

Significantly people of other nationalities, who might not be thought of as obvious visitors, can be seen at Verdun. Thus on my most recent visit I was asked by a middle-aged German couple, lost in Verdun city, how to reach the battlefields; I duly directed them in the direction of Douaumont and Vaux. At Côte 304, I talked with a family of husband, wife and son, who, arriving in a smart Mercedes, turned out be Polish by background but now living in Germany, the wife's grandfather having been a victim of Auschwitz. Such tiny portents suggest that Verdun 1916 is now increasingly matter for history rather than for hatred — indeed the battle is surely becoming, in Wordsworth's famous phrase quoted in this book's first chapter, 'an old unhappy far-off thing' that should not be forgotten, rather seen in a new light.

Even Verdun itself seems changed, as compared with my own first visits there, over twenty years ago. The city bustles with traffic that hurries with an almost, though not quite, Parisian speed; given a touch of summer weather (for which the area has not been renowned) people are out drinking and dining in the pavement cafes or the terraces of restaurants, and the last thing on their minds is the strategy of Falkenhayn or the folly or otherwise of the determination to reclaim Douaumont at whatever cost. What is surely Verdun's ugliest memorial, the Victory Monument overlooking the city's busiest shopping thoroughfare, the Rue Mazel, seems oddly incongruous at the top of its great flight of steps, which are less used by ascending pilgrims than as convenient perches for school-children waiting for family cars to arrive or shop-workers relaxing during a lunch-break. The Verdunois have other things on their minds.

As for the battle zone, it can send out mixed signals according to the weather or the season. I have seen it under snow. Cross-country skiers gliding elegantly by or children happily cavorting on toboggans can make such places of ill repute as Froideterre and Thiaumont look like the pistes of a thriving winter resort: no history here surely. Return when the snow is melting, however, and its last relics can bring out jagged, ominous shapes in the broken ground. Go there in spring or summer, and of course if you look for them you can easily discover the old trenches and the shell holes, but much of the area is under a rich canopy of trees that make it — even though one knows the ground beneath is riddled with the detritus of war — look almost beautiful. The tall Ossuary tower, however, is omnipresent: a raised reminding finger on the skyline: 'do not forget'.

It is perhaps the old destroyed villages which most catch at the heart: each one with its immaculate shrine, its token modern church — used perhaps just once a year — whose very neatness and cleanness of line make the demise of the old rural communities that once thrived there seem the more poignant. One almost wishes they had been just left to grass and nature; that might have been a kinder death. These live in the mind, as does the remarkable view from the high vantage-point of the battered roof of Fort Douaumont, which, by a curious paradox, seems to me to be Verdun at its most reassuring.

Look north and east from it over the long wide landscape before you, stretching many miles to a distant forested horizon, and then try to imagine the Germans advancing in force across it in 1916 to bleed France white and destroy what Falkenhayn thought was 'England's best sword'. The very thought emphasizes how absurd and unreal such a concept seems now, and helps to make it evident that, whatever troubles Europe takes into the twenty-first century, this corner of it will, assuredly, never see the like of that again.

Sources

For full details of works referred to see Bibliography

Preface
Quotation by German Werth, from his book *Verdun, Die Schlacht und der Mythos*, p.209.

1. The name
Hitler quotation on Stalingrad, quoted Holger H. Herwig, *The First World War, Germany and Austria-Hungary 1914-1918*, p.198. Quotations by Hindenburg and Paléologue, Richard Thoumin, *The First World War*, p.239. Henry Bordeaux quotation, *The Last Days of Fort Vaux*. Quotations by Rifleman P.H. Jones and Captain E.W.S. Balfour, Imperial War Museum Department of Documents. Comment by Julian Green, *The World at Sixteen*, Vol II., p.26.

2. The background
De Gaulle quotation, from *Vers l'Armée de Métier*, quoted as epigraph by Richard Holmes, *Fatal Avenue*. Verdun history, from *Verdun and the Battles for its Possession*, Michelin Battlefield Guide, 1919. Danton quotation, Alistair Horne, *The Price of Glory*, p.11. Material on Vauban and Louis XIV*Reader's Companion to Military History*, p.271. Richard Holmes quotation re Montmédy, op.cit., p.30. Material on Seré de Rivières, ibid., pp.51-2.

3. The plan
Christmas Memorandum, quoted Erich von Falkenhayn, *General Headquarters and its Critical Decisions, 1914-1916*, p.217. Michelin Guide, caption to map, pp.6-7. Pétain quotation, from his book *Verdun*, p.32. For discussion of date of Christmas Memorandum and Falkenhayn's intentions see Richard Holmes, *The Western Front*, pp.82-3. Holger H. Herwig on Falkenhayn's intentions, op.cit.,p.180. Winston Churchill quotation on German motives at Verdun, *World Crisis*, Vol II, pp 656-7. Crown Prince Rupprecht on Falkenhayn, Alistair Horne, op.cit., p.39. Kaiser's instructions to Crown Prince Wilhelm, Klaus W. Jonas, *The Life of Crown Prince Wilhelm,* p.92. Churchill's assessment of the Crown Prince, op.cit., p.658. Crown Prince Rupprecht on one-bank only attack, Alistair Horne, op.cit., p.156. Operation *Gericht* interpreted as 'execution place', Alistair Horne, op.cit., p.38, as 'scaffold', Richard Holmes, *Fatal Avenue*, p.224.

4. The preparations
German artillery elements arrayed against Verdun, Alistair Horne, pp.42-3. Mike Hibberd, Imperial War Museum. Barbara Tuchman quotation and details of Krupp 420 mm gun, from her book *The Guns of August*, pp.167, 192. Verdun as *Région Fortifiée*, details of withdrawal of guns, etc., Richard Holmes, op.cit., p.223. Jean de Pierrefeu on Joffre's adulation, Richard Thoumin op.cit., pp.201-2. For the Siege of Paris and the Commune; see Alistair Horne, *The Fall of Paris, passim*; for Joffre as a gunner subaltern in 1870, ibid, p.viii. Good Friday story regarding Joffre, Jean de Pierrefeu, quoted Richard Thoumin, op.cit., p.203. Scepticism of Operational Bureau towards Intelligence Bureau, Jean de Pierrefeu, *French Headquarters 1915-18*, pp.49-50. Extracts from Georges Blond, *Verdun,* pp.3-4, 9. Diary of Reserve Lieutenant W. Weingartner, Imperial War Museum Department of Documents. Pre-battle situation on French side and Colonel Driant, Alistair Horne, *The Price of Glory*, Chapter 4, *passim*, Richard Holmes, op.cit., p.224 and *The Western Front*, p.89. French over-confidence before attack, Jean de Pierrefeu, *French Headquarters 1915-18*, pp.50, 51.

5. The battle: first phase
Letter by Otto Heinebach, *German Students' War Letters*, pp.242-3. Quotation by Crown Prince, from his book *My War Experiences,* p.180. Quotations on devastating opening bombardment, Jacques Péricard, *Verdun 1916*, pp.6-7. Trees hurled aside like skittles, Peter Simkins, *World War I*, p.94. General von Zwehl's infantry attack, Alistair Horne, op.cit., p.58. Colonel Driant message 'We shall hold', ibid., p.81. Eye-witness account of death of Driant, from Jacques-Henri Lefebvre, *Verdun,* p.93. Verdun's first hero, Richard Holmes, *Fatal Avenue*, p.225. 'Friendly fire' at

Samogneux, Alistair Horne op.cit., pp.98-9. Fall of Bezonvaux, Jacques Péricard, op.cit., p.70.

6. The seizure of Fort Douaumont

General description of Fort, *Fort Douaumont, story of a fortress,* also *Verdun: Vision and Comprehension,* pp.80-8. Douaumont as the 'defiant fortress', Gérard Canini, from his article 'Sur les pas des combattants de Verdun', *Historia,* February 1996. Details of seizure, Alistair Horne op.cit. and Richard Holmes, *passim.* Confusion following seizure, contemporary newspapers. 'No question of a siege', Jean de Pierrefeu, op.cit., p.60.

7. The nights of the generals

M. Étienne and General Joffre, Jean de Pierrefeu, op.cit., p.56. Variant interpretations regarding Castelnau's actions on 24 February, Henri Castex, *Verdun, Années Infernales,* pp.13-14. Pétain's account of his appointment, Pétain, *Verdun,* pp.70-1. Alistair Horne on Pétain's overnight stay in Paris, op.cit., p.133.

8. The holding of the line

Quotation by Louis Madelin, Jacques Péricard, op.cit., p.71. Pétain watches his troops, op.cit., pp.122-3. Falkenhayn loses his opportunity, Alistair Horne, op.cit., p.154. Quotation from Captain Georges Kimpflin, from Jean-Norton Cru, *Témoins,* p.333. Quotations from Paul Dubrulle, from *Mon Régiment, passim.* Diary entries of German *Feldwebel,* Henry Dugard, *The Battle of Verdun,* pp. 266-9. Fight for Douaumont village, Jean Lacouture, *De Gaulle, The Rebel,* p.38.

9. The battle: second phase

Churchill comment on this phase of the battle, *World Crisis,* Vol.II, p.666. Description of view over left bank battlefield, Pierre Teilhard de Chardin, *The Making of a Mind,* p.104. Account of fighting by French machine gun sergeant, Richard Thoumin, op.cit., p.233. Account of attack by Lieutenant Raymond Jubert, translation from ibid., pp.234-5. The *poilus'* answer to non-combatants' questions, author's translation from Raymond Jubert, *Verdun,* p.180. Pétain's order of the day of 9 April, copy in Souilly Town Hall, translation from Michelin Battlefield Guide, p.16. Possible alternative sources of *'On les aura!'* slogan, Holger H.Herwig, op.cit., p.184.

10. 'The Sacred Way'

American correspondent's description, quoted Richard Thoumin, op.cit., p.232. Dialogue between Pétain and Major Richard, Alistair Horne, op.cit., p.147. Description by René Arnaud, from his book *Tragédie Bouffe,* p.60. Accounts by Jubert, op.cit., and Dubrulle, op.cit. Airpower and Verdun, see Richard Holmes, *The Western Front,* pp.105-6. German failure to disrupt the Sacred Way, Alistair Horne, op.cit., pp 208-9.

11. The helping hand

Background to the American air effort at Verdun, Paul-Louis Hervier, *American Volunteers with the Allies,* pp.76, 96ff., Quentin Reynolds, *They Fought for the Sky,* pp. 135-8. Diary of Charles Hartley, Imperial War Museum Department of Documents. Background to setting up of British Urgency Cases Hospital, article by J.A. Cairns Forsyth, *Le Faux Miroir,* January 1917, p.12. Diary of Nurse Winifred Kenyon, Imperial War Museum Department of Documents.

12. The mill on the Meuse

'The mill on the Meuse, etc', quotation from Crown Prince Wilhelm, *My War Experiences,* p.223. Strategy of Generals Nivelle and Mangin, Mangin, *Comment Finir la Guerre,* p.74. Mangin quotation, 'Whatever you do etc', John Terraine, *White Heat.* p.209. Pierre Rouquet evidence, interview with journalist Françoise Eyraud, 1993. Letter by Christian Bordeching, *Paroles de Poilus,* pp.109-10. Lieutenant Weingartner Diary, Imperial War Museum Department of Documents. Alfred Joubaire, *Pour la France: Carnet de route d'un fantassin,* diary quotations, pp.275-6, 278-9, last letter, pp.283-5.

13. The heroic defence of Fort Vaux

Explosion of 8 May, Fort Douaumont, *Verdun: Vision and Comprehension,* p.62. Account by Stephen Westman, from his *Surgeon with the Kaiser's Army,* pp.92-3. 22 May attack on Fort Douaumont, Alistair Horne, op.cit., p.235ff. Account by Commandant Raynal, quoted from Guy Chapman, *Vain Glory,* pp.290-6 *passim.* Escape from Fort Vaux, Jacques-Henri Lefebvre, *Verdun,* p.275. Quotations by Henry Bordeaux, from his book *The Last Days of Fort Vaux.* Pétain comment on the failure at Fort Douaumont and the gallantry displayed at Fort Vaux, op.cit., pp.168-9.

14. The martyr city

Cynical comment of General von Gallwitz, Holger H. Herwig, op.cit., p.196. Charles Hartley diary, as Chapter 11. Diary entries by Captain Desagneaux, *A French Soldier's War Diary, 1914-1918,* pp.18-20. Account of arriving at Verdun Citadel, René Arnaud, *Tragédie Bouffe,* pp.64-5.

15. The turning-point
'Green Cross Gas' etc., Alistair Horne, op.cit., p.285ff. Henry Bordeaux on waiting for German attack, quoted *Verdun, An Illustrated Historical Guide*, p.74. 'Tragic hour' comment, Jacques Péricard, op.cit., p.389. Background to 'You must not let them pass!' message, Pétain, op.cit., p.179. Comparison with German soldiers near Moscow, 1941, Alistair Horne, op.cit., p.299.

16. The continuing battle
Churchill on inflexibility of French defence, quotation reproduced in *World Crisis*, Vol II, p.667. Letter by Corporal René Pigeard, *Paroles de Poilus*. Hindenburg as a 'hero-god', Cyril Falls, *The First World War*, p.173. Letter by Pierre Prouteau, *Paroles de Poilus*. Letter by Anton Steiger, *German Students' War Letters*, pp.276-7. Rarity of truces at Verdun, Stephen Westman quotation, op.cit., p.93. René Arnaud quotation, op.cit. p.98. Comment by Lieutenant Bordeching, *Paroles de Poilus*. Truce episode at Froideterre, Walter Beumelburg, *Combattants Allemands à Verdun*, quoted Alain Denizot, *Verdun 1914-1918*, pp.324-5. Difficulty of burying the dead, Stephen Westman, op.cit., pp.93-4. René Arnaud quotations, op.cit., *passim*. Henri Desagneaux quotation, op.cit., p.26. Attitude of German soldiers to Verdun fighting, Holger H. Herwig, op.cit., p.193, German Werth, *Verdun, Die Schlacht und der Mythos*, pp.209-10.

17. The recapture of Fort Douaumont
Details of honours conferred on Verdun, Michelin Guide, p.30. Lieutenant Weingartner Diary, Imperial War Museum Department of Documents. Pétain on recapture of Fort Douaumont, op.cit., pp.201-2. Lieutenant-Colonel Picard quotation, from Jacques Péricard, op.cit., p.576. Major Nikolai account, quoted *Verdun, An Illustrated Historical Guide*, p.90. Douaumont the symbol, quoted Alistair Horne, op.cit., pp.105, 308. Accounts of attack by wounded soldiers, G.D., *Le Faux Miroir*, pp.61-2, M., ibid., p.49. Intoxication of victory, Lieutenant-Colonel Picard, as above. Quotations by E. Ashmead-Bartlett, from *Some of my Experiences in the Great War*, pp.157-8, 161-2, 184, 174-5. Pierre Teilhard de Chardin quotations, op.cit., pp.138-40. 'Thoughts of a Night Sister' by Sister S.M. Edwards, *Le Faux Miroir*, pp.17-18.

18. The closedown
Account of 24 October attack by Raymond Abescat, from *Visages de la Grande Guerre*, p.65. Crown Prince quotation, *My War Experiences*, pp. 254-7, abbreviated. For effect of Verdun battle of modern war, see Holger H. Herwig, op.cit., pp.188-98 *passim*. Quotation from John Terraine, *White Heat*, p.208. Historians' summing up of Verdun Battle: Peter Simkins, op.cit., p.107, Richard Holmes, *The Western Front*, p.110, Michael Geyer, quoted Holger H. Herwig, op.cit., p.198, Alistair Horne, op.cit., p.328. Comparison with Stalingrad, Antony Beevor, *Stalingrad*, pp.148-9. Quotation by Marc Ferro, *The First World War*, p.77.

19: The experience
Soldat J. Ayoun's attititude to Verdun, quoted Jacques Péricard, op.cit., p.535. Pierre Rouquet comment, from interview with Françoise Eyraud (as Chapter 12). Comment by Maurice Genevoix, from Alain Denizot, *Verdun 1914-1918*, epigraph. Comment by Raymond Jubert, quoted Alistair Horne, p.326, also, anonymously, Alistair Horne, *To Lose a Battle*, p.23. Quotation by Pierre Teilhard de Chardin, op.cit., pp.119-120. Comment by Raymond Abescat, as Chapter 18. Comment by Werner Beumelburg, Alistair Horne, op.cit., p.326. Extracts from letters by Gaston Biron and Karl Fritz, *Paroles de Poilus*. Paul Dubrulles's comment, Alistair Horne, op.cit., p.177, also (abbreviated) Richard Holmes, *The Western Front*, p.103. René Arnaud's comment, op.cit., p.75. Raymond Abescat, as Chapter 18. A 'sinister brown belt', Alistair Horne, op.cit., p.174. Paul Valéry, quoted Gérard Canini, *Combattre à Verdun*. 'Powerful statement' on Verdun, by Alain Denizot, op.cit., pp.142, 144-5. Comments by contemporary French observers, see Acknowledgements; for more on Abel Gance's film *J'accuse*, see Jay Winter, *Sites of Memory, Sites of Mourning, passim*. Response to the Douaumont Ossuary by Richard Holmes, *The Western Front*, TV Series, Programme 3, BBC-1, 1999.

20: The legacy
Extracts from Paul Husson's *L'Holocauste*, quoted from T.H. Wintringham, *Mutiny*, p.161. Charles Hartley comment, as Chapter 11. Pétain obituary in *The Times*, 24 July 1951. Selection of French Unknown Soldier, *Verdun, Vision and Comprehension*, p.32. Maginot Line, Anthony Kemp, *The Maginot Line: Myth and Reality, passim*

Postscript: Verdun revisited
Extract from Georges Blond, *Verdun*, pp.249-50.

Bibliography

All books published in London unless otherwise stated

René Arnaud, *Tragédie Bouffe, A Frenchman in the First World War*, translated by J.B. Donne, Sidgwick & Jackson,1966

E. Ashmead-Bartlett, *Some of my Experiences in the Great War*, George Newnes, 1918

Antony Beevor, *Stalingrad*, Viking, 1998

Georges Blond, *Verdun*, translated by Frances Frenaye, André Deutsch 1965

Henry Bordeaux, *The Last Days of Fort Vaux*, translated by Paul V. Cohn, Thomas Nelson, 1917

Gérard Canini, *Combattre à Verdun*, Nancy, Presses Universitaires de Nancy, 1988

Henri Castex, Verdun, *Années Infernales*, Paris, Imago, 1996

Guy Chapman, *Vain Glory*, Cassell, 1937

Roger Chickering, *Imperial Germany and the Great War*, Cambridge, Cambridge University Press, 1998

Winston S. Churchill, *The World Crisis 1911-1918*, Thornton Butterworth, 1927, NEL Mentor paperback edition, 1968

Jean Norton Cru, *Témoins*, first edition 1929, Nancy, Presses Universitaires de Nancy, 1993

Alain Denizot, *Verdun 1914-1918*, Paris, Nouvelles Editions Latines, 1996

Henri Desagneaux *A French Soldier's War Diary*, translated by Godfrey J. Adams, Morley, Yorkshire, The Elmfield Press, 1975

Paul Dubrulle, *Mon Régiment dans La Fournaise de Verdun et dans La Bataille de la Somme, Impressions de Guerre d'un Prêtre Soldat*, Paris, Librairie Plon, 1917

Henry Dugard, *The Battle of Verdun*, translated by F. Appleby Holt, Hutchinson, 1916

Erich von Falkenhayn, *General Headquarters and its Critical Decisions, 1914-1916,* Hutchinson, 1919

Cyril Falls, *The First World War*, Longmans, 1960

Marc Ferro, *The Great War 1914-1918*, translated by Nicole Stone, Routledge & Kegan Paul, 1973

Fort Douaumont: story of a fortress, Tourism Office of Verdun, n.d.

Fort Vaux: incredible story, Tourism Office of Verdun, n.d.

German Students' War Letters, edited by Dr Philipp Witkop, Munich, 1928, translated by A.F. Wedd, Methuen, 1929

Julian Green, *The World at Sixteen*, Volume II, New York and London, Marion Boyars, 1993

Paul-Louis Hervier, *The American Volunteers with the Allies,* Paris, Editions de 'La Nouvelle Revue', 1918

Index

Holger H. Herwig, *The First World War, Germany and Austria-Hungary 1914-1918*, Arnold, 1997

Richard Holmes, *Fatal Avenue,* Jonathan Cape 1992, Pimlico 1993; *The Western Front*, BBC Worldwide Ltd, 1999

Alistair Horne, *The Price of Glory*, Macmillan 1962, Penguin Books 1991; *The Fall of Paris*, Macmillan, 1965; *To Lose a Battle, France 1940*, Macmillan, 1969

Klaus W. Jonas, *The Life of Crown Prince Wilhelm*, Routledge & Kegan Paul, 1961

Alfred Joubaire, *Pour la France, Carnet de Route d'un Fantassin*, Paris, Perrin et Cie, 1917

Raymond Jubert, *Verdun (Mars-Avril-Mai 1916)*, Paris, Payot & Cie, Paris, 1918

Anthony Kemp, *The Maginot Line: Myth and Reality*, Frederick Warne, 1981

Jean Lacouture, *De Gaulle, The Rebel*. First published in 1984 by Editions du Seuil. Abridged version first published in English by Harvill, 1990. Copyright ©Editions du Seuil, 1984, 1990. English translation by Patrick O'Brien copyright ©Harvill, 1990. Extract reproduced by permission of The Harvill Press

Jacques-Henri Lefebvre, *Verdun, la plus grande bataille de l'Histoire racontée par les survivants*, Paris, 1960, 12ᵗʰ edition, Verdun, Éditions du Mémorial, 1996

General Mangin, *Comment Finir la Guerre*, Paris, Librairie Plon, 1920

Olivier Morel et Didier Pazery, *Visages de la Grande Guerre*, Paris, Calmann-Lévy, 1998

Paroles de Poilus, Paris, Librio, © Radio France,1998, distributed by Librairie Ernest Flammarion

Jacques Péricard, *Verdun 1916*, Paris, Nouvelle Librairie de France, 1997

Henri Philippe Pétain, *Verdun*, translated by Margaret MacVeagh, New York, The Dial Press, 1930

Jean de Pierrefeu, *French Headquarters 1915-1918*, translated by Major C.J.C. Street OBE MC, Geoffrey Bles, 1924

Reader's Companion to Military History, Boston, Houghton-Mifflin, 1996

Quentin Reynolds, *They Fought for the Sky*, Cassell, 1958

Peter Simkins, *World War I, 1914-1918*, Colour Library Books, 1992

Pierre Teilhard de Chardin, *The Making of a Mind*, translated by René Hague, William Collins, 1965. First published as *Genèse d'une Pensée*, Paris, Bernard Grasset, 1961

John Terraine, *The Great War*, 1965, latest edition Wordsworth Editions Ltd, 1997; *White Heat, The New Warfare 1914-18*, Sidgwick & Jackson, 1982

Richard Thoumin, *The First World War*, edited and translated by Martin Kieffe, Secker & Warburg, 1963

Barbara Tuchman, *The Guns of August*, New York, Macmillan, 1962

Verdun and the Battles for its Possession, Michelin Battlefield Guide; English language edition, Michelin Tyre Company Ltd, 1919; facsimile edition, Easingwold, North Yorkshire, G.H. Smith & Son, 1994

Verdun: An Illustrated Historical Guide, Verdun, Éditions Lorraine, Frémont, n.d.

Verdun: Vision and Comprehension. Editions Mage, Drancy, 2ⁿᵈ Edition 1982

German Werth, *Verdun, Die Schlacht und der Mythos*, Bergisch Gladbach, Gustav Lübbe Verlag, 1979

Stephen Westman, *Surgeon in the Kaiser's Army*, William Kimber, 1968

Crown Prince William of Germany, *My War Experiences,* Hurst & Blackett, 1922

T.H. Wintringham, *Mutiny*, Stanley Nott, 1936

MANUSCRIPT SOURCES

Imperial War Museum Department of Documents:
Collections of
Brigadier E.W.S. Balfour (courtesy of Mr P E G Balfour CBE, Mr John Balfour OBE MC); Charles Hartley, *Croix Rouge Française*; Rifleman P.H. Jones (courtesy of Mr Paul Jones); Nurse Winifred Kenyon (courtesy of Mrs Ann Mitchell), Reserve Lieutenant W. Weingartner, German Army.

JOURNALS AND MAGAZINES

British: *Daily Mirror, Le Faux Miroir* (magazine of the British Urgency Cases Hospital, Révigny), *The Illustrated London News,* Purnell's *History of the 20th Century*, Chapter 21, *The Sphere, The Times*

French: *Historia* February 1996, *Jours de L'Oise* November 1993 (interview with Pierre Rouquet), *L'Illustration*